Decoding the Hidden Market Rhythm

Part 1: Dynamic Cycles

by Lars von Thienen

A dynamic approach to identify and trade cycles that influence financial markets

www.whentotrade.com

Decoding the Hidden Market Rhythm – Second Edition
A dynamic approach to identify and trade cycles that influence financial markets
Part 1: Dynamic Cycles (Release 2014)
All Rights Reserved.
© Copyright 2010-2014 Lars von Thienen / www.whentotrade.com

All materials of this book, including, without limitation, text, software, scripts, illustrations and video are copyrighted intellectual property.

Everything presented in this book is considered licensed to you for your personal, non-commercial home use only. You're not allowed to redistribute or sell the material or convert it to any other form that people can use. You may not copy, reproduce, republish, upload, post, transmit or distribute this material in any way or for any other purpose unless you get the written permission from the author first.

This book is designed to help readers obtain trading education. It discusses ways to trade the markets using cycle analysis in the decision process. There are no warranties implied. This book makes no guarantee that that you will make money trading any market.

The past performance of any shown trading system or methodology is not necessarily indicative of future results. Hypothetical or simulated performance results have certain inherent limitations. Unlike an actual performance record, simulated results do not represent actual trading. Also, since the trades have not actually been executed, the results may have under- or over-compensated for the impact, if any, of certain market factors, such as lack of liquidity.

Trading involves the risk of loss. Please consider carefully which trading instruments are appropriate to your financial situation. The risk of loss in trading can be substantial. However, the ability to assess risk is vital to a trader's survival. Conversely, without risk there is no profit either.

www.whentotrade.com

This book is dedicated to the Wave59 community. A community in which new ideas can thrive. A place where friendship is more than a word and where rampant ideas can be discussed, are accepted and receive constructive feedback.

I would like to personally dedicate this book to Joseph. A Wave59 member who became a dear friend of mine. An exceptionally loyal and helpful person. Joseph, without your support and continual testing, I would not have been able to stay on this path. Thank you, my friend. I am grateful to have found you.

Lars von Thienen, July 2010

Forward: Second Edition – Part 1: Dynamic Cycles

This second edition of "Decoding The Hidden Market Rhythm" comes in three parts with extended content. Part 1 is about "Dynamic Cycles", Part 2 about "Metonic Cycles" and Part 3 about "Genetic Algorithm & Cycles".

The concepts presented can be replicated using the Standalone WTT Charting Module or the Wave59 Cycles Plug-In.

The original cycles tools were applied prior to the first release in 2010 and they remain the same in this second release. Additional examples have been added for explanatory and demonstration purposes. The additional content can also be reviewed in the video library ("Academy") on the WhenToTrade Website.

After the initial release in 2010, the standalone WTT Charting Module was introduced in 2012 and it marked a significant milestone. It enabled the implementation of cycle analysis supplementary tools. A new genetic algorithm was implemented as a precursor to the next dimension of cyclic analysis. Researchers can now advance cycle research and push the boundaries.

New tools, such as the Genetic Algorithm, is already available within the WTT Charting Module for our community. The first part of "Dynamic Cycles" introduces the underlying basic cycles approach.

Lars von Thienen, February 2014
www.whentotrade.com

Contents

1. **Introduction - It's all about cycles** 9
2. **How to detect and measure cycles in the stock market** 15
   - 2.1 The cyclic approach put into practice 15
   - 2.2 The Cycle Scanner: Introduction of a new & proprietary cycle detection algorithm 17
   - 2.3 Example 1: Dataset with 2 cycles 20
   - 2.4 Example 2: Dataset with 2 cycles + trend 24
   - 2.5 Example 3: Dataset with 2 cycles + trend + noise 26
   - 2.6 Step-by-step guide: How to build a forecast based on cycle detection 29
   - 2.7 Example 4: Dataset with 4 cycles + trend + noise 38
   - 2.8 Building the forecasting model for Example 4 based on the detected cycles 45
   - 2.9 Example 5: Dataset with 5 cycles + noise + changing trends and forces 49
   - 2.10 The Cycle Scanner: Algorithm overview 54
   - 2.11 Final summary – A new area of cyclic analysis at your fingertips 55
   - 2.12 The Cycle Scanner: A step-by-step guide 56
   - 2.13 The Cycle Plotter 61
3. **The Dominant Market Vibration** 65
   - 3.1 Definition of the dominant cycle 65
   - 3.2 Definition of the Dominant Market Vibration 65
4. **Fine-tuning technical indicators using the Dominant Market Vibration** 69
   - 4.1 The basic idea 69
   - 4.2 A step-by-step guide: Trading the S&P 500 E-mini futures contract intraday 71
   - 4.3 Trading the S&P 500 E-mini futures contract intraday – Example 2 79
   - 4.4 Summary 83
5. **Cycles Are Not Static: The Dynamic Nature of Cycles** 85
   - 5.1 Effect A: Shifts in Cycle Length 86
   - 5.2 Effect B: Shifts in Cycle Phase 87

    5.3   The Combined Effects 88

    5.4   Video Lesson – Dynamic Cycles Explained 91

6. Forecasting the next important market turn – Time, direction & polarity... 93

    6.1   Introducing a new forecasting method based on the Dominant Market Vibration 93

    6.2   Introduction of the Dynamic Cycle Explorer method 94

    6.3   Using the Cycle Explorer as a quality check for static cycle frameworks... 104

    6.4   The Cycle Explorer as a visual confirmation tool 105

    6.5   Building a forecast based on the Dynamic Cycle Explorer 106

    6.6   A step-by-step guide to building a tradable forecast model / Daily S&P Index 107

    6.7   Updating the forecast after the projected turning point / Polarity forecast 117

    6.8   Updating the polarity forecast and the next ETA CIT projection 120

    6.9   Review of polarity and ETA and updating the next forecast 120

    6.10 Complete review of all forecasted CIT dates and polarity windows 121

    6.11 Combining a semi-static and purely dynamic forecasting model for trading 123

    6.12 The combined semi-static and dynamic trading approach in action on the S&P 500 125

    6.13 Video Lesson – Dynamic Cycles: S&P500 bar-by-bar review 142

7. Measuring and trading Dominant Sentiment Cycles 143

    7.1   The long-term Dynamic Cycle Explorer 144

    7.2   The short-term Dynamic Cycle Explorer 145

    7.3   Sentiment Cycles Follow-up progressions 150

8. Cycles within Cycles: Combining price and sentiment cycles 153

    8.1   The Dynamic Cycles Approach 154

    8.2   The dominant carrier wave on the price chart – October 2010 155

    8.3   The peak is detected in advance - May 2011 157

    8.4   Following the vibration of the dominant cycle – September 2011 158

  8.5 Cycles within cycles – Sentiment in September 2011 159

  8.6 Current sentiment cycle fits into the long-term wave – October 2011..... 162

  8.7 Video Lesson... 165

9. Dynamic Cycles in Silver and Gold 167

  9.1 Dynamic Cycles Projection: April/May 2011 168

  9.2 Dynamic Cycles Projection: August 2011 172

  9.3 Dynamic Cycles Projection: 2012 and March 2013 175

  9.4 Video Lesson – Silver Cycles Live Calls.. 180

10. Trading the swing of the dominant cycle – Next level momentum trading. 181

  10.1 Calculation of the cycle acceleration... 182

  10.2 Evaluation criteria for the new Cycle Swing Indicator 184

  10.3 Super smooth with no lag – The cycle's acceleration is the leading price momentum 187

  10.4 Adaptive divergence detection on any market: Repeating patterns at cycle tops and bottoms 199

  10.5 Trading the turns of the cycle swing – Staying in vibration with the market... 206

  10.6 Developing automated trading systems based on the Cycle Swing Indicator... 209

  10.7 Cycle Swing Indicator parameter and usage 213

11. Multiple Cycle-Frame Trading.. 215

  11.1 Volume Cycles.. 215

  11.2 Price Range Cycles.. 217

  11.3 Time Cycles & Cycle Cluster.. 219

12. The CSI and cRSI Combo Trading Technique (Intraday) 221

  12.1 Day 1: March 21, 2012.. 222

  12.2 Day 2: March 22, 2012.. 225

  12.3 Day 3: March 23, 2012.. 229

13. Cycles Toolbox and Charting Platform 231

14. Bibliography 235

1. Introduction - It's all about cycles

This book is about cycles. Cycles that influence our life here on Earth. Cycles that represent energy flows that influence people's moods and emotions. Cycles that represent energies originating from outer space. Cycles that manifest themselves in the measurable value of the stock market.

I want to introduce an approach on how to identify relevant cycles and how to use this information for trading. This approach is not entirely new. But the way I use the "cyclic approach" is. Moreover, I throw a few of the universe's energy cycles into the mix. This combination is truly unique in that all details are explained and that this approach is deciphered into a complete trading approach.

Cycles are important.

Cycles surround us and influence our daily lives. Many events are cyclical in motion. There is the ebb and the flow of waves and the inhaling and exhaling of humans.

Our daily work schedule is determined by the day and night cycles that come with the rotation of the Earth around its own axis. The orbit of the Moon around the Earth causes the tides of the oceans. Cycles also have an impact on women from their teenage years on – the menstruation cycle.

Gardeners have long understood the advantages of working with cycles to ensure successful germination of seeds and high-quality harvest. They work in harmony with the cycles to attain the best results, the best crops.

We experience four seasons every year, namely the changes in climate, resulting from the rotation of the Earth around the Sun. This seasonal cycle creates the changes in conditions that affect all living beings on Earth. One common cycle based on seasonal conditions is the bird migration, a regular seasonal journey undertaken by many species of birds.

You would wait until early spring to plant new seeds to take advantage of the rise in pulsing energy of the warming spring temperatures. Knowing when the sun will rise may not seem like a prediction, because we associate prediction with uncertainty and risk, but it is, nonetheless, a prediction of future events that is highly accurate.

These cycles are largely based on the cyclical movements of the Sun and Moon.

However, there is strong evidence that other additional energy cycles in the universe influence our life here on Earth. Independent research by the University of California and the University of Kansas has revealed that the rise and fall of species on Earth seems to be driven by the motions of our solar system as it travels through the Milky Way. Some scientists believe that this cosmic force may provide the answer to some of the biggest questions about Earth's biological history (Schwarzschild, 2007). Finally, cycles have a long history in explaining our behavior on Earth. We can go back a long time in history to recognize that life follows a path of time cycles. We can even find reference to this in the Bible.

ಸಂ A Time for Everything ಲ

There is a time for everything,
and a season for every activity under heaven:

a time to be born and a time to die,
a time to plant and a time to uproot,

a time to kill and a time to heal,
a time to tear down and a time to build,

a time to weep and a time to laugh,
a time to mourn and a time to dance,

a time to scatter stones and a time to gather them,
a time to embrace and a time to refrain,

a time to search and a time to give up,
a time to keep and a time to throw away,

a time to tear and a time to mend,
a time to be silent and a time to speak,

a time to love and a time to hate,
a time for war and a time for peace.

Ecclesiastes 3:1-8

Introduction - It's all about cycles

If there is indeed a time for everything that explains and predicts our behavior, this must also be applicable to people's economic hopes, which manifest themselves in the value of the stock market.

Two well-known pioneers who applied cyclic analysis in the stock market are W.D. Gann and J.M. Hurst. Gann used cyclic and geometric time and price patterns, but did not elaborate the details of his approach. His work is still a mystery to many of us.

Hurst was the first to introduce cycle analysis to the technical analysis of the stock market. Even today, a lot of cycle forecasters, like Peter Eliades, successfully use the techniques of Hurst's approach outlined in his seminal work "The Profit MAGIC of Stock Transaction Timing". For example, Hurst demonstrated that the only difference between a head and shoulders pattern and a double top pattern is the phasing of the cyclic components.

Additionally, a paper published by three authors from the MIT Laboratory for Financial Engineering in 2000 concludes that "technical patterns do provide information. It does raise the possibility that [pattern] analysis can add value to the investment process." (Lo; Mamaysky; Wang; 2000)

Today we have evidence that detecting patterns adds value to the investment process and that all technical patterns can be rebuilt by means of cyclic components. In this regard, it should be valuable to think in terms of cycles rather than using a framework that consists of static chart patterns.

If this is the case and has already been widely acknowledged, why are only a few traders and investors using cyclic analysis in the stock market?

The likely answer to that question is because cyclic analysis is extremely difficult to put into practice. It requires a great deal of work and some complex mathematics that is not easy for everyone to apply. Additionally, a number of obstacles exist that hamper the use of cycle analysis by traders:

1. <u>The gap in speech/language between cycle researchers and traders</u>

   One reason cycle analysis is often limited to scientific researchers is the linguistic barrier. This becomes clear in the following example:

   - "The actual support level identified, coupled with Fibonacci retracement, suggests the presence of strong buying opportunities in the near-term."

   - "The magnitude of the first six frequency patterns and the statistical significance of the Q-score suggest the presence of a high-frequency predictable component in the stock market."

   Despite the fact that both statements have the same meaning, most readers will understand the first statement but find the second puzzling.

2. <u>Gap in knowledge: Trading expertise (visual) vs. cycles calculation (mathematical)</u>

   The second gap is attributable to different knowledge areas. Technical analysis is primarily visual while cycle analysis is mostly numerical.

   The visual mode of technical analysis is one of the few human cognitive activities where computers do not yet have an absolute advantage over us. Numerical analysis involves the study of data sets *after* the fact. But in real-time environments, traders and investors have to decide in the now and their decisions are mainly based on visual pattern recognition from charts. In many cases, the human eye can perform this "signal extraction" quickly and accurately. There are no, or more precisely, only few available cycle tools that are able to present the visual information extracted from numerical cycle analysis to the trader and function as a visual guide.

3. <u>Gap: Forecasting vs. trading (different types of market approaches)</u>

The third reason cyclic analysis is something of a rarity in trading is the distinction between forecasting and trading.

Most traders are not interested in predicting the future; instead, they enter a trade based on probabilities, apply money management and exit the trade sticking to clear rules. They claim that this is "the real way of trading". Traders are convinced that they can make money by simply entering the trade randomly and by applying money management and exit rules.

On the other end of the spectrum are the "forecasters". This group of experts is not interested in money management and exit strategies. They solely base their trading on predicting future market behavior. A gap exists in the mindsets of these two groups characterized by an ongoing debate about trading versus forecasting.

Cyclic analysis is more of a forecasting method. It is therefore not surprising that this tool cannot be found in an active trader's toolbox. The active trader is not interested in "forecasting". He manages his trade.

I want to try to bridge these gaps with this publication. At least a little bit. Because in the end, the essence of cyclic analysis for trading is pretty straightforward.

You don't have to dwell on how to arrive at these results on your own. It is all ready for use in the trading arena for the trader who wants it all in "visual" form. And the explanations I provide will give you the necessary insights and background on how to effectively use these tools.

This book differs from traditional ones on cycle approaches, because it does not deliver a static framework of cycles that data need to be squeezed into.

That is, I do not try to make the market "fit" into a particular cycle framework which has at least two different possible outcomes. "Failures" within static frameworks are often explained with a complex set of named exceptions and deviations. The listing of exceptions after a static cycle framework fails (such as: "A cycle inversion took place") is of little comfort to the investor who has made investments based on one of the delivered predictions.

I will begin with the raw data and search for those cycles that actually exist. We will not follow the path of static cycles with a fixed length or phase.

I will present a dynamic approach on how to use cycle analysis for trading. This cycle approach can be adjusted to the current vibration in the stock market.

All cycle tools are included and can easily be dragged 'n dropped onto the chart. But always remember that a fool with a tool is still a fool.

I hope you treat this newly gained knowledge with respect and wisdom.

2. How to detect and measure cycles in the stock market

In this chapter I will introduce a completely new proprietary algorithm to detect active cycles in any financial instrument for any time frame. All my research results have been integrated into a comprehensive digital signal processing engine for cycle analysis. This engine works together with WhenToTrade Charting Platform and Wave59. The robustness and reliability of this algorithm will outperform all existing engines I personally am aware of. So you will get the best toolkit available on the market for detecting cycles. With this "weapon", you will be able to discover new areas to apply cyclic information to trading.

2.1 The cyclic approach put into practice

Most approaches try to identify cycles based on known reasons / forces and apply them to the actual price chart by selecting the last visual trough or crest and plotting the known cycle length into the future.

Such approaches have two main problems:

1. You have to be able to "detect" the right high or low to establish the starting point for the cycle forecast. But markets are usually not so clear-cut and it is very difficult to identify the correct highs/lows with your eyes on the chart. The market does not only consist of one cycle – there are always lots of cycles active at the same time making it virtually impossible to detect the right ones.

2. You have to know the reasons/forces behind each cycle and which ones to select (like tidal movements, planetary positions/aspects, etc.). However, there simply are too many cycle factors that *could* be active. It is always easy to say one was right or wrong *after* the fact. There are also far too many cycles that have a potentially high

probability of influencing the markets. In hindsight, it is always easy to identify which cycle was active at a given time and why. But this approach is only of limited utility for identifying the right moment in time to trade in real-time. Retrospectively, it also seems highly probable that such active cycles relate to important turning points in the market. However, there are simply too many potential cycles that would have to be taken into consideration in real-time, i.e., when looking forward. Assessing the probability in advance that a given cycle will actually be active at a particular time is like buying the winning lottery ticket.

From a research perspective, I include a large number of these approaches in the analysis of planetary movements and their influence on financial markets.

However, my own experiences also tell me that these approaches are not suitable for trading in real-time, i.e., for planning ahead.

I would therefore like to present an alternative approach. In principle, I am convinced that astrological cycles have an influence on us, in particular those connected with the Sun and Moon.

With reference to trading the stock market, however, I am less interested in determining precisely which astrological cycle based on which constellation, ephemeris and planetary aspects is currently exercising influence on the market. Rather, I am interested "simply" in identifying the cycles that are actually active in select financial instruments (the index) and their relevance for trading the stock market. One could compare this approach to reverse engineering. The end point as it is (the index) is taken and broken down into its basic components to understand how everything is linked together. Insights gained thereby are then used for one's own purposes. In terms of the final outcome, it is of no significance why this or that basic component is used. In other words, the reason *why* specific cycles are active is not important - the fact of the matter is that they are. And this insight alone is significant to further process this information to conduct successful trading.

The pivotal point of this approach, therefore, is a method that can accurately determine which cycle is currently active with regard to the length, amplitude, and duration of the last high and low of a data series.

2.2 The Cycle Scanner: Introduction of a new & proprietary cycle detection algorithm

To borrow from the language of engineering, frequency analysis is used to measure cycles. As traders, however, we should not be deterred by these "technical" terms. Frequency is nothing other than "oscillations (cycles) per time frame". In technical-mathematical analysis, the measurement of frequency is therefore repeatedly described. Time-frequency analysis identifies the point in time at which various signal frequencies are present, usually by calculating a spectrum at regular time intervals.

The application of frequency analysis to financial data is in principle nothing new and has already been described in numerous articles. However, current methods often come up against barriers in terms of application in financial markets. This is attributable to the specific features of the financial markets. Financial markets are influenced by numerous overlapping waves, whose strength and phases vary over time and are consequently not constant. The data are also overlaid by significant one-off events (noise) and quasi-linear trends. The classical methods of frequency analysis are not designed for the special characteristics of financial markets. Hence, the established methods are largely unable to provide reliable results as far as practical trading signals are concerned.

However, this book is designed for practical application in trading and forecasting and is not intended to be a scientific publication on new algorithms. Against this background, I would like, on the one hand, to abstain from the academic debate about the advantages and disadvantages of individual methods and, on the other, to avoid repeating what has already been said in other publications. For readers with an academic inclination and who are interested in the aspects addressed here, the publications by Meyer Analytics (www.meyeranalytics.com) and John Ehlers (www.mesa.com) are recommended as introductory reading.

I have experimented with nearly all approaches and algorithms of frequency analysis, in particular with the algorithms of the Discrete Fourier Transform (DFT), Maximum Entropy Spectral Analysis (MESA), and wavelets.

Ultimately, however, none of these methods reliably and adequately identified cycles to meet my requirements. It has taken me approximately three years of intensive research and development to mold these methods for the purpose of cycle detection in financial instruments in a truly reliable way.

My method is specially designed for analysis of the financial time series datasets. It combines the advantages of current methods but tries to the extent possible to eliminate the disadvantages of the individual approaches with reference to the specific features of the financial time series.

By combining special DFT methods (including the Goertzel algorithm), validation by means of statistical measurement methods (including the Bartels Test) and my own approaches to pre-processing (detrending), I have been able to develop my own reliable method for measuring cycles in financial time series datasets.

Building on my expertise as an engineer, software developer, and trader, I have been able to develop and integrate this method into a standalone Charting Platform.

My proposed method provides the spectrum of frequency analysis for every possible financial instrument and every possible time frame. The following results are thereby provided:

1. Presenting a visual spectrum of the wave analysis of a length of 5 - 300 price bars;

2. Determining the peaks in the spectrum analysis - i.e., the relevant and significant cycles;

3. Filtering of the values derived from the frequency analysis through statistical validation, i.e., identifying the cycles that are actually "active";

4. Determining the precise phase and amplitude of every active cycle;

5. Output of the data in a form comprehensible to traders, i.e.,

- the phase in the form of the date of the last low point

- the amplitude in the form of the current price-scale, and

- the length of the wave in the form of the number of bars on the chart;

6. Determining the "strength" of a cycle by establishing the price movement per bar ("cycle strength").

In classical cycle analysis, the waves with the largest amplitude are usually described as dominant. However, for us as traders the relative influence of a cycle per time unit - i.e., per bar on the chart - is of much greater interest. Therefore, the so-called cycle strength is ultimately used as a measurement value for the cycle with the greatest influence per price bar. The value with the highest cycle strength will be used again later as representing the dominant cycle.

These results and the mathematical method alone would fill an entire book on their own. As this publication is designed for more practical purposes and aims to advance the method's successful application in trading, I prefer to focus on *how* the method is actually applied.

The following examples serve to illustrate the application of this analytical algorithm.

2.3 Example 1: Dataset with 2 cycles

This example is of a more theoretical nature, considering that this type of "pure" data is not, of course, available in financial markets. I would like to, however, begin with this example for illustrative purposes.

Before we turn to actual financial series, independent test data are used for verification. These test data are produced separately and read into WhenToTrade Charting Platform again for analysis as simple daily charts.

This case involves two simple, combined waves:

- Cycle 1: Length of 30 / Amplitude of 40
- Cycle 2: Length of 95 / Amplitude of 55

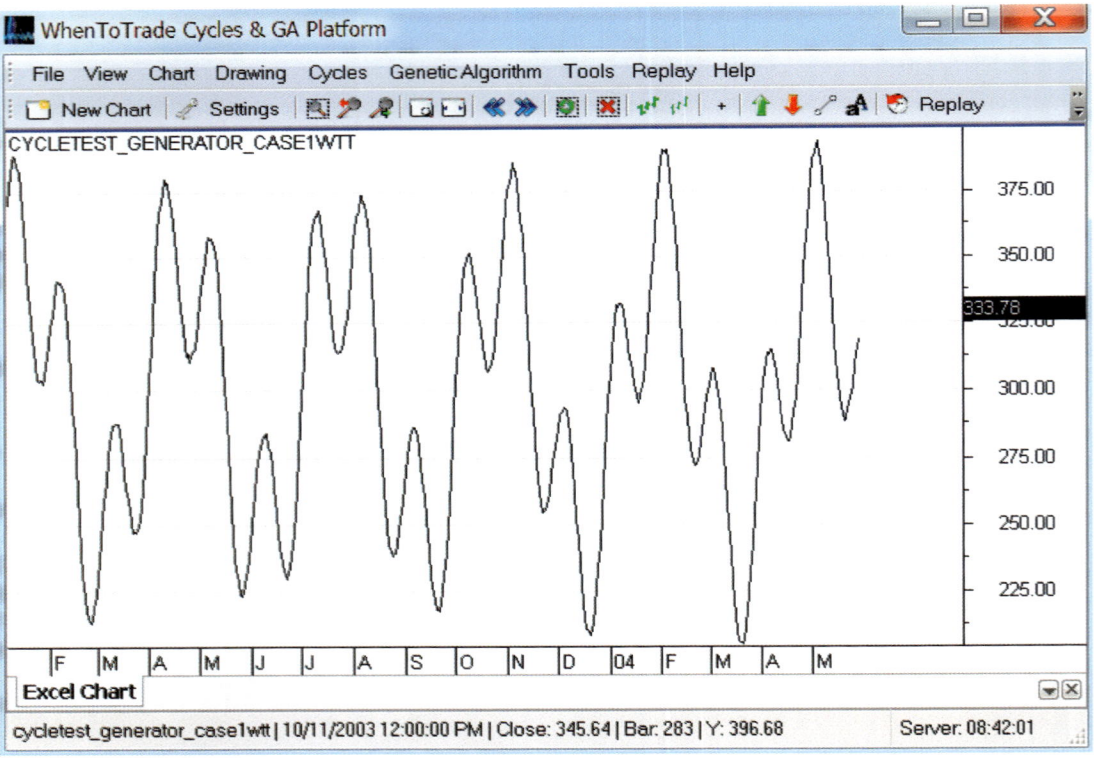

Figure 2-1: Sample Dataset 1

The indicator in the lower part of the chart shows the complete spectrum of the wave analysis. Two peaks can be clearly identified. The first lies at a length of precisely 30 and the second at a length of exactly 95 days.

The data are also found in detail in the log:

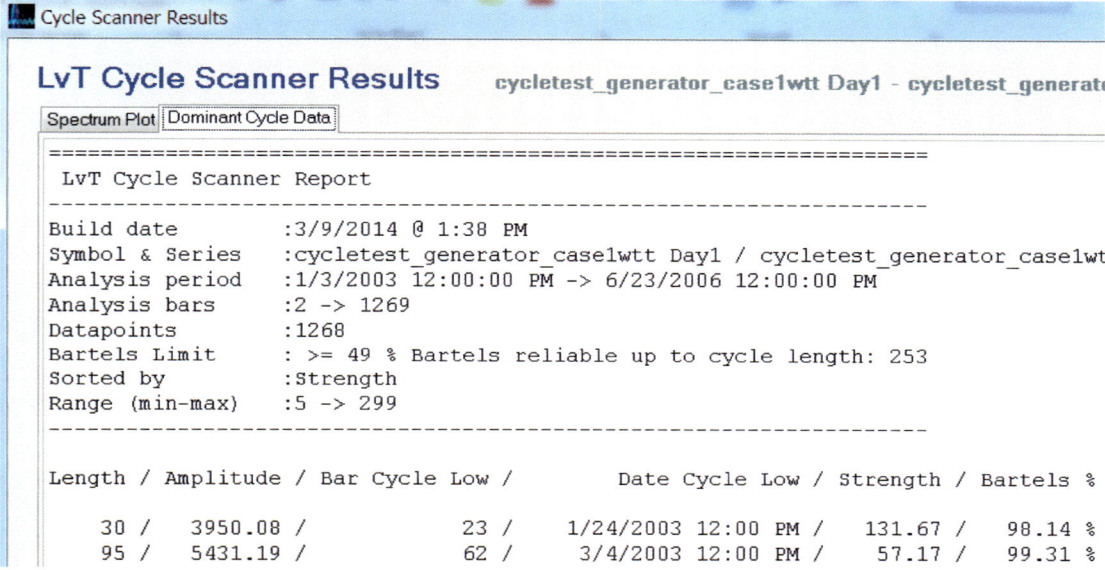

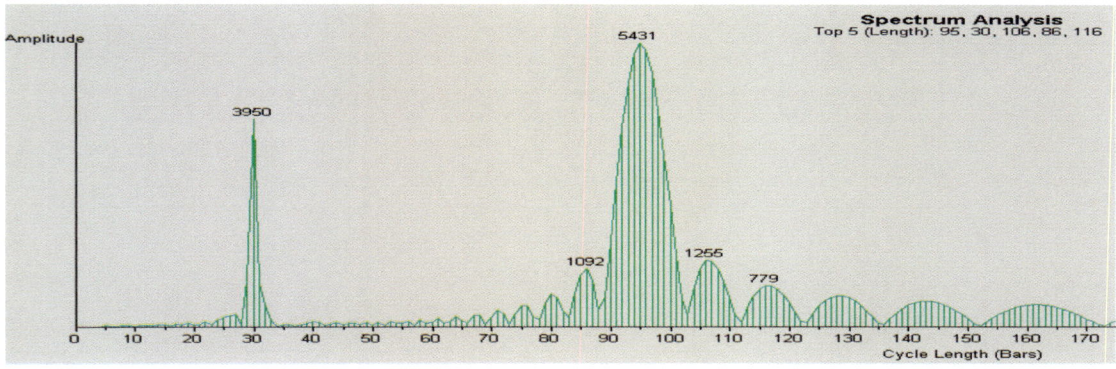

Figure 2-2: Cycle Scanner log file & spectrum plot for sample Dataset 1

The method was thus able to identify the two waves with absolute precision with respect to their length and amplitude. You will also be able to identify the output of the phases based on the date of the first low.

The additional statistical test result (Bartels score) of over 98% also confirms the actual presence of the cycles in the data series. When working with cycles in financial data, I recommend disregarding identified cycles with a Bartels score below 50%. A lower value indicates that this wavelength does not have a reliably stable presence in the data series over a specific period of time. Such information is particularly relevant for later use in trading. Although a cycle may have been correctly identified by spectrum analysis, it may very well be that that this cycle only occurs (or occurred) once or twice in the entire data series. We do not want to use cycles that only "appear once" as our trading signals. The Bartels Test is thus a measure that indicates whether the presence of the cycle statistically identified in the data series over several runtimes could be confirmed.

The fact that these two waves can be identified despite the use of a time frame for the analysis that does not even cover two complete wave lengths (in relation to 95 days) is of further significance. Below is the test analysis when only approximately 170 data points (i.e., approximately five months of daily data) are used for analysis:

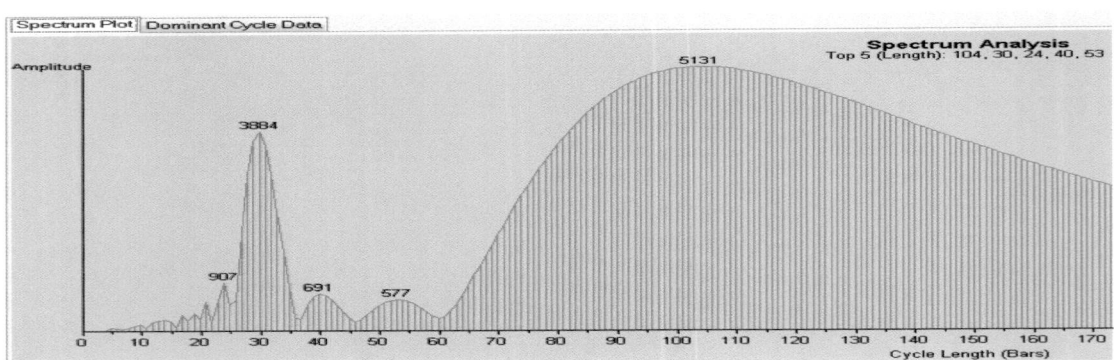

Figure 2-3: Spectrum plot for Dataset 1 with small amount of data

```
Spectrum Plot | Dominant Cycle Data
================================================================
 LvT Cycle Scanner Report
----------------------------------------------------------------
 Build date          :3/9/2014 @ 1:45 PM
 Symbol & Series     :cycletest_generator_case1wtt Day1 / cycletest_generator_case1wt
 Analysis period     :1/3/2003 12:00:00 PM -> 6/23/2003 12:00:00 PM
 Analysis bars       :2 -> 173
 Datapoints          :172
 Bartels Limit       : >= 49 % Bartels reliable up to cycle length: 34
 Sorted by           :Strength
 Range (min-max)     :5 -> 299
----------------------------------------------------------------

 Length / Amplitude / Bar Cycle Low /       Date Cycle Low / Strength / Bartels %
     30 /   3884.18 /           24 /    1/25/2003 12:00 PM /   129.47 /   97.93 %
    104 /   5131.13 /           60 /     3/2/2003 12:00 PM /    49.34 /   63.21 %
```

Figure 2-4: Detected cycles with small amount of data

Even the cycle with a length of 95 days (three months) is thus identified at a measured length of 104 days in this short data series (a range of analysis of just five months) with an accuracy of over 90%.

This is another major advantage of this new combined method. Whereas classical methods often require four or more complete waves to be present and the range of analysis to be at least 3-4 times as long as the largest wavelength to be identified, less than twice the longest wavelength of analytical data suffices to complete the analysis in this case.

2.4 Example 2: Dataset with 2 cycles + trend

In this example, we add trends of various strengths to the previously determined waves. This reflects a key characteristic of financial markets and will therefore be of crucial importance later. The algorithm does not necessarily have to be affected by trends.

We have to ensure that the cycles can still be correctly identified despite the additional trends.

Here we will combine two waves again and add up, down, and sideways trends of varying strengths.

The following wavelengths were used for the test data:

- Wave 1: Length 30 / Amplitude 20
- Wave 2: Length 200 / Amplitude 80

Accordingly, the chart looks like this:

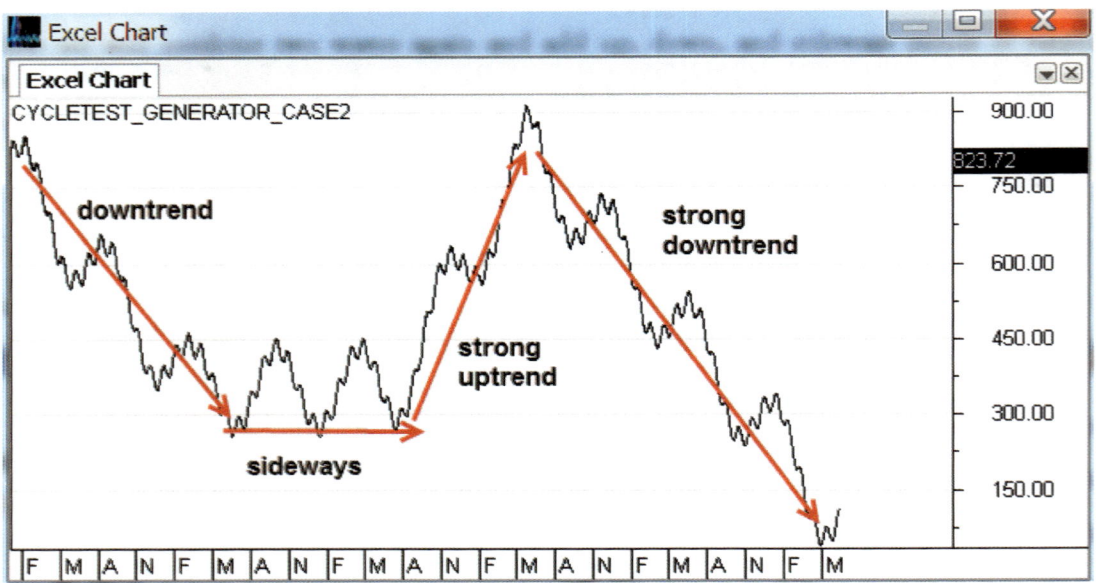

Figure 2-5: Sample Dataset 2 / Two waves with linear trends of different forces

The spectrum analysis over a short predefined time frame now provides the following result:

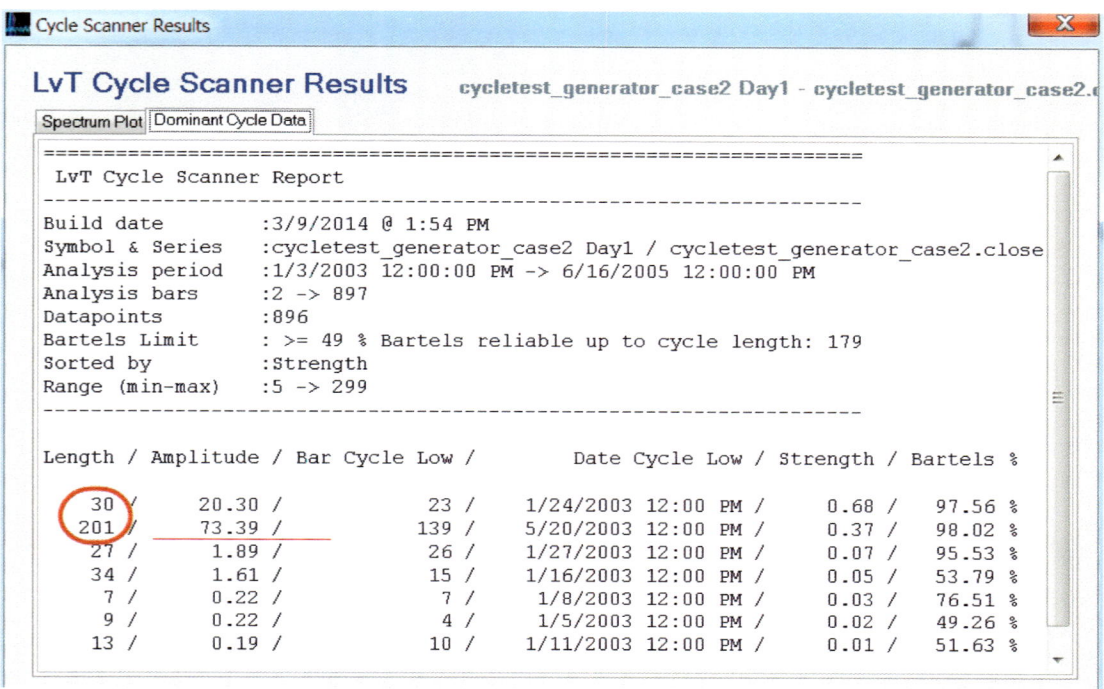

Figure 2-6: Result of the spectrum analysis for Dataset 2 in the script log

It is clearly visible that the algorithm was able to detect both cycles. The algorithm was not affected by the trends that were included. It was successful in "detrending" the data prior to the frequency analysis. That is, the algorithm has a proprietary detrending function because it can deal with different forms of trends and forces. As this example shows, we have included four different trends in the analysis. Notwithstanding, the algorithm was able to filter out all of these trends.

The other identified cycles printed in the log with a length of 27 and 34 days can easily be classified as non-relevant noise. This is clearly discernible when looking at the amplitude information. The first two had a price amplitude of 20 and 74 (as was precisely the case for the input cycles). And then there is a huge jump in the detected amplitudes, from 74 down to 1 and below. This is a clear signal that you can disregard this information, because the "low" amplitude will have no effect.

Conclusion:

The Cycle Scanner is able to deal with different trends.

2.5 Example 3: Dataset with 2 cycles + trend + noise

Now we will increase the complexity and add the third feature of financial markets: A lot of random noise. This "noise" may, for example, be generated by news that compels the market to "jump" in one direction or the other.

We will use the same dataset from Example 2 (wavelength of 30 and 200 with trends) for this example and add a lot of noise to the data.

This is what our test dataset looks like now. Go ahead and compare it with the chart above. You can clearly see how distorted the price data looks and that the smaller cycle is lost in all the noise.

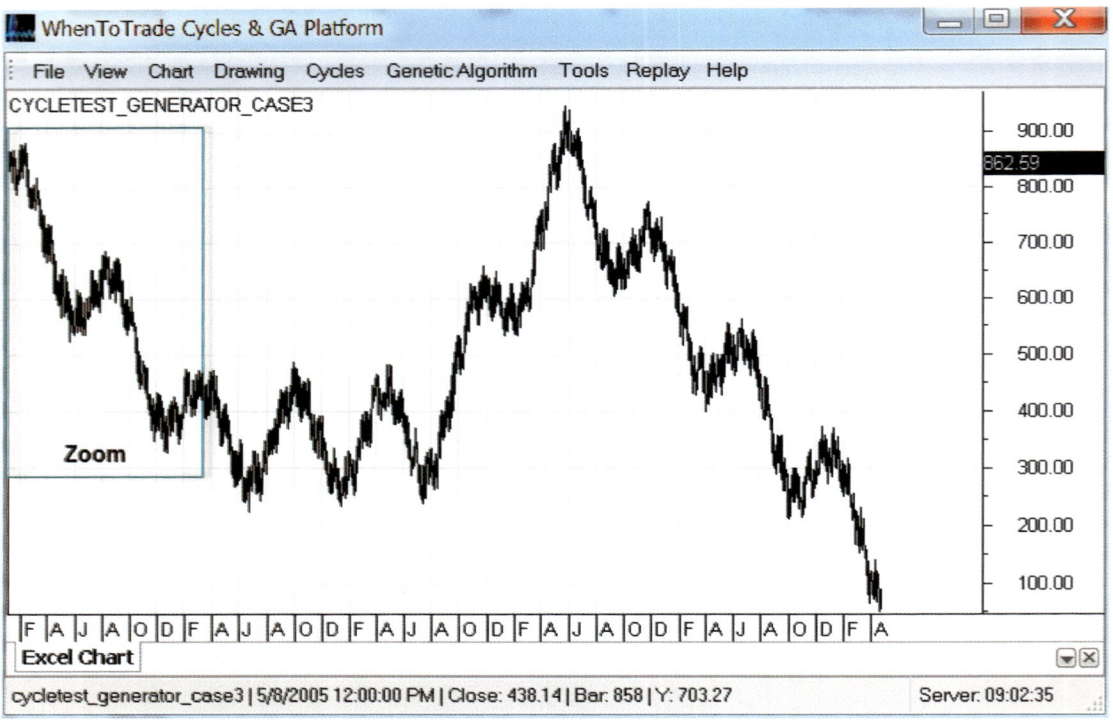

Figure 2-7: Sample Dataset 3 – 2 waves + trends + noise

On a side note: The noise level is a lot higher than the amplitude of the smaller cycle. So we have a low signal-to-noise ratio here with regard to the smaller cycle. A closer look at the data demonstrates what I am talking about:

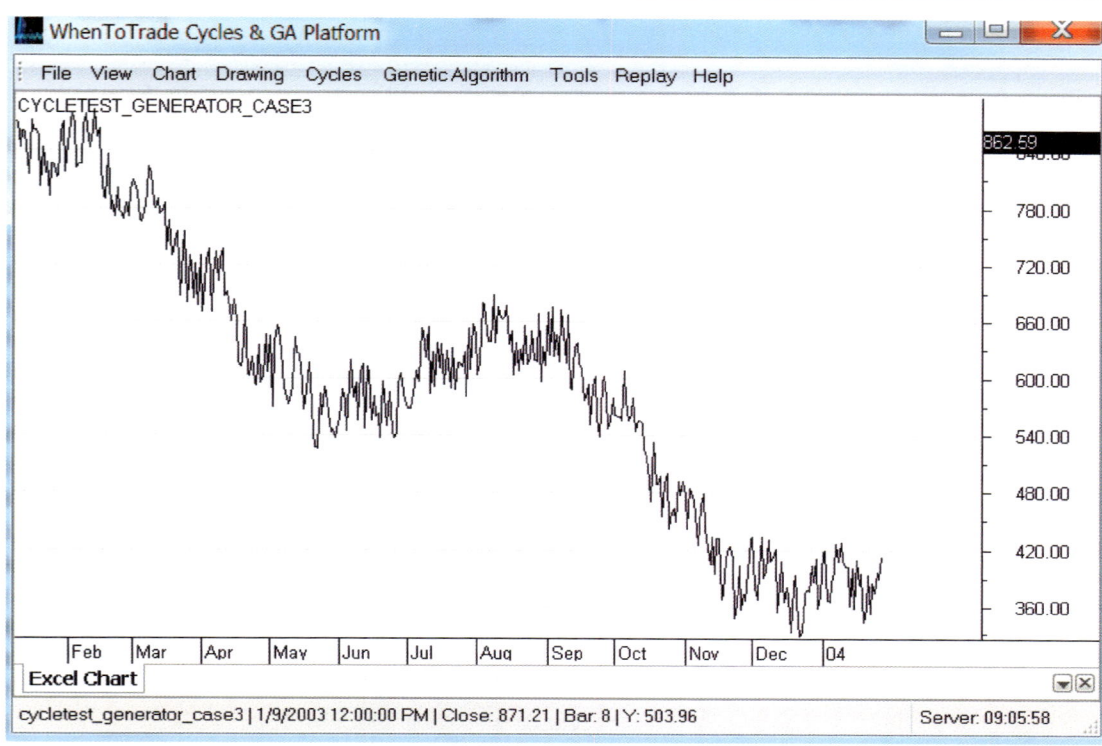

Figure 2-8: Close-up of the same data

Here comes the challenge for our new algorithm:

1. The longer-term cycle with a length of 200 days only occurs 1.5 times in the one-year dataset. It would therefore be difficult to detect the running 200 bars cycle if we only have such a short history of data to analyze.
2. The short-term wave with a length of 30 days is completely "lost" in the high noise ratio.
3. The actual downtrend also distorts and stretches the dataset.

Let's see if our algorithm is still able to detect the two cycles.

Here is the result of the analysis:

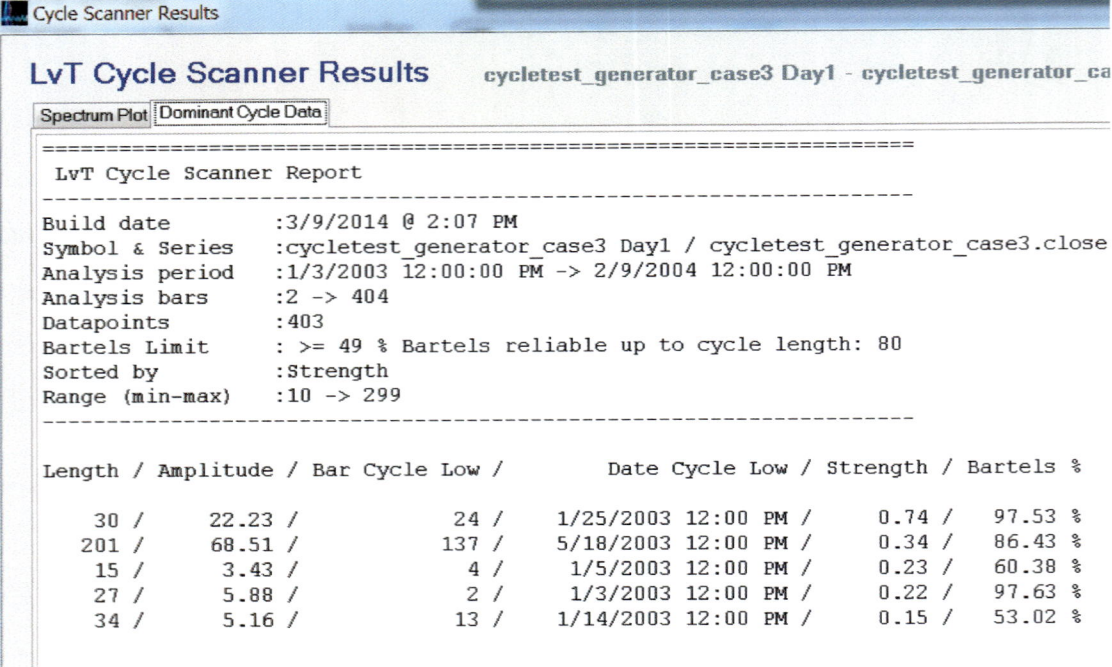

Figure 2-9: Analysis results for sample Dataset 3

And again:

The algorithm was not affected by all the noise and trend information. It correctly identified the two cycles with a length of 30 and 201 days. The other cycles with a length of 15,27 and 34 days can be "overlooked" if you compare the amplitude with the first two cycles.

Conclusion: The algorithm is able to handle a high noise ratio!

Before we move on to real financial data, let me give you a brief outlook on why this information is so important and of particular interest for trading.

2.6 Step-by-step guide: How to build a forecast based on cycle detection

When we know which cycles are driving the market, we are able to use this information to build a forecast based on cycles. Let's now go over this forecasting technique step-by-step.

Step 1: Cycle analysis

At any given point in time, perform a cycle analysis based on your favorite market/index and time frame. We will use the example from case 3 for this particular scenario. So let's say it's February 9 and we're looking at the actual chart.

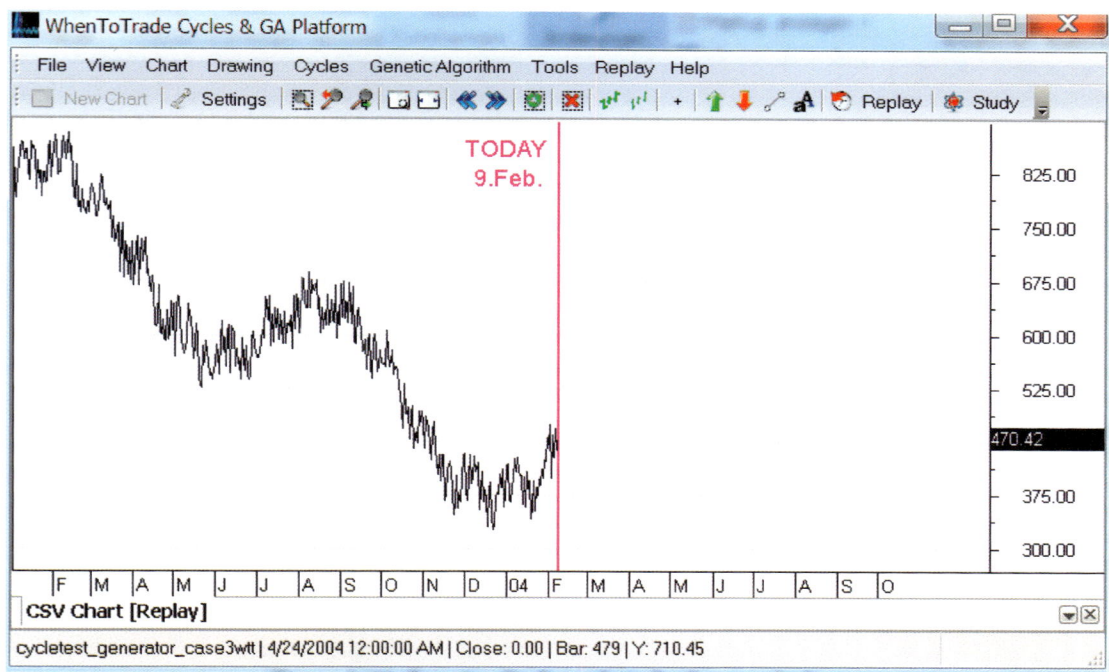

Figure 2-10: Step 1 – Cycle analysis for last year's data

Start the Cycle Scanner which will perform the cycle analysis following the steps explained in the examples above. For an analysis of a daily chart, I would recommend using 1 – 2 years of daily data. In the present example, we are "only" using one year for our analysis.

Results of this analysis:

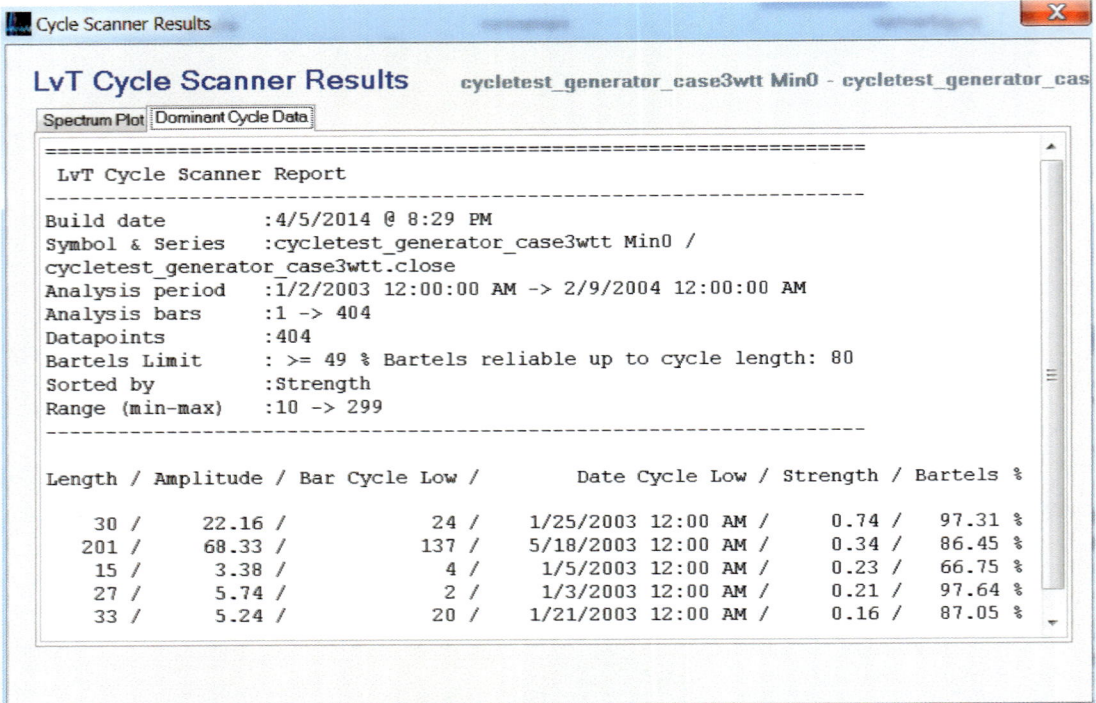

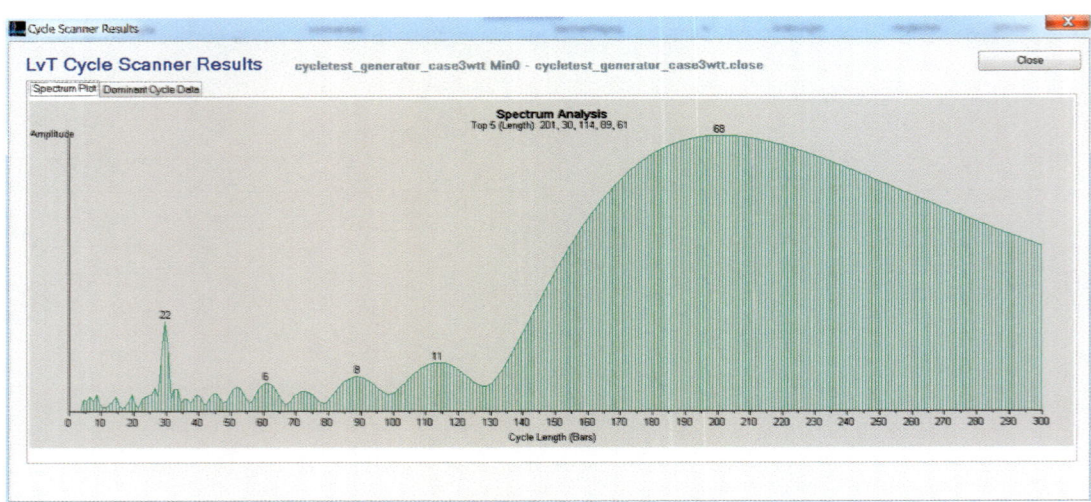

How to detect and measure cycles in the stock market

Step 2: Plot active cycles and expand them into the future

Now that we know that the cycles with a length of 30 and 201 days are active, we can start developing a forecast. Hence, we will plot each cycle according to the information provided by the Cycle Scanner.

Open the Cycle Plotter via the Cycles Menu and the scanner results can be loaded into the plotter toolkit just by pressing the "Load Scanner Peaks" button in the upper right corner of the window.

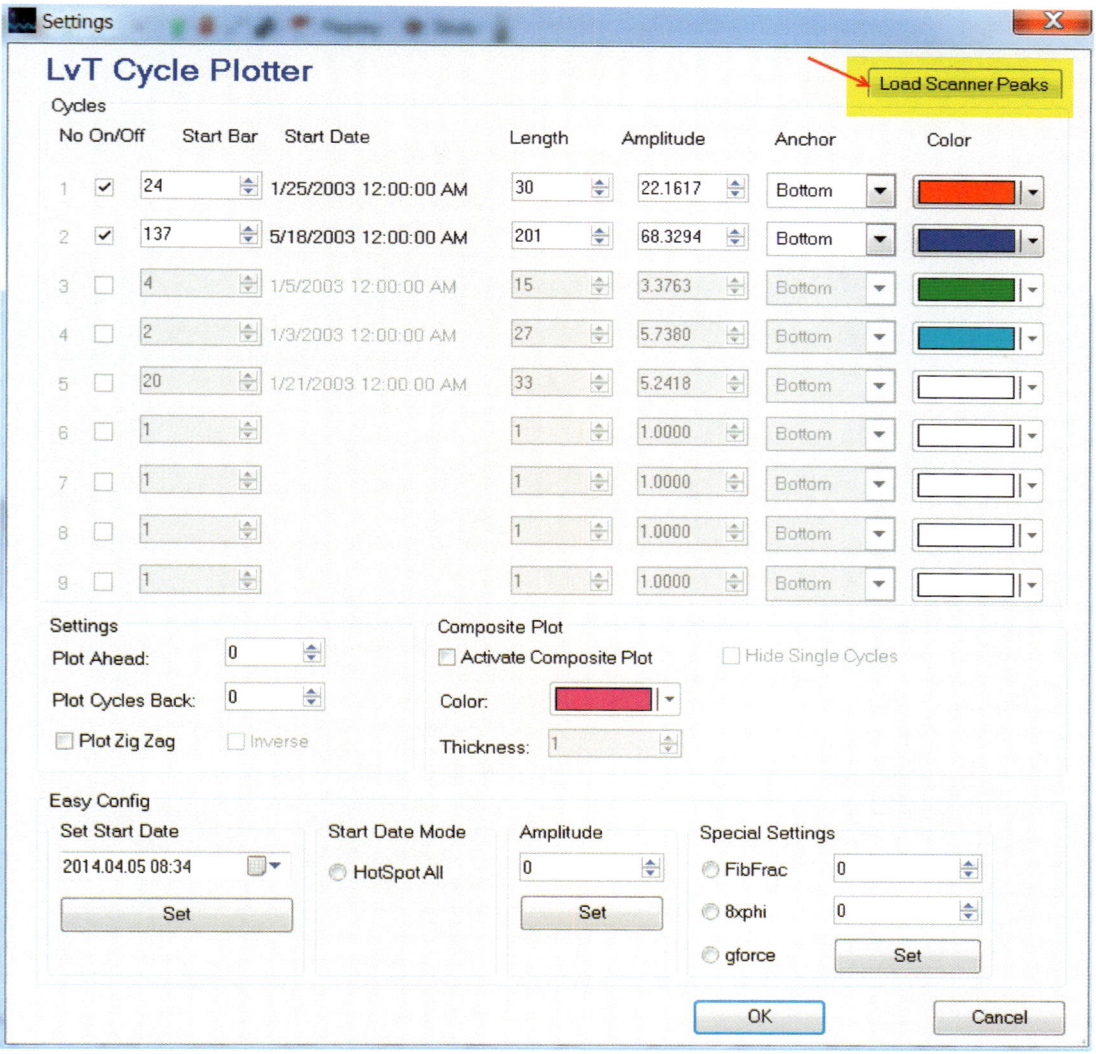

The first wave is plotted in line with the start date, amplitude, and length information. The second wave is also plotted in accordance with the given start date, amplitude, and length information.

As the illustration below shows, you can now plot the cycles in the future.

Figure 2-11: Plotting the cycles identified in the chart and in the future

Step 3: Build a composite cycle based on the cycles identified

If more than one cycle is active, you have to add all individual cycles into one "big" composite cycle. All you have to do is simply add the information of each cycle into one composite cycle. First, select one plotted cycle with the left mouse button. Once selected, press the right mouse button to display the context menu:

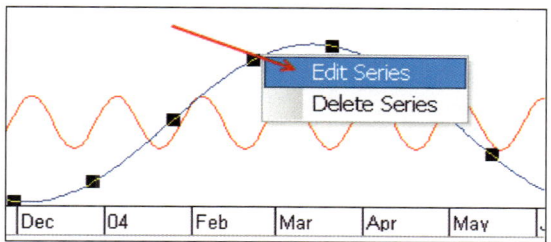

Choose "Edit Series" to open the configuration panel again. Now select the option to plot the cycles as one composite cycle "Activate Composite Plot". Choose if you want to see the individual signal cycles, select the color and thickness.

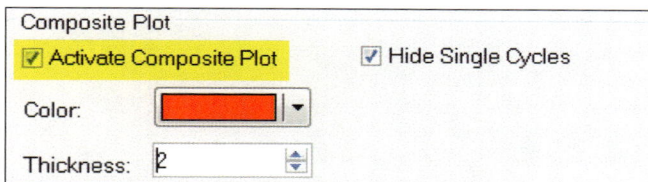

The following illustration presents the composite cycle derived from these two cycles.

How to detect and measure cycles in the stock market

Figure 2-12: Composite cycle based on two separate cycles.

Step 4: Mark expected future turning points

Now we are able to see how this composite forecast will perform in the future. And we are also able to spot incidences where we expect a change in trend. This information is important for going long or short selling in the market.

I have marked some incidences on the next chart which denote a turn in the composite cycle.

These turns forecast market turns. The cycles have to, of course, remain active during the next few days/weeks.

We have just created our first forecast based on cycles!

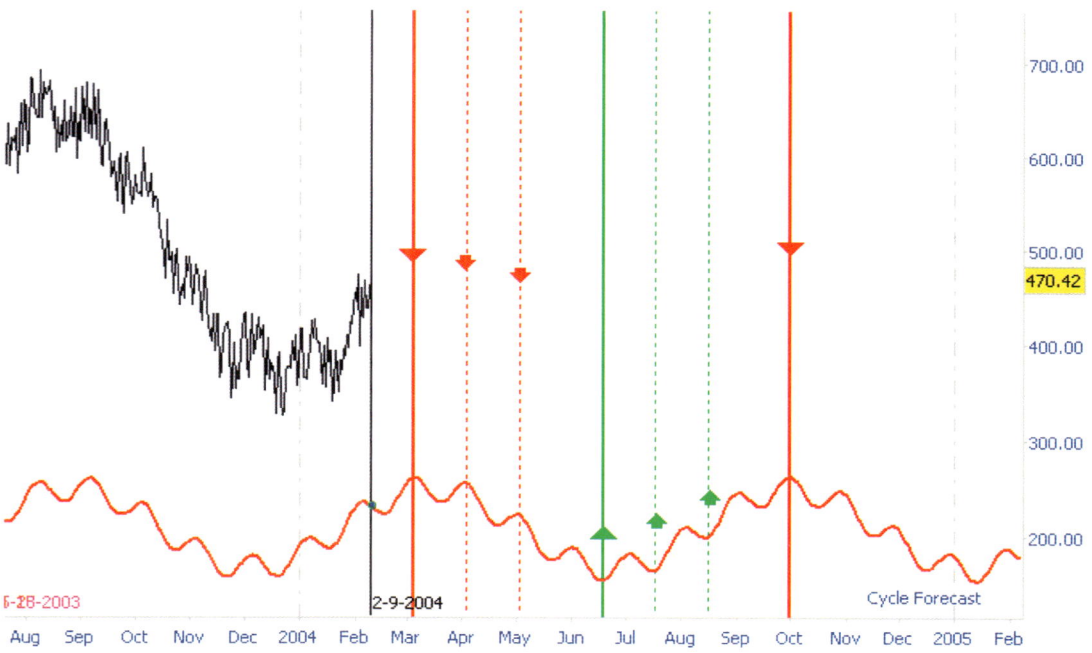

Figure 2-13: Mark expected turning points forecasted by the composite cycle

Step 5: Just see how it plays out...

Now we can move ahead in time. Our forecast will stay put. The forecast was done on February 9. And as you can see, the forecast was able to spot future turning points all the way up to the exact date.

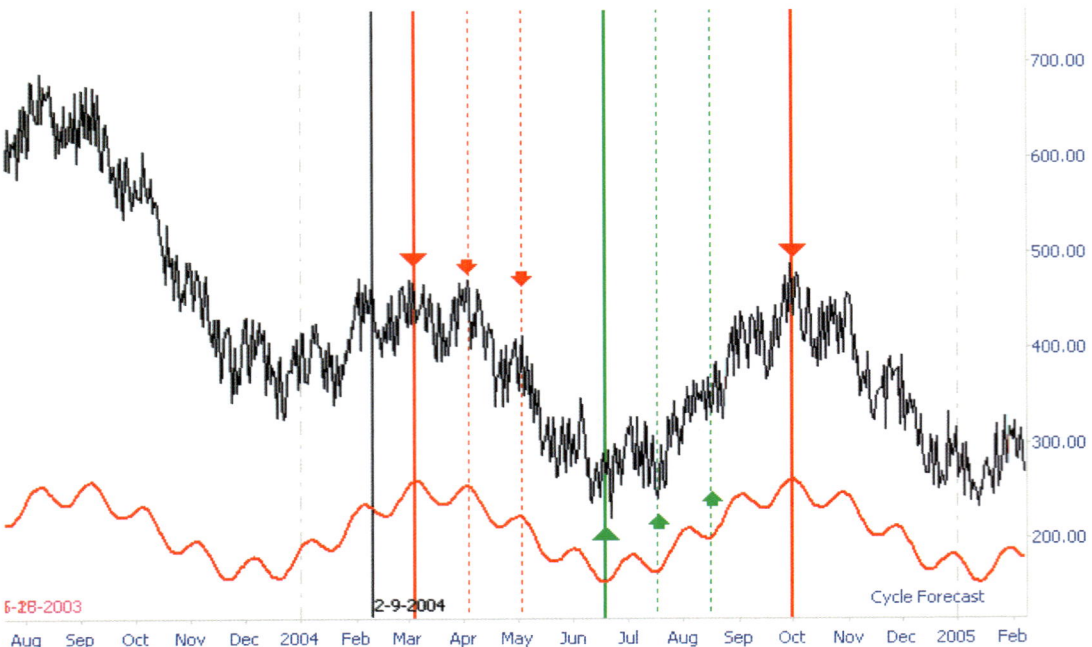

Figure 2-14: Real dataset and forecast of February 9

Here with a smoothed plotted price curve for better illustration:

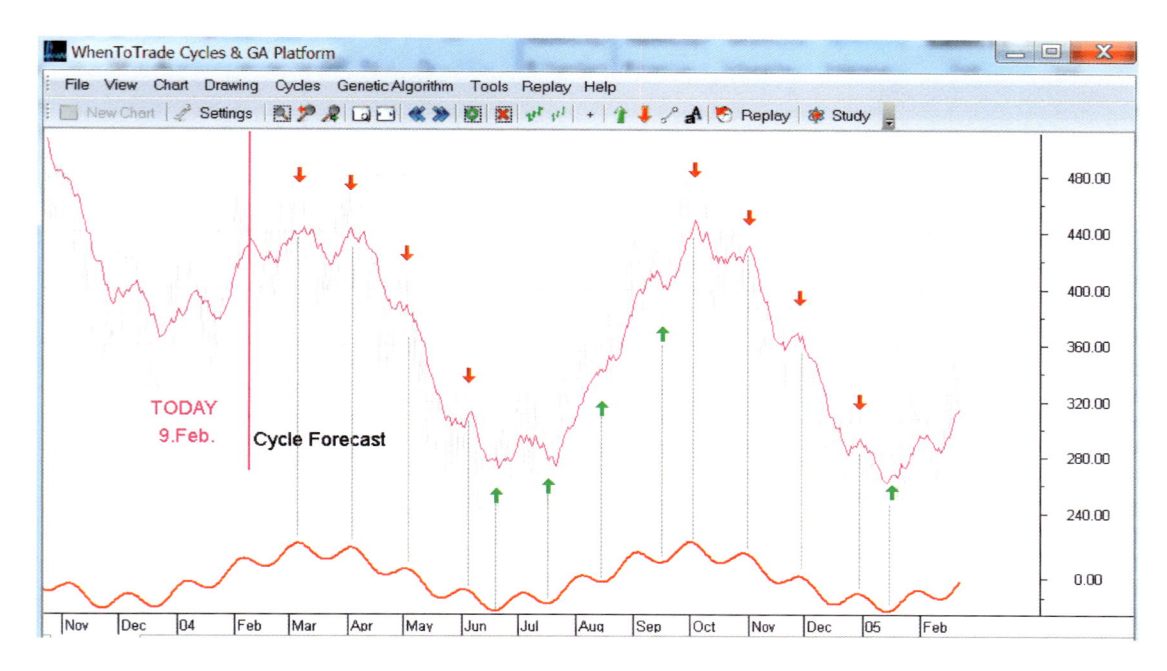

Figure 2-15: Real dataset and forecast: How it played out

As you can see, the cycles forecast is a detrended forecast. It is evident that the main trend changes from a downtrend to a sideways trend – but the cycles forecast has provided us with reliable information for trading. The trend change was not known at the time of the analysis.

This is, of course, only a theoretical example. The purpose of this example is to demonstrate how to build cycle forecast models. And you can see that if you have a reliable engine for identifying cycles, you will be able to build highly accurate forecast models. Despite a trend change and a lot of noise in the signal, our engine was able to detect the right cycles.

Using this forecasting method, you will now be able to plot cycles in the future to spot future turning points.

2.7 Example 4: Dataset with 4 cycles + trend + noise

Let's increase the degree of complexity once more with the next dataset. We will use four different cycles with different phase offsets:

Wave	Length	Amplitude
1	12	40
2	31	70
3	54	90
4	82	65

We will add different trends and a lot of noise. In this example, the average noise level is 1.5 higher than the max. amplitude of the wave with a length of 12 days. It will thus be difficult to see whether the engine can detect this small cycle despite all the noise and trend change.

This is what Dataset 4 looks like:

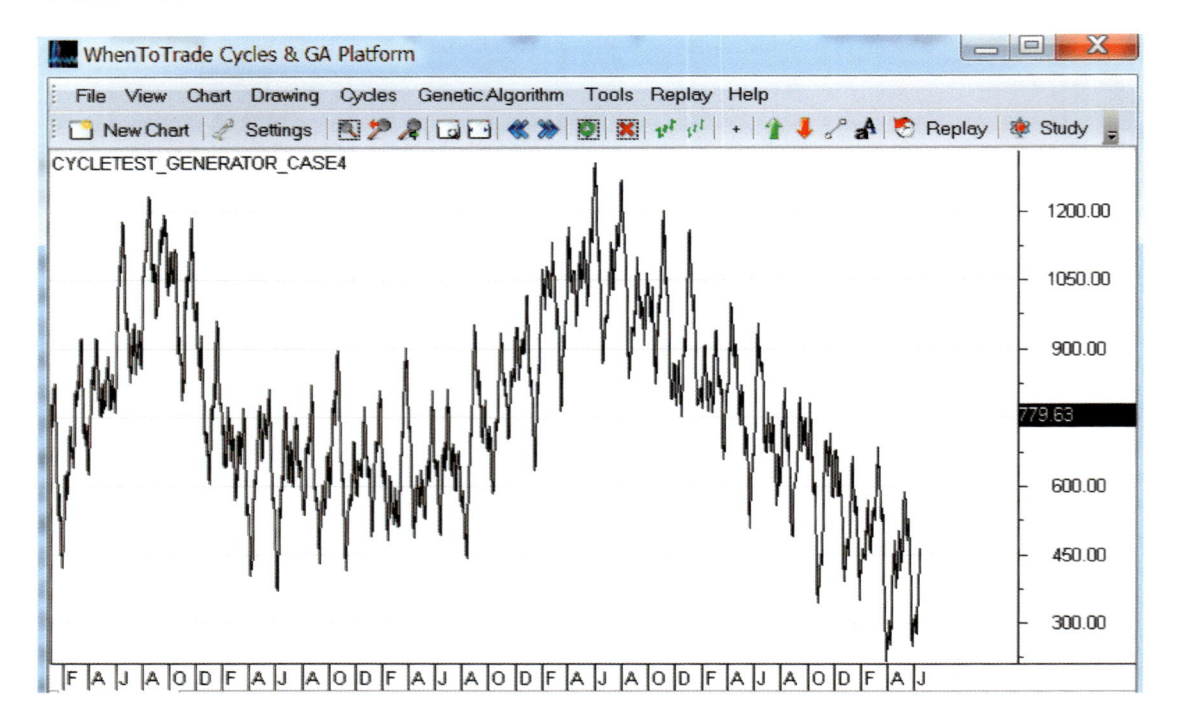

Figure 2-16: Sample Dataset 4

For our test we will again only use one year of data history. This corresponds with reality later on. I would recommend using 1-2 years of data history if you are analyzing cycles on a daily time frame.

Let's take a closer look at what I am talking about:

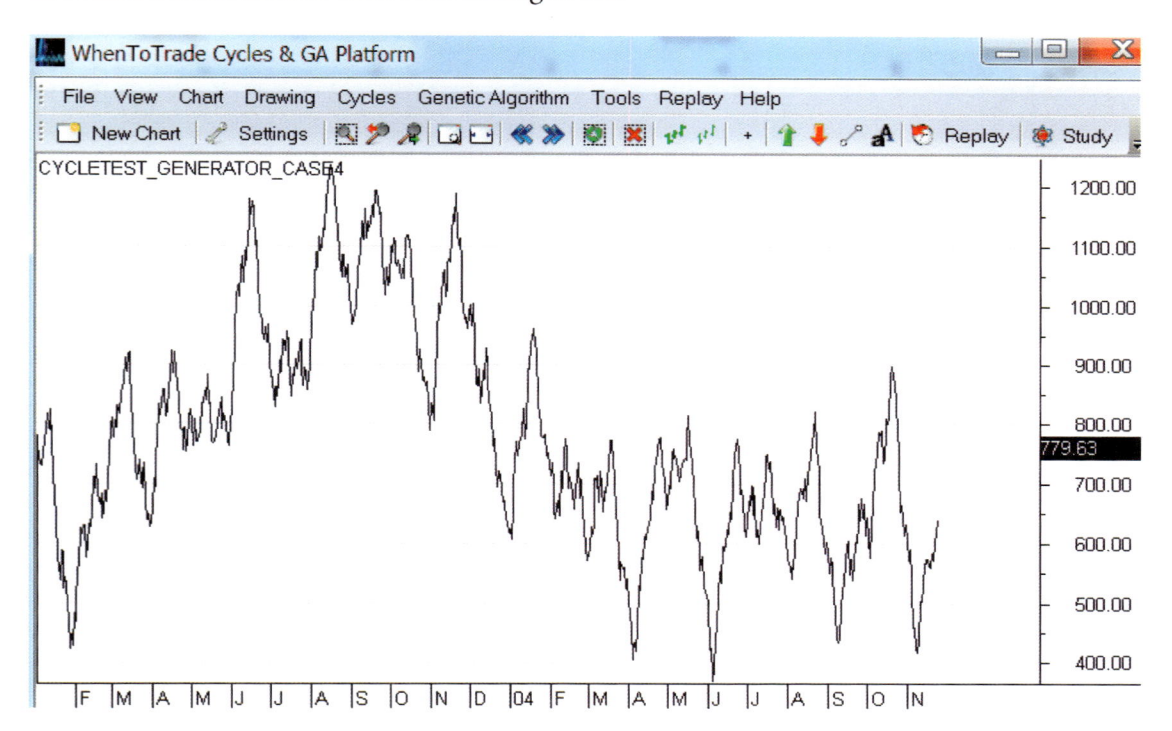

Figure 2-17: Zoom-in of Dataset 4

This example is also interesting, because we can compare traditional methods of detecting cycles. If you connect the high-high and low-low CIT on the chart, it seems we have a running cycle of around 65 calendar days.

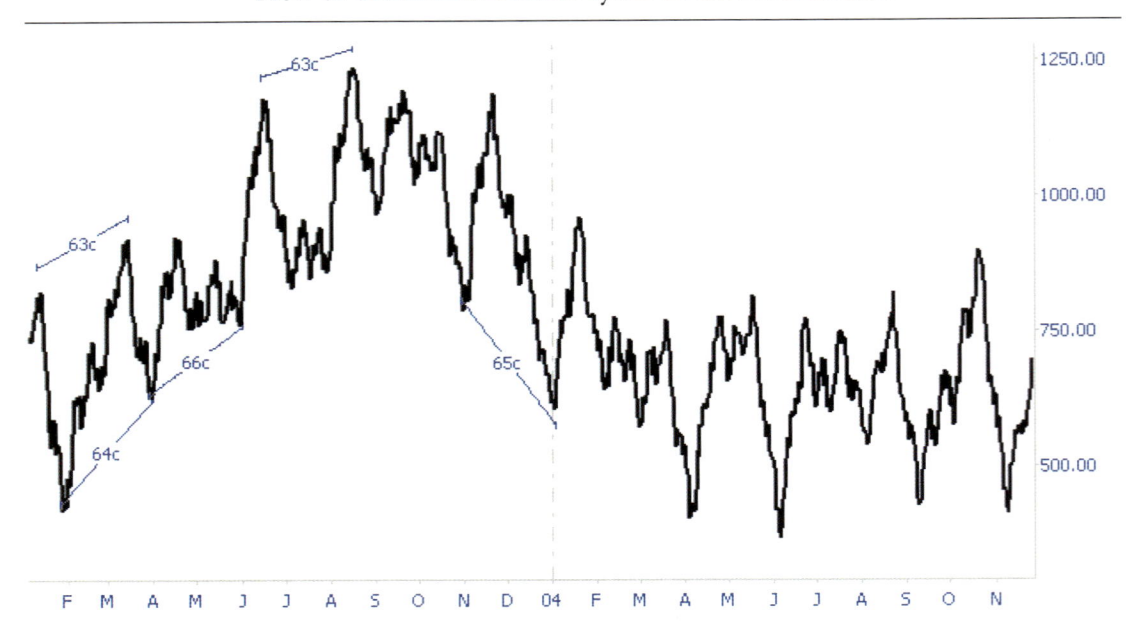

Figure 2-18: Dataset 4 – Visual impression of a cycle with a length of 65 days

However, we know that this is sample data with no cycle of 65 days! In other words, you cannot identify cycles using this "simple" method. It looks like we have an active 65 day cycle. But we will see shortly that this cycle is not useful for forecasting or trading.

To demonstrate this, let's plot a 65 CD cycle from the last low of January 4 and see whether this is useful for future trading. The standard approach would be to use this 65 CD cycle that has been visually identified and plot it in the future:

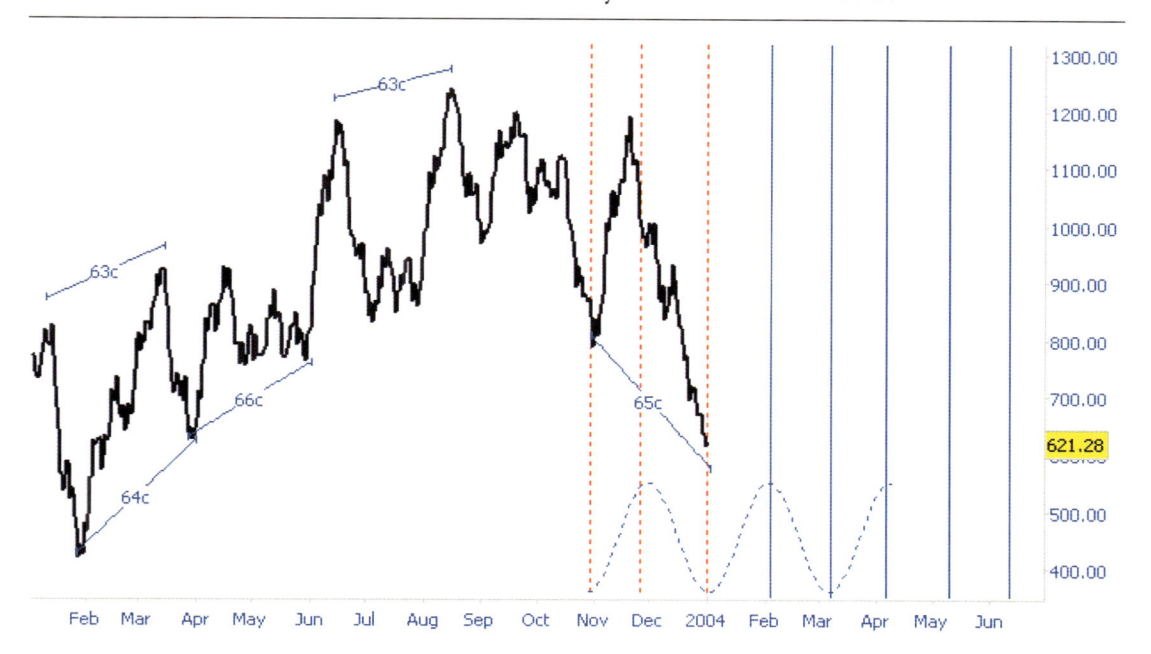

Figure 2-19: 65 CD cycle plotted ahead

The blue lines in the chart indicate the expected turning dates of this particular cycle. The information on the turning dates predict a:

- high at the beginning of February
- low during the first half of March
- high at the beginning of April.

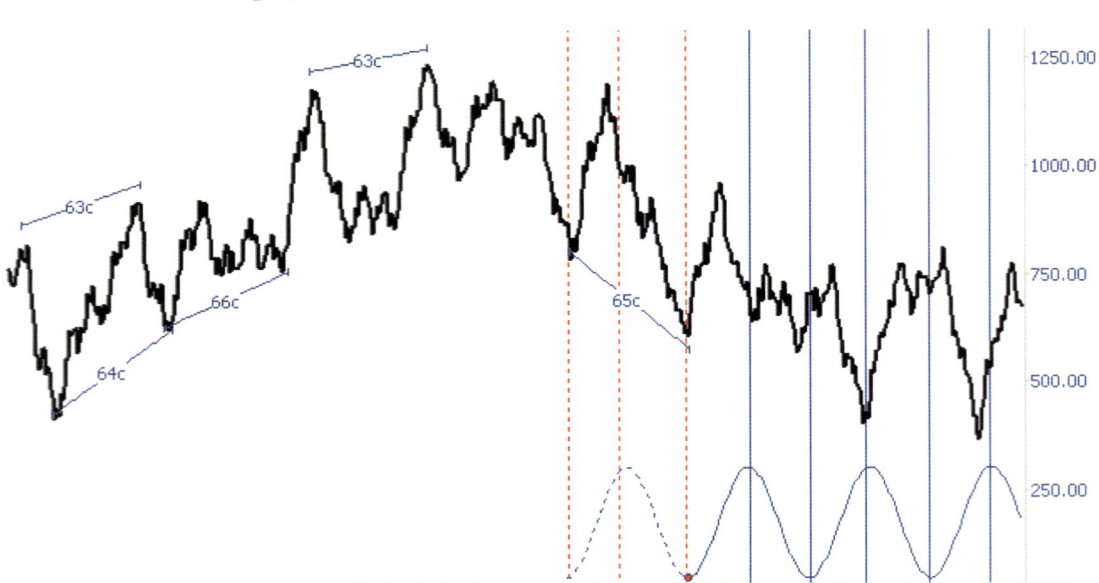

Now let's see how it played out:

Figure 2-20: Dataset 4 – 65 CD cycle forecast and how it played out

As you can clearly see, there is no correlation between the 65 CD cycle we have "detected" and actual price behavior. If we had performed a cycles forecast using this classical method, we would have been totally wrong. Normally, you would deduce: "Ok, the 65 CD cycle was inverted", because April did not have a high, but a low. So you would argue *after* the fact that the 65 CD cycle was inverted.

But we know from our example that this line of reasoning is totally wrong! There is no 65 CD cycle and there is no inversion. The detection of cycles by visual recognition of the highs/lows was completely wrong.

I want to use this example to show that the key component of all cycle models is a reliable and robust cycles detection method. And as I have already demonstrated, most of the common methods simply do not work.

Now let's use our new algorithm to determine the active cycles using only one year of data history.

Let's start with the plot of the spectrum from the cycle analyzer for the same dataset:

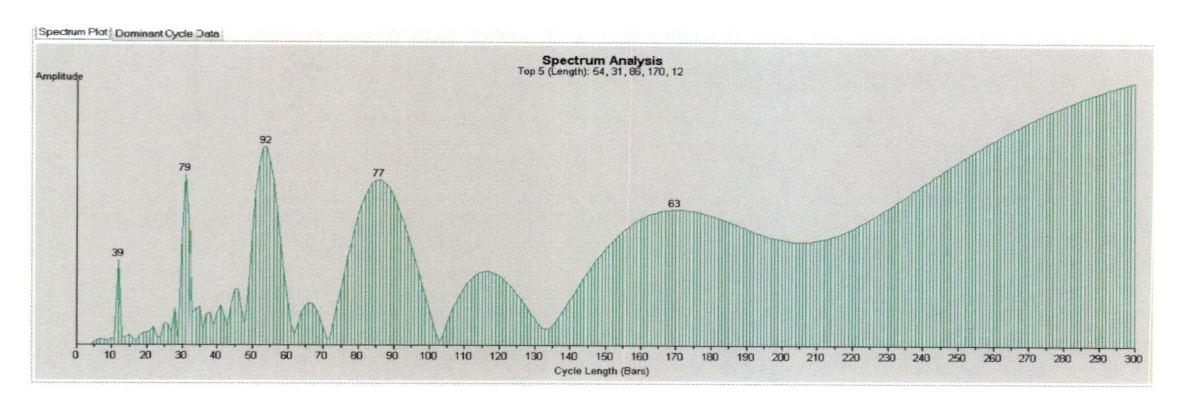

Figure 2-21: Cycle Scanner plot of Dataset 4

We can clearly see the obvious peaks of the cycles that were used to generate the dataset. Even our small cycle of 12 days was recognized accurately with a sharp peak on the spectrum plot. Despite all the noise in this data.

The question now is what we should do with the detected cycles 117 and 170? After all, these cycles are not present in the dataset.

This is the printout from the script log:

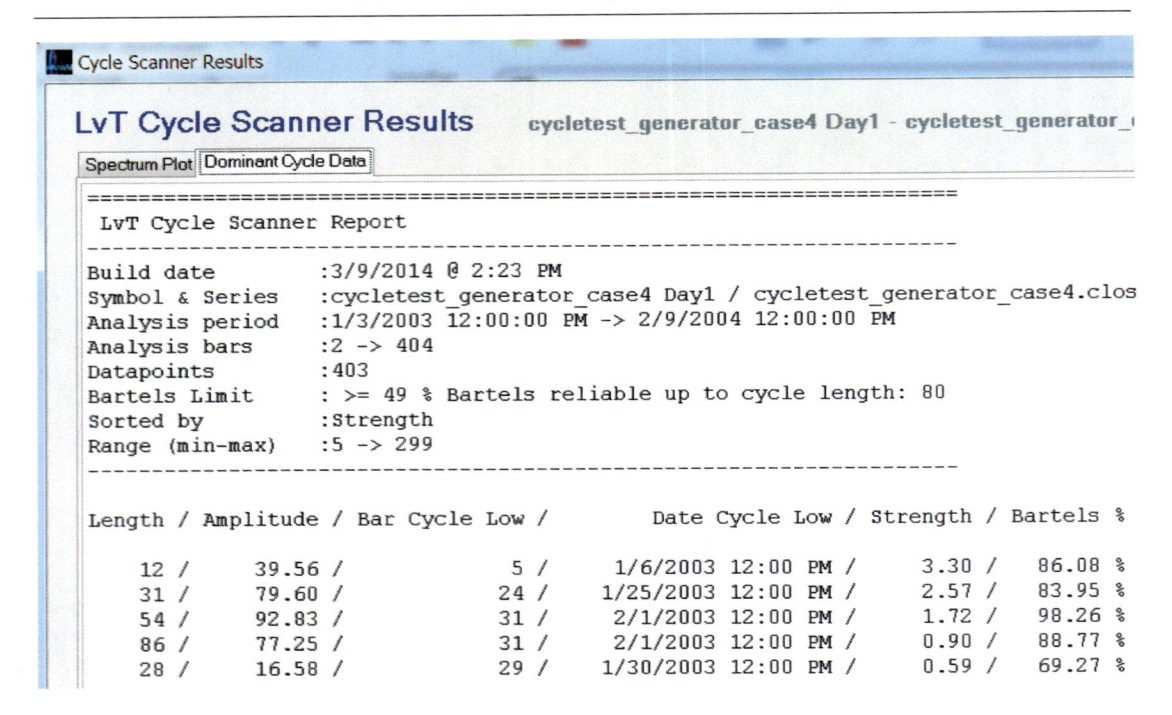

```
LvT Cycle Scanner Report
------------------------------------------------------------------
Build date       :3/9/2014 @ 2:23 PM
Symbol & Series  :cycletest_generator_case4 Day1 / cycletest_generator_case4.clos
Analysis period  :1/3/2003 12:00:00 PM -> 2/9/2004 12:00:00 PM
Analysis bars    :2 -> 404
Datapoints       :403
Bartels Limit    : >= 49 % Bartels reliable up to cycle length: 80
Sorted by        :Strength
Range (min-max)  :5 -> 299
------------------------------------------------------------------

Length / Amplitude / Bar Cycle Low /   Date Cycle Low / Strength / Bartels %
   12  /   39.56  /     5  /  1/6/2003 12:00 PM  /  3.30  /  86.08 %
   31  /   79.60  /    24  /  1/25/2003 12:00 PM /  2.57  /  83.95 %
   54  /   92.83  /    31  /  2/1/2003 12:00 PM  /  1.72  /  98.26 %
   86  /   77.25  /    31  /  2/1/2003 12:00 PM  /  0.90  /  88.77 %
   28  /   16.58  /    29  /  1/30/2003 12:00 PM /  0.59  /  69.27 %
```

Figure 2-22: Result of the cycle analysis for Dataset 4

These cycles obviously do not appear on our result list, the reason being our post-processing using the statistical engine built into the algorithm. These cycles are "sorted out" because they have a low Bartels score (below 49). And that demonstrates the power of the combined algorithm that was created for this Cycle Scanner.

The list accurately displays the real cycles: 12, 31, 54, and 86 days (the actual length would be 85 days). If you take a look at the 28 day cycle, you can see the low "amplitude". This is also a full derivative of the 12er cycle (4 * 12). We can therefore skip the 28er cycle here.

The result is as clear as can be! All cycles have been identified correctly in terms of cycle length and amplitude. And the algorithm (correctly) did not detect a 65 day cycle as we have seen in the chart.

So, the next step would be to apply the cycle forecasting method I have introduced in case 3. Let's apply it to this case now.

2.8 Building the forecasting model for Example 4 based on the detected cycles

Step 1: Cycle analysis

We have just completed this step. The report above was published on February 9 using the data history of the year 2003. The engine provided us with information on the four cycles (12, 31, 54, and 86 days) including their LOW dates and amplitude. We will enter them into the chart in the next step.

Step 2: Plot active cycles and expand them into the future

We are now able to plot the four cycles with their correct low offset dates and perform a projection of these cycles in the future. The data is derived from the output of the Cycle Scanner and imported into the Cycle Plotter via the "Load Scanner Results" button as shown below.

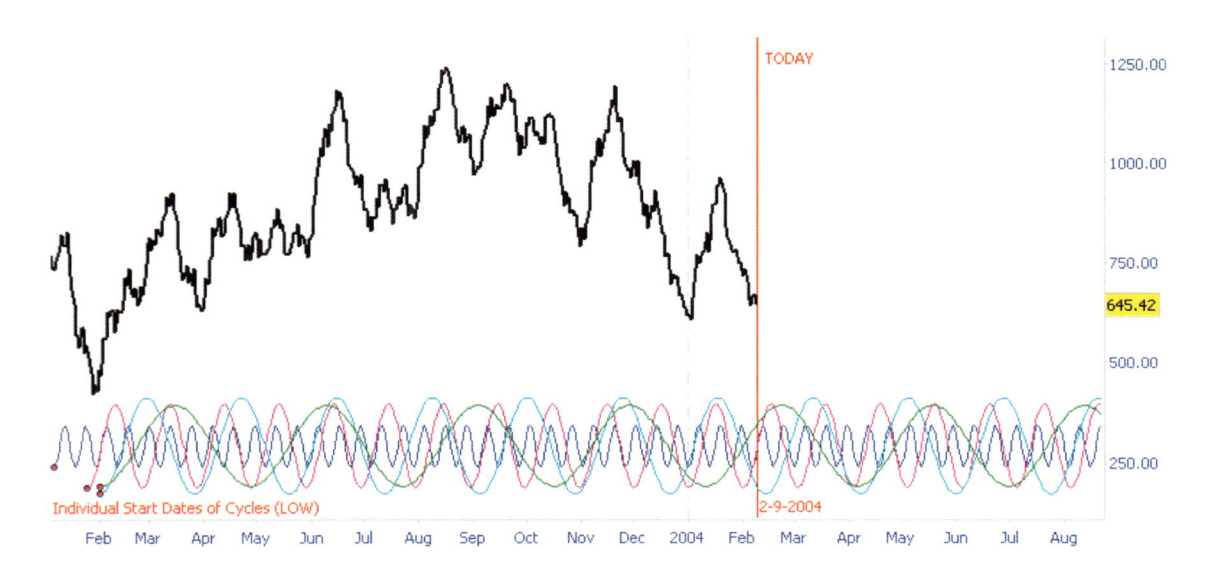

Figure 2-23: Dataset 4 – Single cycles forecast for detected cycles

Step 3: Build a composite cycle from the detected cycles

It'll get more complicated now when we enter four cycles into the chart and build a forecast based on these cycles. Of course you can plot each cycle individually to determine when they are in "alignment" in terms of their lows and/or highs in order to spot turning points. To do so, you will need to build a composite model. But that involves nothing more than simply adding together all four cycles. It's easy. So let's see what the composite of these four cycles looks like.

Figure 2-24: Composite cycle forecast for Dataset 4

Step 4: Mark expected future turning points

The next step involves identifying the main future turning points of the composite cycle. These incidences are the dates when we expect a major change in market trend. For easier reading, I have only marked the expected major lows and highs. There is, of course, more to it. But why don't you just take a closer look!

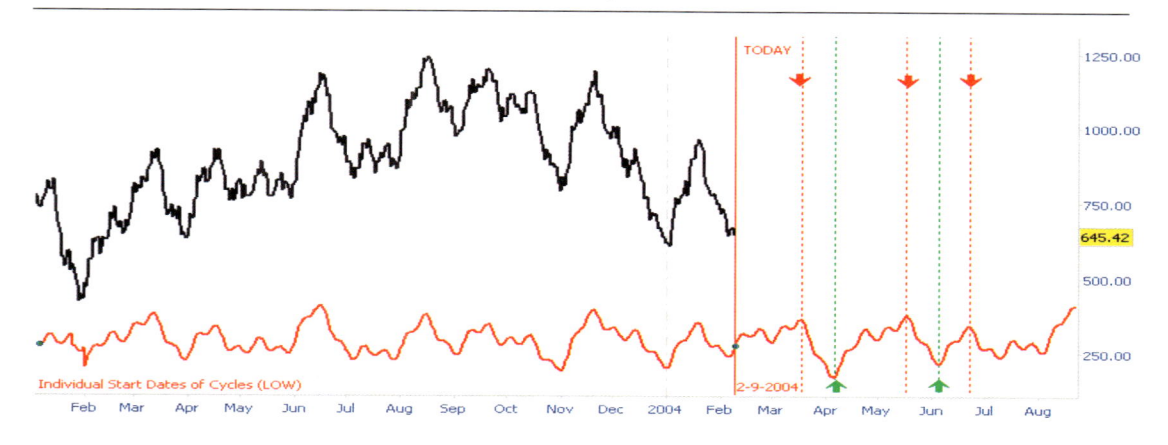

Figure 2-25: Forecasted turning points (CITs) in the coming months

Step 5: Just see how it plays out…

Now let's check how this forecast would have played out.

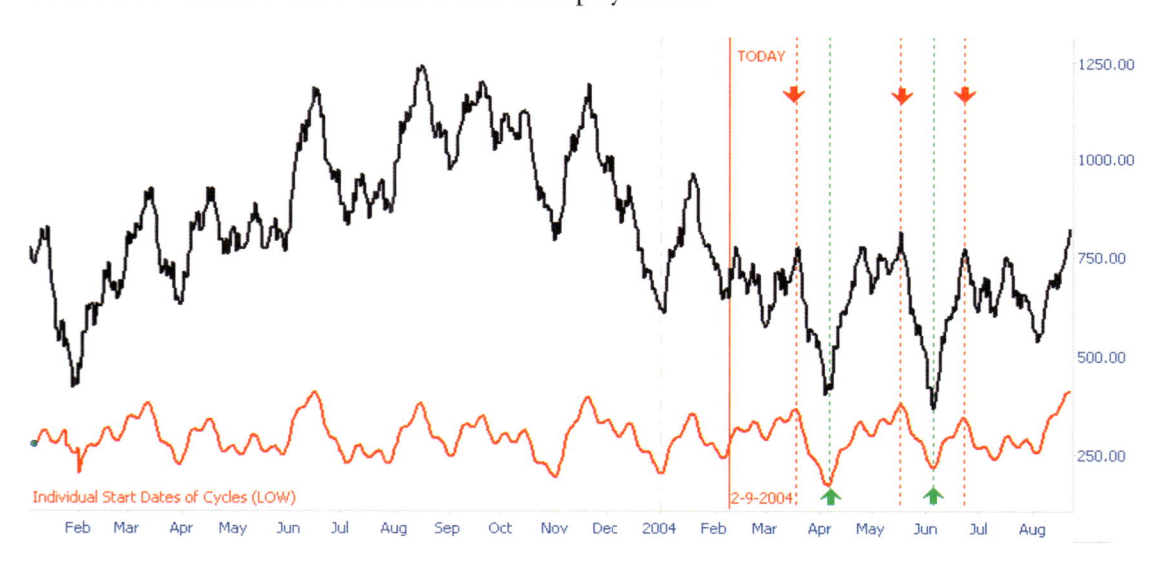

Figure 2-26: Composite forecast and result

I think there is no need to comment on this chart. You can see for yourself how accurate the composite forecast spotted the correct turning points. And not only are the marked ones correct. Each single turning point in the composite forecast corresponds with a turn in the sample market.

Take a closer look at the chart and study it a little.

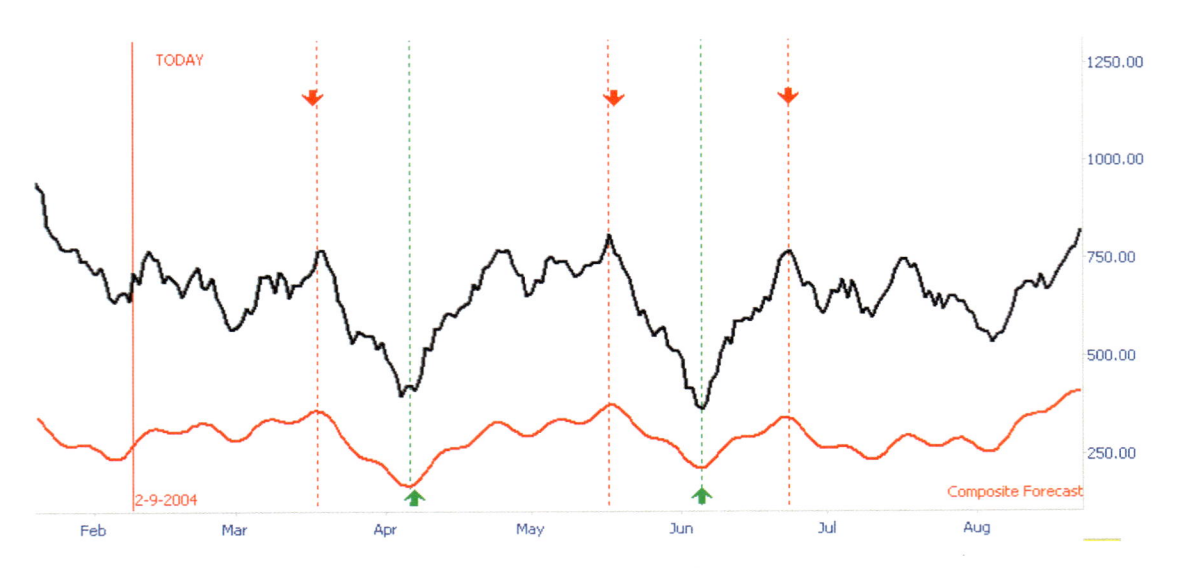

Figure 2-27: Comparison between composite forecast and sample dataset

Compare this result with the visual cycles detection method illustrated above on the 65 CD cycle. The benefits of the Cycle Scanner results are clearly visible.

This is, of course, only sample data and not real market data. But there are two important things I would like to mention about all these test data:

1. It is important to prove that the algorithm is able to detect cycles in simulated market conditions with noise, trends, and different cycles running in parallel.
2. You should gain a general understanding of a simple cycles forecasting method using the detected cycles to forecast future turning points.

Before we move on to real markets, let's conduct one last heavy stress test using our engine to see whether the new algorithm can master this test as well.

2.9 Example 5: Dataset with 5 cycles + noise + changing trends and forces

We will again increase the complexity by adding another cycle and by increasing the trend levels and trend changes. We will, of course, also add random noise on top of it all. We will use the following five cycles for the next dataset:

Wave	Length	Amplitude
1	30	40
2	50	60
3	95	55
4	195	110
5	230	150

Just to demonstrate that you can use any time frame with this engine, I have chosen an intraday time frame similar to normal trading times from 09:30 to 16:00 on a one minute chart. Here is what it looks like:

Figure 2-28: Sample Dataset 5

You can see that this sample dataset looks very similar to real markets. And it is based purely on the five cycles, different trends, and noise. Therefore, it reveals that all features that come close to real markets are included in the model. Now let's see what cycle information the new algorithm will be able to offer.

In the first run, we will only use one day of data history to analyze the cycles. This is also the way it would be done in real markets —the last trading day is used to extract cycles and this information is then used to forecast the next turning points.

Below is the analysis report for the intraday data of May 6.

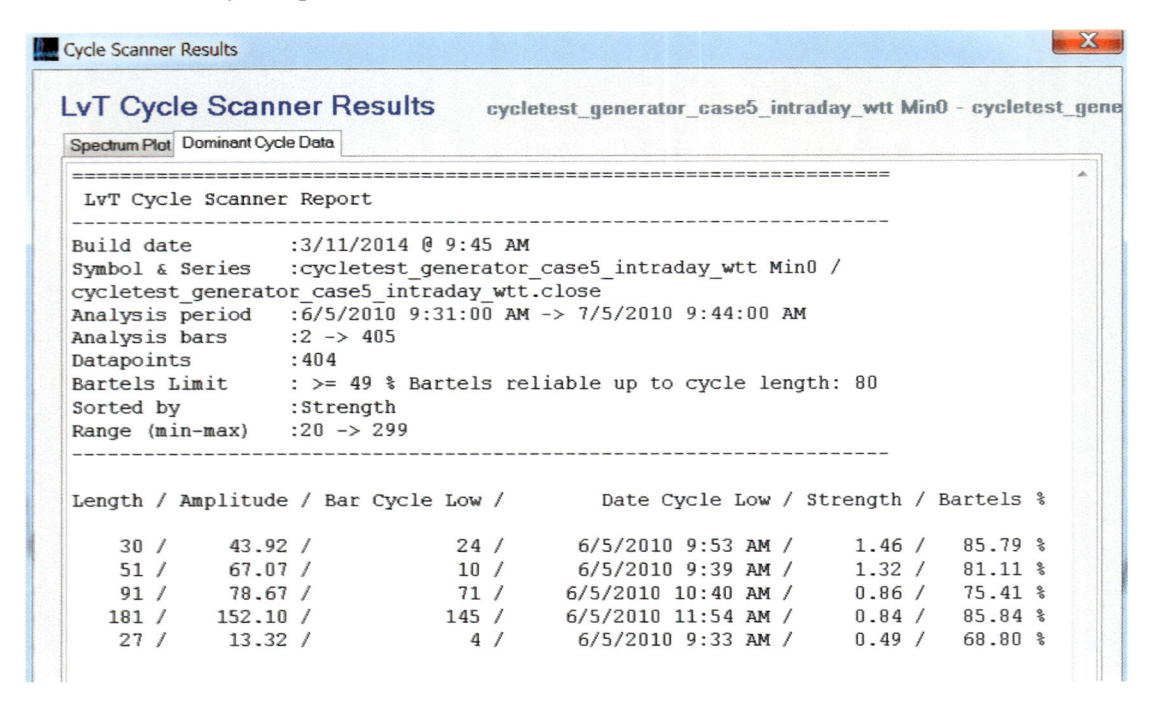

```
LvT Cycle Scanner Results      cycletest_generator_case5_intraday_wtt Min0 - cycletest_gene
Spectrum Plot  Dominant Cycle Data
=================================================================
  LvT Cycle Scanner Report
-----------------------------------------------------------------
  Build date          :3/11/2014 @ 9:45 AM
  Symbol & Series     :cycletest_generator_case5_intraday_wtt Min0 /
  cycletest_generator_case5_intraday_wtt.close
  Analysis period     :6/5/2010 9:31:00 AM -> 7/5/2010 9:44:00 AM
  Analysis bars       :2 -> 405
  Datapoints          :404
  Bartels Limit       : >= 49 % Bartels reliable up to cycle length: 80
  Sorted by           :Strength
  Range (min-max)     :20 -> 299
-----------------------------------------------------------------

Length / Amplitude / Bar Cycle Low /    Date Cycle Low / Strength / Bartels %
    30 /    43.92 /        24 /         6/5/2010  9:53 AM /   1.46 /   85.79 %
    51 /    67.07 /        10 /         6/5/2010  9:39 AM /   1.32 /   81.11 %
    91 /    78.67 /        71 /         6/5/2010 10:40 AM /   0.86 /   75.41 %
   181 /   152.10 /       145 /         6/5/2010 11:54 AM /   0.84 /   85.84 %
    27 /    13.32 /         4 /         6/5/2010  9:33 AM /   0.49 /   68.80 %
```

Figure 2-29: Cycle Scanner result for Dataset 5 (one day of data history)

There is some information here we are seeing for the first time: The Cycle Scanner provides the exact LOW dates (phase offset) precisely to the minute when using intraday charts!

The scanner now was able to extract four cycles. The 30, 51, 91, and 181 minute cycles. The 27 minute cycle were skipped owing to their low amplitudes in comparison with the other four cycles. That is, the maximum error ratio here with reference to the longer cycle of 195 minutes (real) as compared to 181 minutes (detected) is only 8%. The cycle with a length of 230 minutes was not detected because we did not have sufficient data in the analysis windows (only one day). It is thus not surprising that the scanner was not able to detect the cycle with a length of 230 minutes (approx. 4 hours) in only 8 hours of test data.

In other words, we are now faced with the situation that the scanner did not detect all cycles and that one cycle with an error ratio of 8% was among those cycles identified. This is similar to reality –there will always be some errors in detection and we will inevitably miss some longer-term cycles. So this is not really surprising from an analytical point of view.

But now let's see what happens if we use these four detected cycles including the erroneous cycle in a forecasting model. Will it be reliable enough for trading purposes?

Hence, we will enter the four detected cycles with their given LOW dates and amplitudes into the chart. This would have been the situation had we entered them just after the open on May 7 with one day of data history.

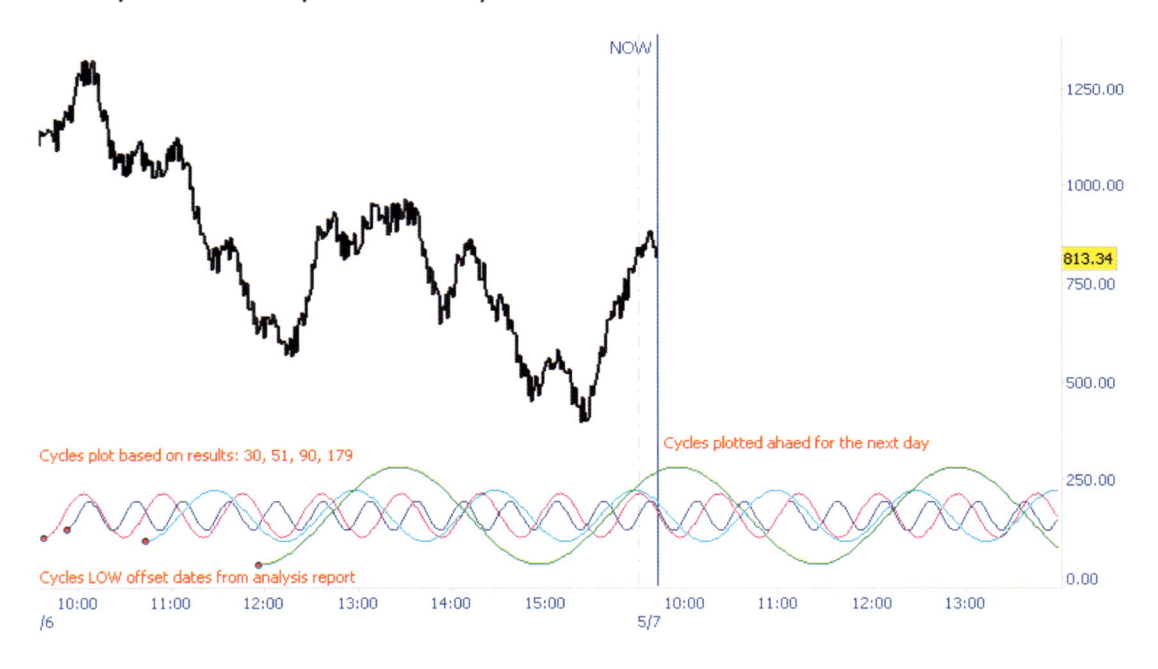

Figure 2-30: Dataset 5 and single cycles forecast

Again, the method needs to sum up all individual cycles into one composite. This is the composite picture for the detected individual cycles with the major turning points already indicated in the chart. This is the method used to build a trading forecast for the next day.

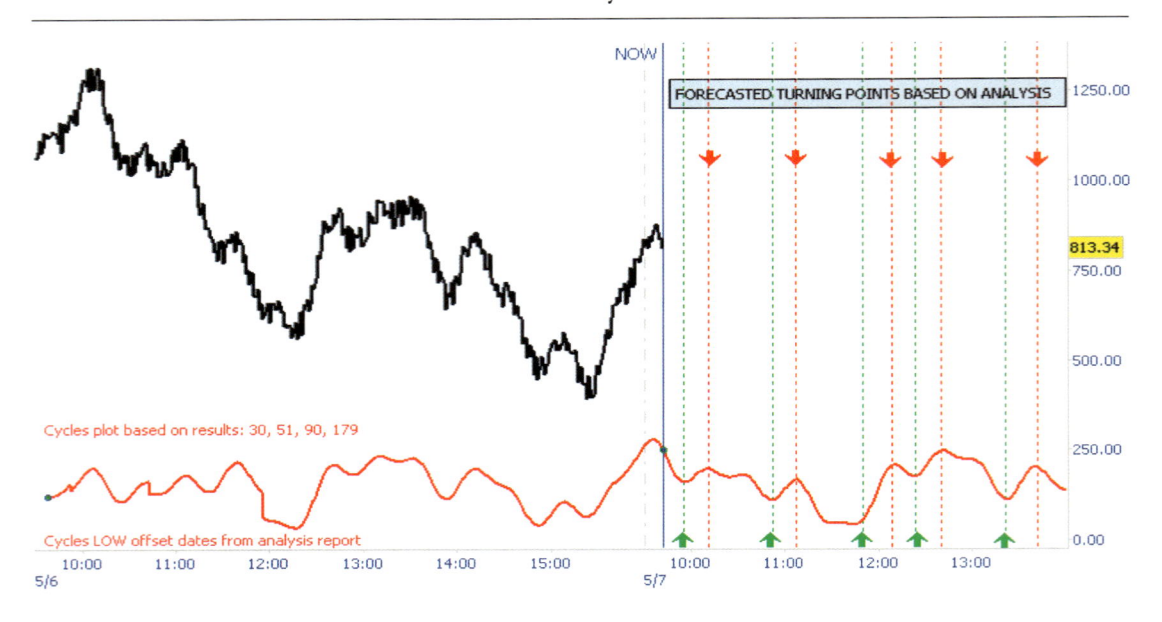

Figure 2-31: Dataset 5 with composite cycle forecast based on Cycle Scanner

This chart would have been our trading forecast for May 7. We would have identified the future times for the day on which we would expect the market to turn. Let's see what this forecast brings:

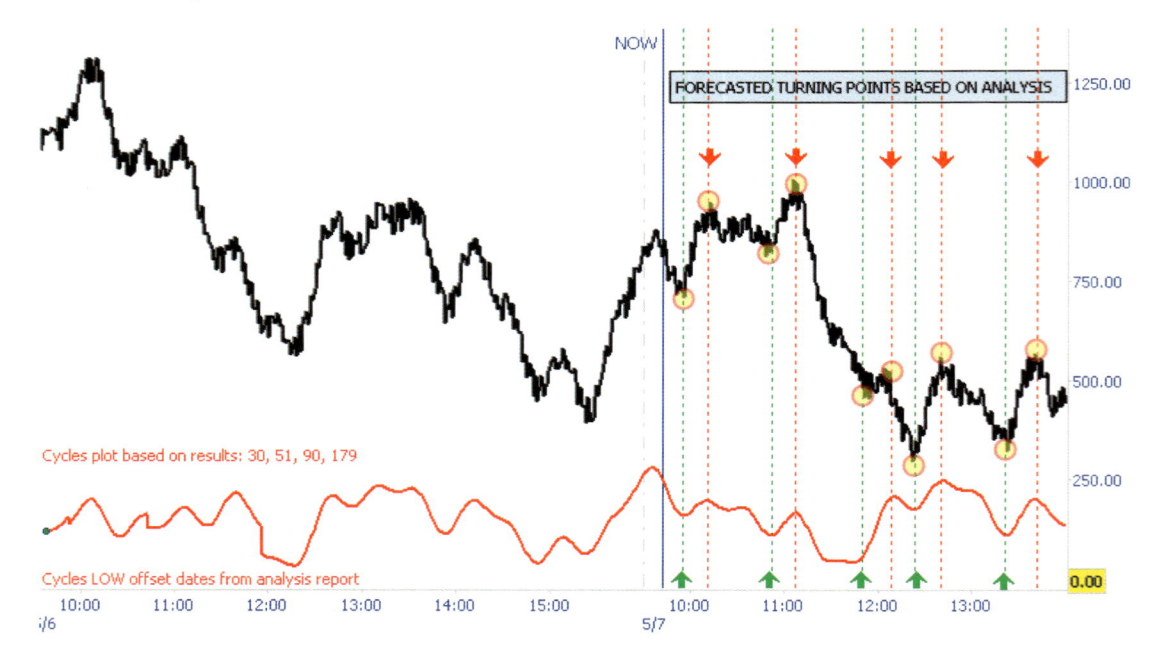

Figure 2-32: Composite forecast based on scanner and sample Dataset 5

Again, the Cycle Scanner was highly accurate in forecasting the turning points up to the minute! This example shows what you can expect in a real market. Even if there is an error in the correct cycle length and even if we "miss" one cycle, the forecast based on the Cycle Scanner results is reliable and robust for building tradable forecasts. And that's just it. We need tradable forecasts. And we will get them.

This was the last example to demonstrate the potential of the new algorithm using sample data. This last sample dataset comes very close to real market conditions. And we have seen now that the results of the Cycle Scanner are highly accurate for building forecasts.

2.10 The Cycle Scanner: Algorithm overview

If you are an engineer, you can imagine how difficult this course was; a full workload on all the mathematical stuff, the coding, the testing, and the individual development to optimize the existing algorithms. If you are into trading, it doesn't matter in the end.

Just keep this figure in mind to gain an understanding of how the Cycle Scanner works:

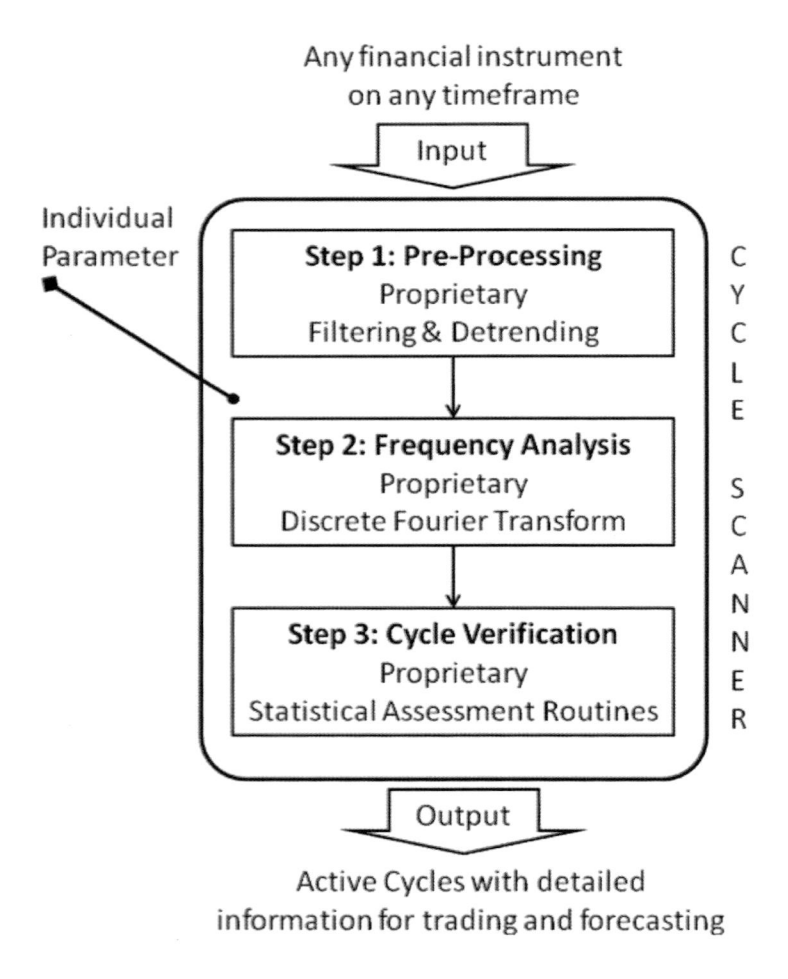

Figure 2-33: Overview "Cycle Scanner"

2.11 Final summary – A new area of cyclic analysis at your fingertips

So far, I have shown and proven how reliable and robust this new engine is. It is very important to test the engine on sample data for which we know the cycle information. But all examples and stress tests have demonstrated that this new algorithm is able to tackle all features of financial data sets including noise, trends, and changing cycles over time. It can overcome the problems of all known individual analysis routines. The combination and adaptation of different algorithms produce this great result.

All sample datasets are included on the CD. I can assure you that I have carried out thousands of such examples. It is, after all, very important for you to be able to trust a new engine before you apply it to financial markets. I hope you have realized by now that you can trust this new algorithm. In the following chapters, I will show you how to use it for real trading purposes. You will then be able to test and rebuild all shown examples. I have included this data in order for you to be able to become familiar with the Cycle Scanner before you apply it to real data.

This powerful toy is lying right in front of you. You can attach the Cycle Scanner to any device and use any time frame. The full algorithm is built into the WTT software. It's just a few clicks away.

You are now also able to use the results of the Cycle Scanner to build the forecasts for future turning points.

You have only just arrived at Chapter 2 of this book. And you already have the most powerful cycle detection engine for financial markets at your fingertips.

2.12 The Cycle Scanner: A step-by-step guide

The Cycle Scanner was developed in C++ to deliver the best analytical performance in a real-time environment. The engine is already integrated and works with all WhenToTrade "WTT" and Wave59 versions.

LvT Cycle Scanner

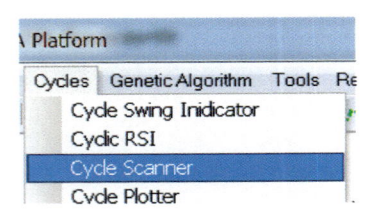

This tool has the following parameter options:

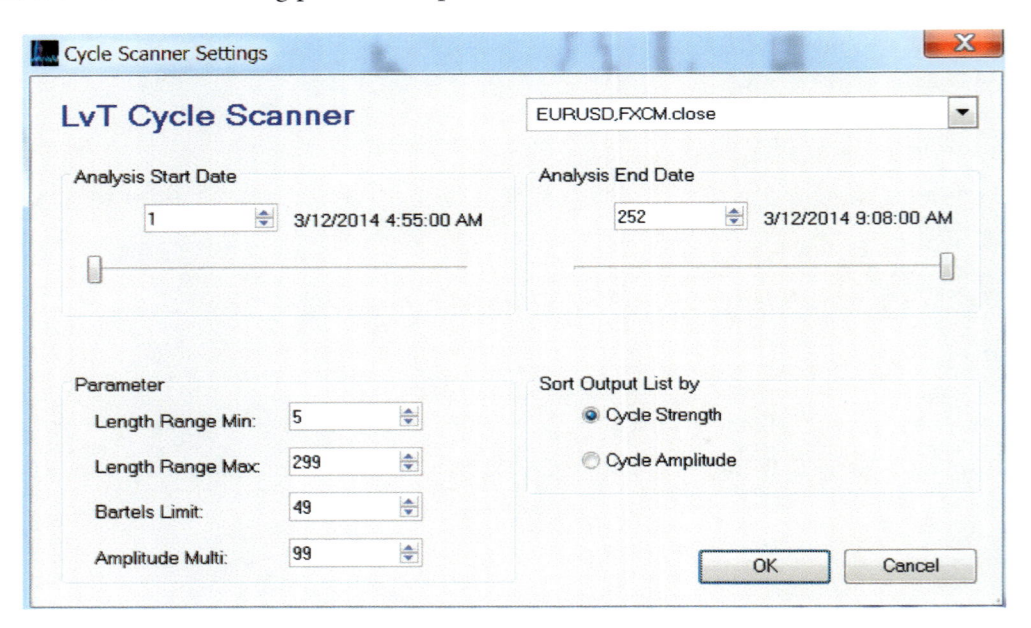

Figure 2-34: Cycle Scanner parameter input box

Comments for usage within Wave59:

All functions can be called directly from the new Wave59 Cycles menu. The Cycles menu will be visible once you have been activated. I have created all scripts required for carrying out cycles detection. You won't have to write a single line of code. But I have left the

QScript code readable for you. If you like, you can use the functions for your own scripts and trading systems at a later point. You just need to import the cycle QScript functions which are provided with the software purchase as separate download.

- **Startdate and enddate**

    The startdate and enddate define the period of data to be used in the algorithm to detect the cycles. These are very important parameters because they determine which dataset should be used for the analysis engine. As was the case in the examples, I recommend using 1-2 years of data when analyzing daily charts and 1-2 days of 1-minute data history when analyzing intraday charts. The best start- and end dates are highs and lows in the current market. So select the highs and/or lows for the start/enddate and try to build a period of 1-2 years (daily) or 1-2 days (intraday).

- **Bartels limit**

    The post-processing engine applies a cycle verification engine based on statistical routines. The Bartels score indicates the "reliability" of the presence of a cycle in the current data. The value is measured in percent. A low value implies a low statistical alignment between the cycle and the real data. A high value indicates a high statistical alignment between the cycle and the real data.

    This post-processing engine should be used as a second filter of the results. The frequency analysis delivers all cycles detected by this procedure. Subsequently, only cycles with a high Bartels score should be detected by the engine.

    That is, I would recommend skipping cycles with a Bartels score lower than 40%.

- **Length min / Length max**

    This defines the cycle lengths that you want the data to be scanned for. If you only want to scan cycles with a length of between 50 and 100 days, enter 50 for length_min and 100 for length_max. You can define the range the Cycle Scanner should search. The maximum length of cycles is 299 and the minimum length is 5 (always measured in number of bars).

- **Sort by: Strength or Amplitude**

    Cycles have two key features: Length and amplitude. Usually, cycles are sorted by amplitude because the cycle with the highest amplitude will have the highest influence on the movements of the market. But when it comes to trading, we are interested in the cyclic force per time unit, which is measured in bars on the price chart. A better value can be obtained if we sort the cycles according to level of influence with reference to price movement per bar. This value can be very easily calculated: Simply divide the amplitude by cycle length. You will then obtain the price change in terms of cycle per bar. This is termed "cycle strength" in my algorithm.

    When set to "Strength", the cycles in the script log will be sorted according to cycle strength value. When set to "Amplitude", they will be sorted according to amplitude.

- **Amplitude Multi:**

    You can set a value which works as a multiplier for the detected amplitudes. While working with small price changes (e.g. Forex data), you want to stretch the small amplitudes with a constant factor. You can set this constant factor here as multiplier value. It will not disrupt the cycle analysis and only help to visually plot cycles with larger values for the amplitudes.

The result of the cycle analyzer is printed onto the script log. There you will find all relevant information about the detected cycles. It consists of a spectrum plot and a detailed data result tab:

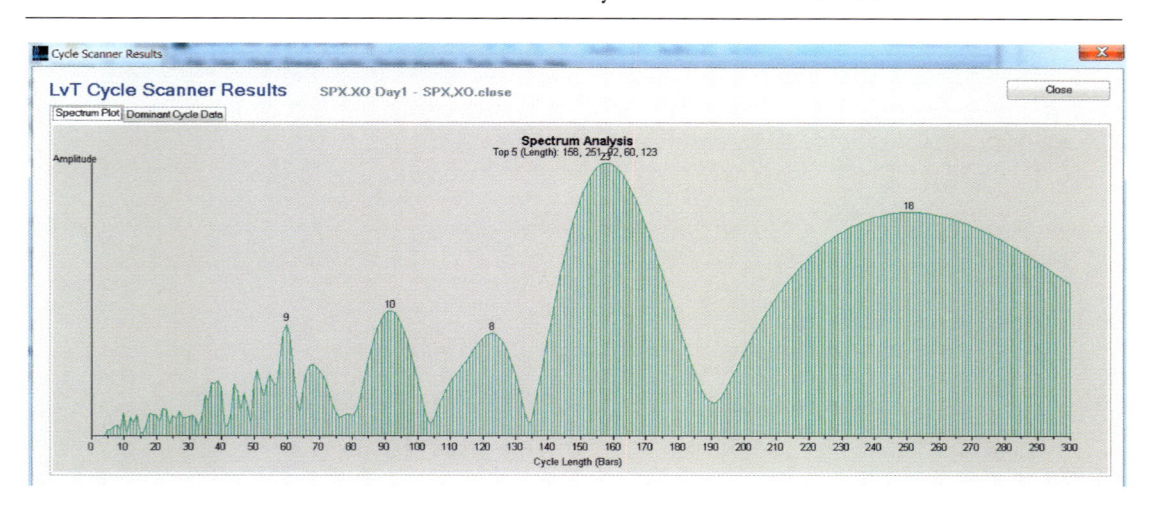

How to detect and measure cycles in the stock market

Figure 2-35: Cycle spectrum plot

The header of the Cycle Data tab provides basic information on when the analysis was done, which data was used for the analysis, and on the set-up.

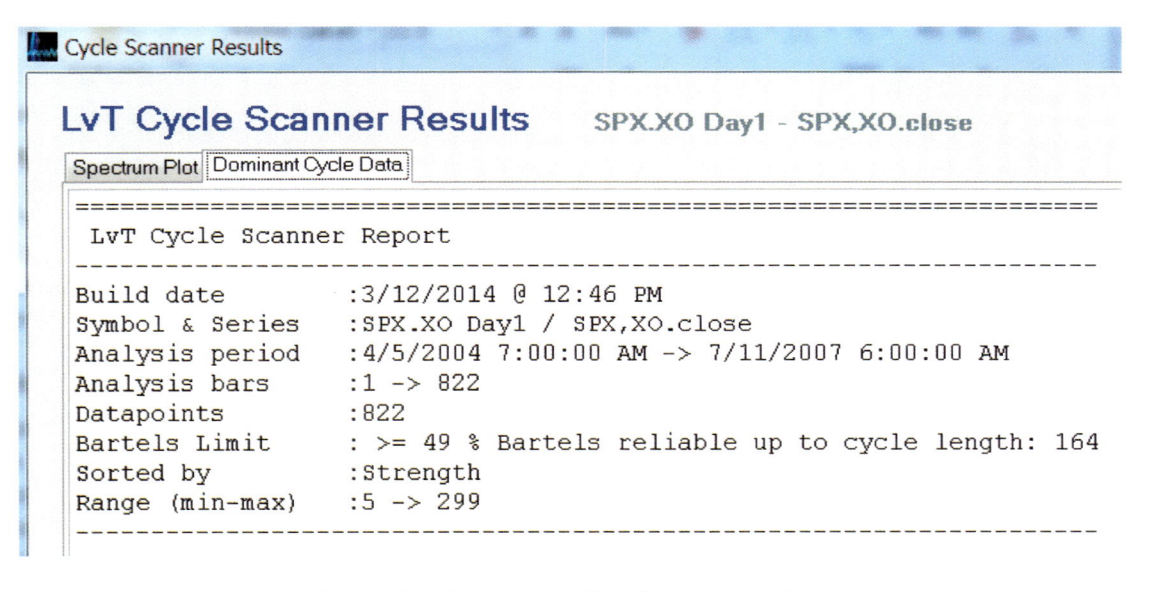

Figure 2-36: Header of cycle analyzer log

The second part of the cycle data tab comprises the table with the results of the spectrum analysis. The detected cycles are sorted by cycle strength or amplitude (as indicated in the header).

Each cycle line includes the following information:

```
Length / Amplitude / Bar Cycle Low /    Date Cycle Low / Strength / Bartels %
    60 /      9.38 /           25 /  5/10/2004 7:00 AM /     0.16 /    93.12 %
   158 /     23.10 /          102 /  8/30/2004 7:00 AM /     0.15 /    95.86 %
    12 /      1.56 /            9 /  4/16/2004 7:00 AM /     0.13 /    55.62 %
    14 /      1.70 /            5 /  4/12/2004 7:00 AM /     0.12 /    49.56 %
    51 /      5.52 /           36 /  5/25/2004 7:00 AM /     0.11 /    81.17 %
    18 /      1.83 /           13 /  4/22/2004 7:00 AM /     0.10 /    88.42 %
    55 /      5.13 /           33 /  5/20/2004 7:00 AM /     0.09 /    90.15 %
    20 /      1.72 /           15 /  4/26/2004 7:00 AM /     0.09 /    79.80 %
   251 /     18.95 /           89 /  8/11/2004 7:00 AM /     0.08 /    88.70 %
```

Figure 2-37: Cycle parameter

2.13 The Cycle Plotter

The cycle plotter is able to plot up to eight individual cycles on the chart. The plotter is also able to build a composite from all cycles. The plotter is used for the sample datasets and to "verify" the results of the Cycle Scanner. You can use the plotter to manually plot different cycles on the chart. You can also use it for learning purposes and rebuild the examples presented here.

LvT_Cycle_Plotter

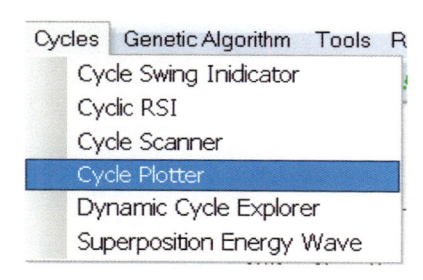

Parameters:

The parameter should be self-explanatory. Just play with it a little. I want to mention one important benefit, however: You can directly roll over the results from the Cycle Scanner's data tab into the cycle plotter. Just press the button located in the upper left corner of the Settings window called "Load Scanner Peaks" and the results will be populated into the settings screen from the last cycle scanner analysis run.

This makes it very easy to check the results of a detected cycle on the chart.

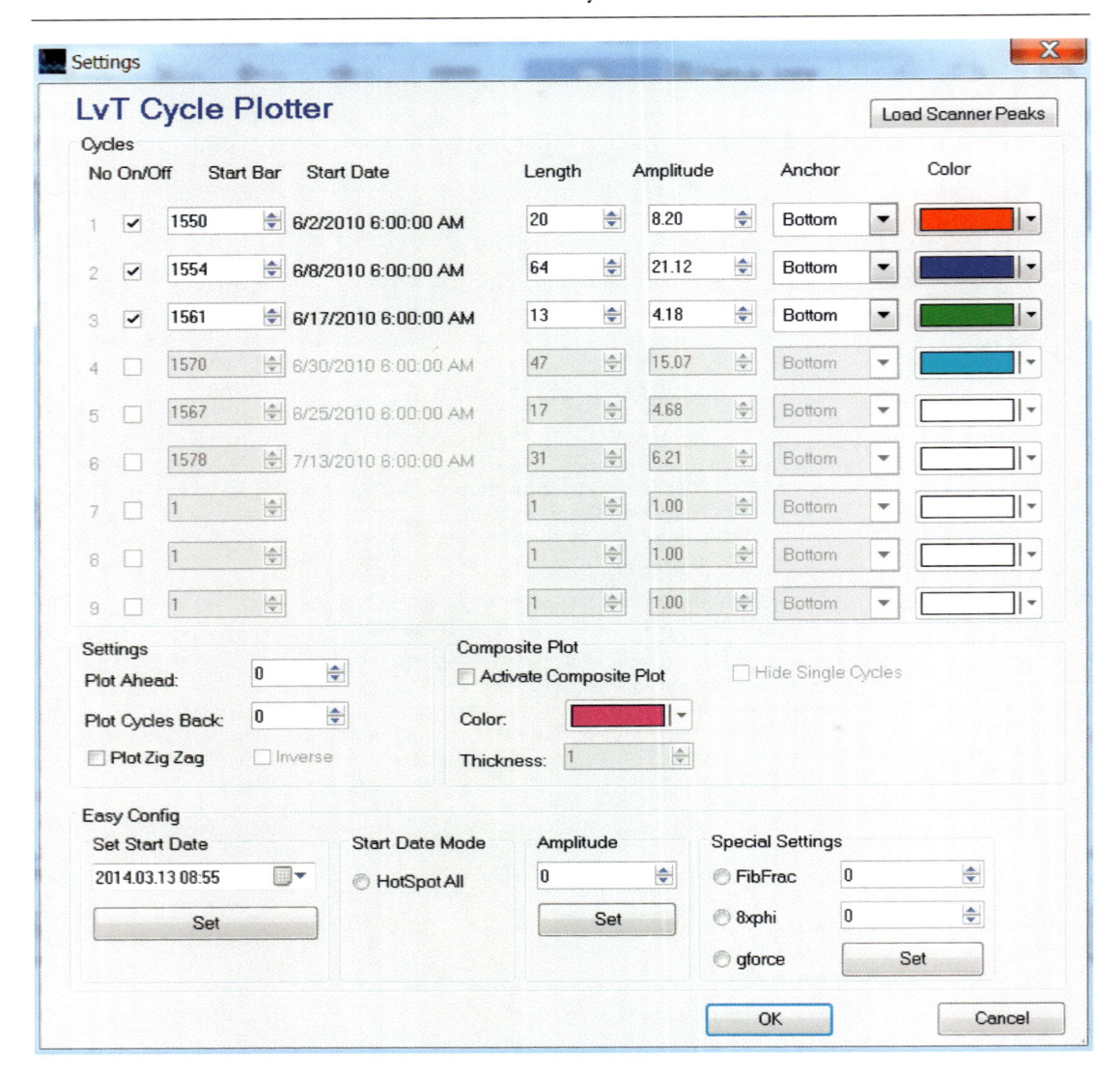

Figure 2-38: Cycle plotter parameter

Finally, the cycle will plot based on all of the information derived from the Cycle Scanner. And using the option "Activate Composite Plot", you can switch between a composite plot of all cycles or an individual plot.

It is a little different to do it within the Wave59 Cycles Plug-In. However, you can copy and paste the results from the script log into the cycle plotter manually. Here is how to do it:

Step 1: Copy full line for cycle from script log

First, select one full line including the quotation marks and press CTRL + C or click the right mouse button.

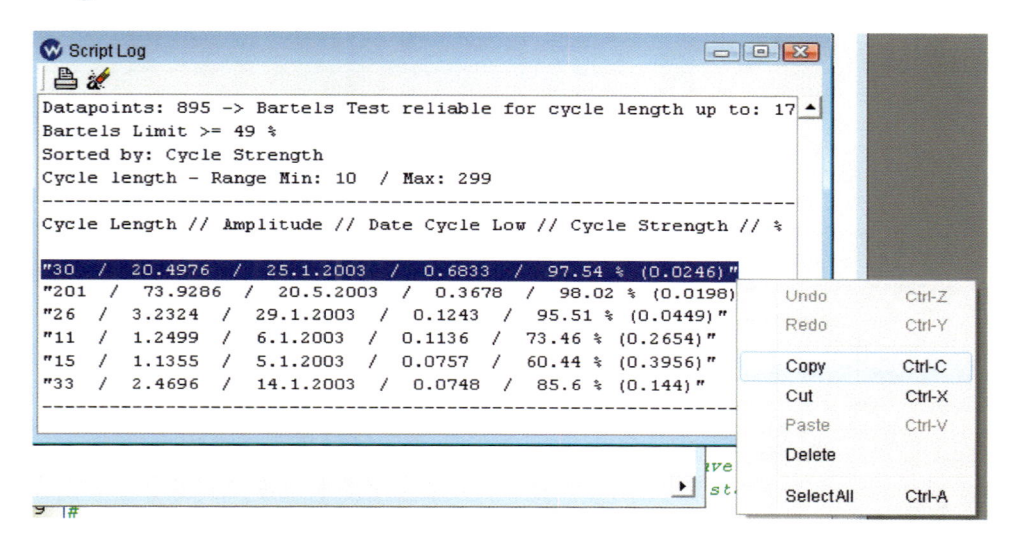

```
Script Log
Datapoints: 895 -> Bartels Test reliable for cycle length up to: 17
Bartels Limit >= 49 %
Sorted by: Cycle Strength
Cycle length - Range Min: 10  / Max: 299
--------------------------------------------------------------
Cycle Length // Amplitude // Date Cycle Low // Cycle Strength // %
"30   /  20.4976  /  25.1.2003  /  0.6833  /  97.54 % (0.0246)"
"201  /  73.9286  /  20.5.2003  /  0.3678  /  98.02 % (0.0198)"
"26   /   3.2324  /  29.1.2003  /  0.1243  /  95.51 % (0.0449)"
"11   /   1.2499  /   6.1.2003  /  0.1136  /  73.46 % (0.2654)"
"15   /   1.1355  /   5.1.2003  /  0.0757  /  60.44 % (0.3956)"
"33   /   2.4696  /  14.1.2003  /  0.0748  /  85.6  % (0.144)"
```

Context menu: Undo Ctrl-Z, Redo Ctrl-Y, Copy Ctrl-C, Cut Ctrl-X, Paste Ctrl-V, Delete, Select All Ctrl-A

Step 2: Open parameter startdate in cycle plotter

Switch to the chart and insert the cycle plotter or configure the cycle plotter indicator and open the startdate of the wave you want to use. Mark or delete the information.

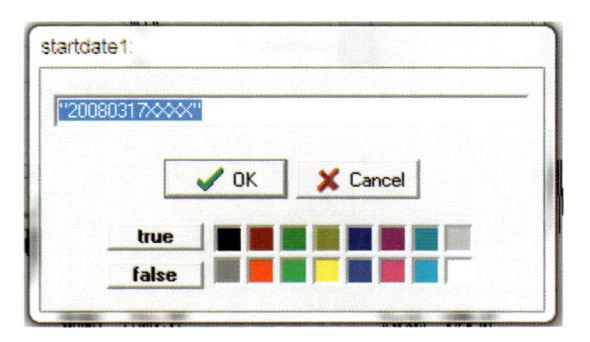

startdate1: "20080317XXXX"

63

Step 3: Paste full line from cycle analyzer log

Press CTRL + V or click the right mouse button and "Paste" to insert the full line.

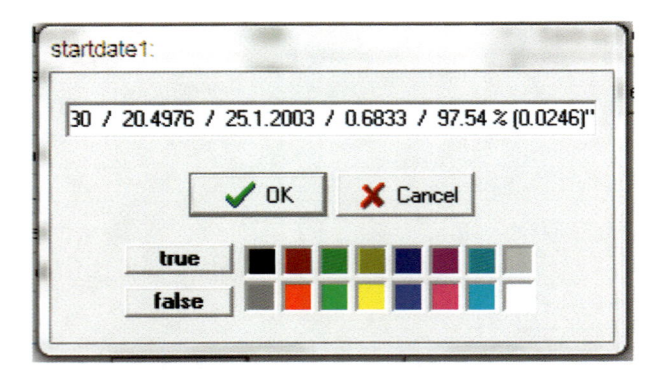

Subsequently, the script will recognize that all cycle information has been entered into this line and the next individual fields for cycle length and amplitude will therefore be disregarded.

3. The Dominant Market Vibration

Now that we are able to detect cycles with surgical precision, we can start to apply our new Cycle Scanner engine to real markets.

3.1 Definition of the dominant cycle

The most important information with reference to trading and cycles is the so-called "dominant cycle". The most straightforward definition of the dominant cycle is the identified cyclic component with the greatest amplitude. The dominant cycle is described by its wavelength, measured in bars.

3.2 Definition of the Dominant Market Vibration

To arrive at more reliable and robust information on the dominant cycle, our new engine filters the dominant cycle with more proprietary algorithms.

Step 1:

The algorithm has a dynamic filter for detrending, which is included for pre-processing. This ensures that our data is not affected by trending information. This algorithm is one of the best detrending filters I have found in digital signal processing.

Step 2:

Subsequently, the engine performs a spectral analysis based on an optimized Discrete Fourier Transform and then isolates those cycles that are repetitive and have the largest amplitudes. The second step gives us the dominant cycle.

The second step includes the proprietary frequency analysis routines. Research results have shown that an adapted Goertzel algorithm is most suitable when it comes to detecting cycles in financial time series. Since this book is about trading, I do not want to publish my mathematical and statistical results here. For those who want to know more about the differences between the various algorithms, read Dennis Meyers' paper "MESA vs. Goertzel-DFT" (meyersanalytics.com/publications/MesaVsGDFT.pdf)

I have adapted Goertzel's algorithm for my own cycles engine, specifically in terms of the characteristics of financial time series datasets, but we will take it a lot further in the next step.

Step 3:

In the third step, the statistic reliability of each cycle is evaluated. The goal of the algorithm is to exclude cycles that have been influenced by one-time random events (news, for example).

One of the algorithms used for this is a more sophisticated Bartels Test. The test builds on detailed mathematics (statistics) which measures the stability of the amplitude and phase of each cycle.

Bartels' statistical test for periodicity, published at the Carnegie Institution of Washington in 1932, was embraced by the Foundation for the Study of Cycles decades ago as the best single test for a given cycle's projected reliability, robustness, and consequently, usefulness.

The Bartels Test is based on von Neumann's Ratio Test for Randomness. Bartels introduced a way to build ranking scores for cycles in a dataset according to their measured ratio of randomness.

The method provides a direct measurement of the likelihood that a given cycle is genuine. The higher the Bartels score is (above 70%, up to 100%), the higher the likelihood that the cycle is genuine and has not been influenced by one-time events.[1]

Step 4:

An important final step in making sense of the cyclic information is to establish a measurement for the strength of a cycle. Once the third step is completed, we have cycles that are dominant (based on their amplitude) and genuine with reference to their driving force in the financial market. But for trading purposes, this does not suffice. The price influence of a cycle per bar on the trading chart is the most crucial information.

Let me give you some examples by comparing two cycles. One cycle has a wavelength of 110 bars and an amplitude of 300. The other cycle has a wavelength of 60 bars and an amplitude of only 200.

So, if we apply the "standard" method for determining the dominant cycle, namely selecting the cycle with the highest amplitude, we would select the cycle with the wavelength of 110 and the amplitude of 300.

But let's look at the following information - the force of the cycle per bar:

- Length 110 / Amplitude 300   → Strength per bar: 300 / 110 = 2.7
- Length 60 / Amplitude 200   → Strength per bar: 200 / 60   = 3.3

For trading it is more important to know which cycle has the biggest influence to drive the price per bar, and not only which cycle has the highest amplitude!

That's the reason why I am introducing the measurement value "Cycle Strength". The Cycle Scanner automatically calculates this value in the script log.

---

[1] For further reading of the last official version, see: "The Rank Version of von Neumann's Ratio Test for Randomness", Author: Robert Bartels, Journal of the American Statistical Association, Vol. 77, No. 377, (Mar., 1982), pp. 40-46.

Step 5:

Sort the outcome according to the calculated cycle strength score. Now we have a top to bottom list of cycles which have the highest influence on price movements per bar. And that's precisely what we need!

Summary: The dominant market vibration

After our new engine has completed all five steps, the cycle at the top of the list (with the highest cycle strength score) will give us information on the dominant market vibration. In fact, the wavelength of this cycle is the dominant market vibration, which is very useful for trading.

I will use the definition of the Dominant Market Vibration because this full algorithm and the idea behind it go far beyond the classical definition of a dominant cycle as found in the literature.

4. Fine-tuning technical indicators using the Dominant Market Vibration

It does not suffice to only measure cycles accurately. Cycles and the measured Dominant Market Vibration must be applied in real trading environments. Let's start with a very old approach equipped with a brand new algorithm.

The first and easiest way to use the Dominant Market Vibration is to "fine-tune" technical standard indicators. This is not a new idea – but with the details presented in the last chapter, we can empower old ideas with a robust and dynamic cycle detection algorithm.

I will present a combination strategy that pairs the popular RSI oscillator with the cyclic concepts of the Dominant Market Vibration. This combination resolves the problem of flawed trading signals so common to traditional oscillator analysis by filtering them out.

The usage of the Cycle Scanner in combination with the RSI will show how the incorporation of cycle analysis greatly enhances the accuracy and value of oscillator signals.

4.1 The basic idea

A lot has already been written about the fine-tuning of technical indicators using information on the dominant cycle length. I will explain the basics next.

The reason we only use the technical indicators with their standard length setting of, for example, 13,is attributable to the lack of knowledge about how to set the correct length value ahead of time. One of the major drawbacks of using technical indicators with their standard length setting is the problem of filtering out flawed trading signals.

Fine-tuning technical indicators using the Dominant Market Vibration

Based on the logic of the calculation algorithm, standard indicators perform best when their "inner" setting (the length parameter for the calculation) is aligned with the Dominant Market Vibration of the price movement that is to be tracked. 'Aligned' means that the length input parameter is a harmonic number of the full dominant wavelength. The easiest would be to use the full or half harmonic of the Dominant Market Vibration measured.

Statement 1: Set the length parameter of technical indicators to a full or half harmonic of the Dominant Market Vibration.

Another common approach (when you're not sure how to detect the dominant cycle) would be to apply some back-optimizing to determine which length setting would have performed best in the past and use this setting for future trading. But even a back-optimized setting is a fixed setting that is not able to adjust to the actual market characteristics.

The usage of back-optimized or standardized fixed length periods in technical indicators leads to inaccurate results on the right-hand side of the chart where all trading is done.

Since the dominant cycle lengths and phase offsets that drive the market change over time, the adjustment of the indicators to these lengths must be done dynamically.

Statement 2: The length parameter must be adjusted dynamically.

However, the key for putting this idea into practice is to have a reliable and accurate method for detecting the dominant cycle at any given time. Most articles usually only explain how to adjust the standard length parameter of technical indicators and then leave you on your own when it comes to putting it into practice, i.e., how to detect the actual dominant cycle on your own. You can subscribe to newsletters or pay a lot of money to obtain this type of information. However, I will focus on putting this idea into practice. This publication will provide you with all the know-how you need to use this method on your own.

In the previous chapter, I introduced the proprietary algorithms needed in order to detect the dominant market cycle. This algorithm is included here and has been significantly simplified so you can apply it to any chart with only two mouse clicks. The last chapter has already indicated that you now have a powerful engine right at your fingertips that will deliver the wavelength.

Equipped with these tools, you are now able to dynamically detect the actual cycle length at any given point in time. You can start using this information to fine-tune your indicators right away.

Let's start by reviewing some examples.

4.2 A step-by-step guide: Trading the S&P 500 E-mini futures contract intraday

Let's review the market on an intraday chart using standard indicators. We will choose May 18, 2010 for this test (which is yesterday, i.e., the day before writing these lines, so no cherry picking here!). First, let's take a look at the chart based here on a normal standard RSI indicator:

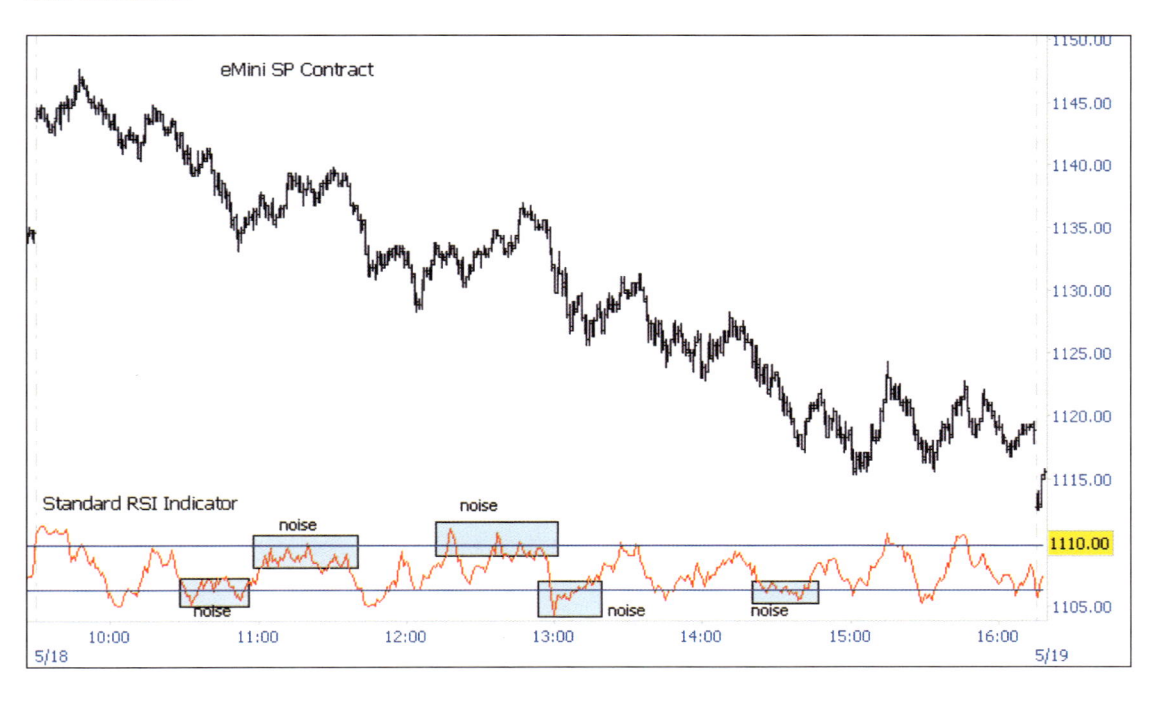

Figure 4-1: E-mini with standard RSI on May 18 – Not tradable information

You can clearly see from the noise information of the RSI that we would have had a lot of whipsaw trades with a great loss at the end of the day. Now let's see whether we are able to fine-tune the RSI indicator with the information derived from the Dominant Market Vibration.

Fine-tuning technical indicators using the Dominant Market Vibration

We will now go over the entire method in detail. Let's assume that it's the start of the trading day on May 18. Hence, we will have to prepare for the trading day in the morning just after the market has opened.

Step 1: Open chart and run cycle analyzer using (approx.) one day of data history

We have attached the Cycle Scanner toolkit to the chart. The period from the start date of the trading on May 17 until the morning of May 18 was chosen, i.e., one complete day of data history.

Next, let's have a look at the scanner results window:

```
Chart format: 1 bar = 1 minutes
Analysis Begins On: 201005170939   and   Ends On: 201005180949
Datapoints: 415 -> Bartels Test reliable for cycle length up to: 83
Bartels Limit >= 49 %
Sorted by: Cycle Strength
Cycle length - Range Min: 10  /  Max: 299
-----------------------------------------------------------------
Cycle Length // Amplitude // Date Cycle Low // Cycle Strength // %
'Real' Cycle Percent (Bartels Value)

"45  /  1.829   /  17.5.2010.1003.T  /  0.0406  /  86.9 %  (0.131)"
"40  /  1.4226  /  17.5.2010.1004.T  /  0.0356  /  85.8 %  (0.142)"
"36  /  1.1885  /  17.5.2010.1007.T  /  0.033   /  64.3 %  (0.357)"
"12  /  0.3314  /  17.5.2010.947.T   /  0.0276  /  77.63 % (0.2237)"
"57  /  1.4412  /  17.5.2010.1015.T  /  0.0253  /  84.95 % (0.1505)"
```

Step 2: Detect the Dominant Market Vibration

If we follow the definition of the Dominant Market Vibration presented in the introduction of this chapter (highest score of cycle strength), the Dominant Market Vibration detected has a wavelength of 45 bars (minutes). The idea now is to use this information to fine-tune the indicators. The most effective approach is to take half of the identified wavelength as input for the length parameter of standard indicators. In this case, the score of 22 would be the half-length of the Dominant Market Vibration (45 / 2 = 22.5 -> but we will use only full integer values for the length settings, here 22).

Step 3: Use the market vibration to fine-tune indicators

At the start of the trading day, we knew that the market vibration was about 45 minutes. Therefore, we will use 22 as the length input for standard indicators in the chart (1 minute chart). Accordingly, we will enter the standard RSI indicator into the chart with an individual length of 22.

We have now completed our "cyclic" fine-tuning of the RSI indicator. That is it. It's all very straightforward if you know the dominant market cycle and vibration score. It is just about setting the right length value for the indicator to be in sync with the market vibration.

Performance review of the cyclic fine-tuned RSI indicator:

Let's review whether this fine-tuned RSI indicator is able to perform better. The next chart shows the trading day including the cyclic fine-tuned RSI. The trading signals – a break below/above the upper/lower lines (30 and 70) – are marked as blue lines in the chart for easy reading.

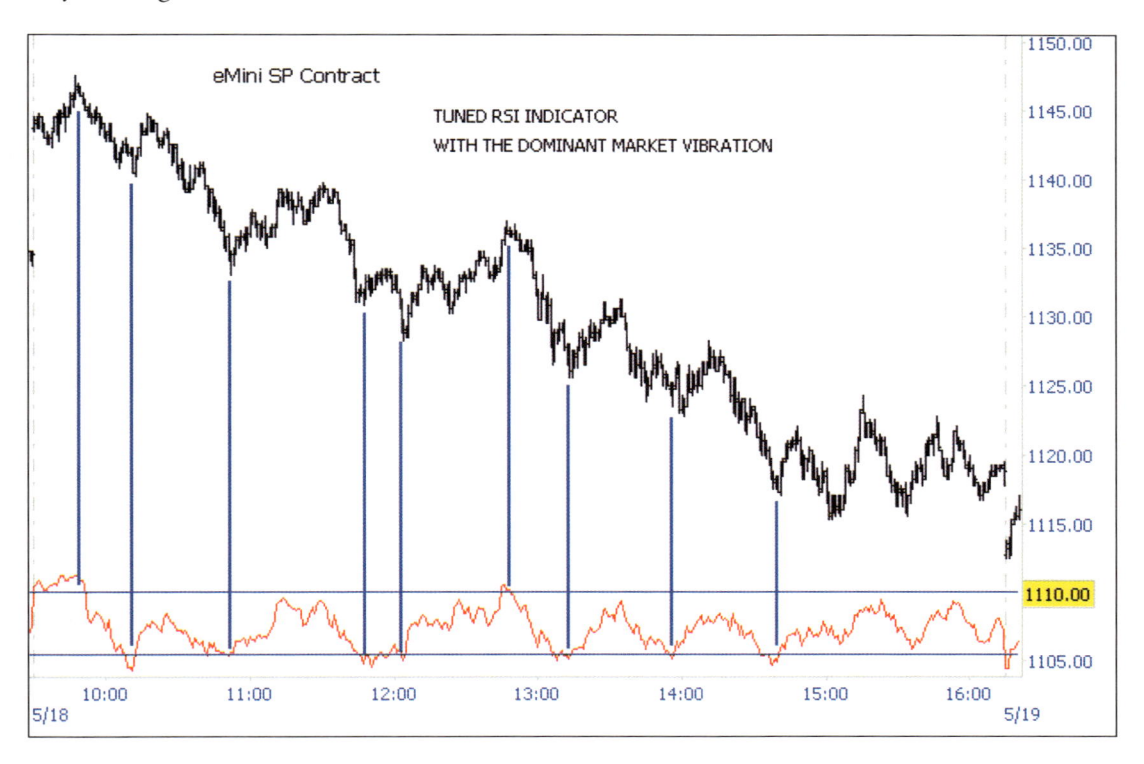

Figure 4-2: E-mini with cyclic fine-tuned RSI on May 18 – Clear trade signals

You can see that each RSI signal was in alignment with important market highs/lows. Now the RSI is able to perform its duty because it is now vibrating to the beat of the market. This is very important for standard indicators. Normally, no one knows how to set the "length" parameter of most of the technical indicators. Or, alternatively, you are able to see immediately *after* the fact which length input would have performed best. But in trading, what *would* have been the best parameter for the indicator is irrelevant after the fact.

Therefore, we need information on what the best parameter is ahead of time. The Dominant Market Vibration, which we can identify using our new engine, is able to deliver this information.

If you only use the standard length setting, which is not in alignment with the Dominant Market Vibration, the output of the indicator will be useless with regard to reliable trading signals. You can compare both charts at the end of this chapter. You will clearly see what I am talking about (Figure 4-4 and Figure 4-5 on page 77).

But let's take it even one step further.

Once we know the cyclic component of the market, we are also able to apply some noise filtering with nearly zero lag. Therefore, I have integrated a cyclic smoothing engine into the RSI indicator. It is the same RSI indicator, only that the RSI signal is smoothed by this new "cyclic super smoother".

The next chart shows the same RSI with a length setting of 22, supplemented by the smoothing engine. One major advantage becomes evident now: The signals referring to the break above/below the lower/upper indicator lines remain the same, the nearly zero lag filtering notwithstanding.

We are now able to clearly see the divergences between the price and the cyclic fine-tuned RSI indicator. These divergences would not have been easy to see in the normal RSI indicator. But in this cyclic fine-tuned version, the divergences are easily visible. And these signals are even more important than the line breaks. The divergences of this indicator are highlighted in the chart below.

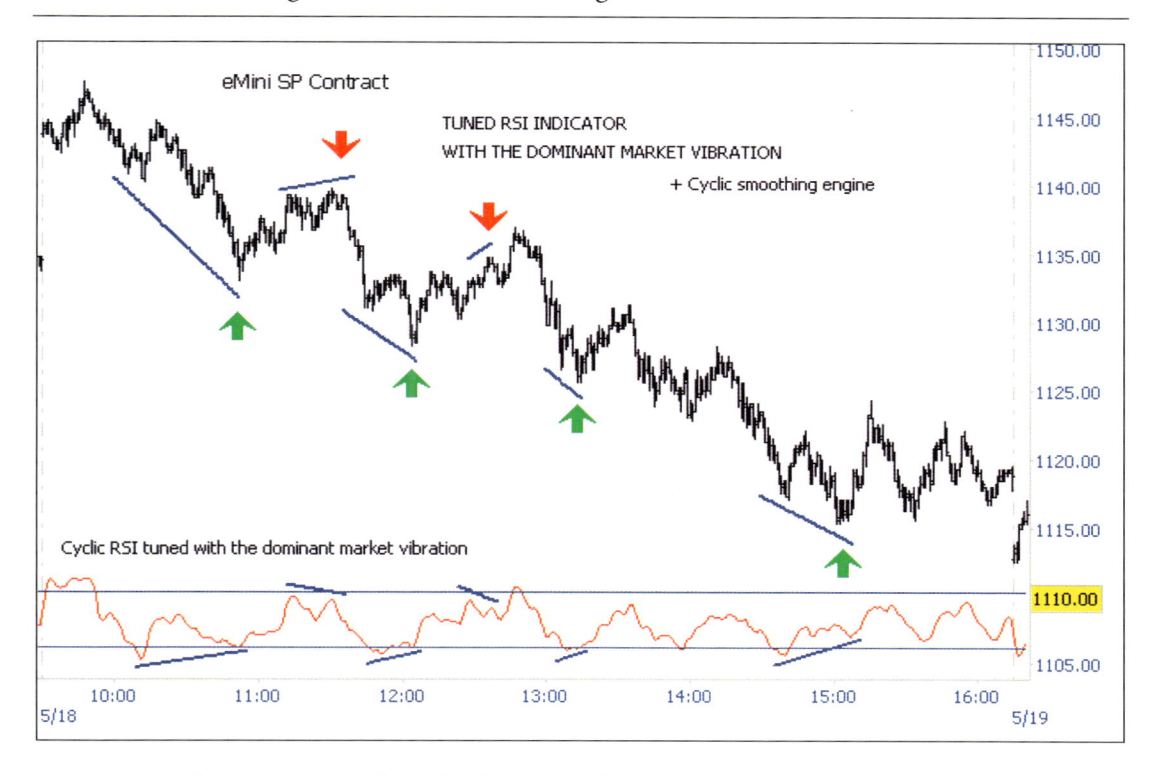

Figure 4-3: E-mini with cyclic fine-tuned & smoothed RSI on May 18 – Clear divergence signals

The most powerful signals are attained when there is a divergence AND a break of the upper/lower signal line as previously detected.

The cyclic tuned RSI indicator can be activated via the main menu:

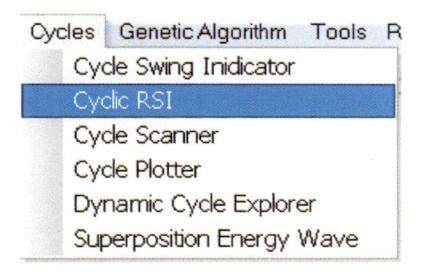

The following additional parameters are available: "Vibration" specifies the sensitiveness for the dominant cycle detection and "Range1" and "Range2" the Adaptive Bands behaviour.

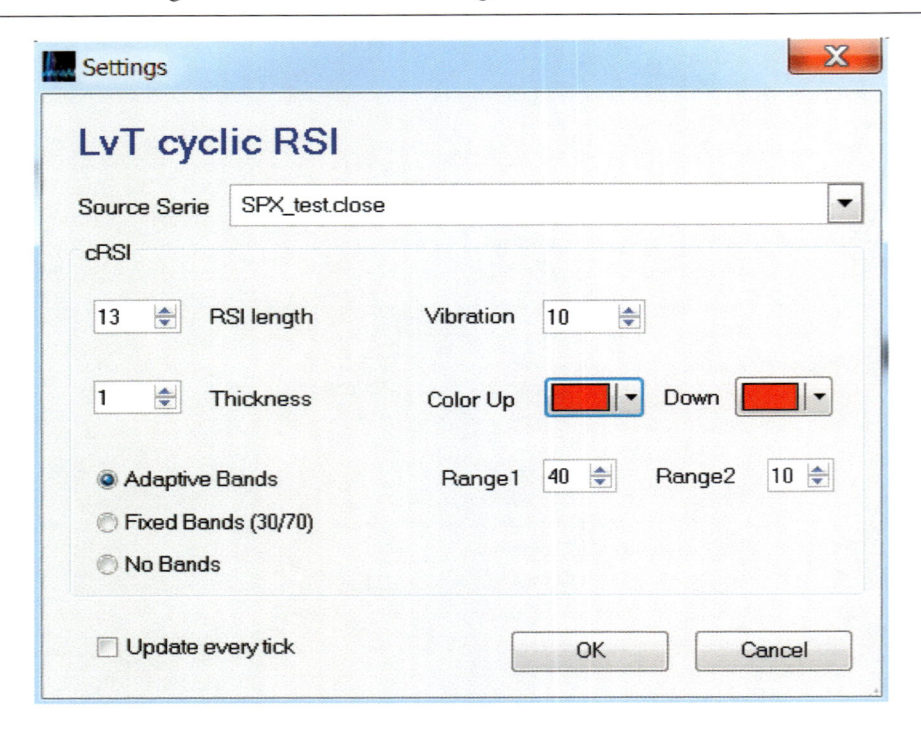

[Settings dialog: LvT cyclic RSI — Source Serie: SPX_test.close; cRSI: RSI length 13, Thickness 1, Adaptive Bands / Fixed Bands (30/70) / No Bands; Vibration 10, Color Up, Down, Range1 40, Range2 10; Update every tick; OK / Cancel]

Please review these signals with the standard RSI indicator on the next page (Figure 4-4 and Figure 4-5 on page 77). You would not have been able to see these signals with the standard RSI settings.

To better understand, I have included a large chart here including both indicators. You can thus review the details of the chart on your own and compare these two RSI signals more closely (Figure 4-6, Page 78).

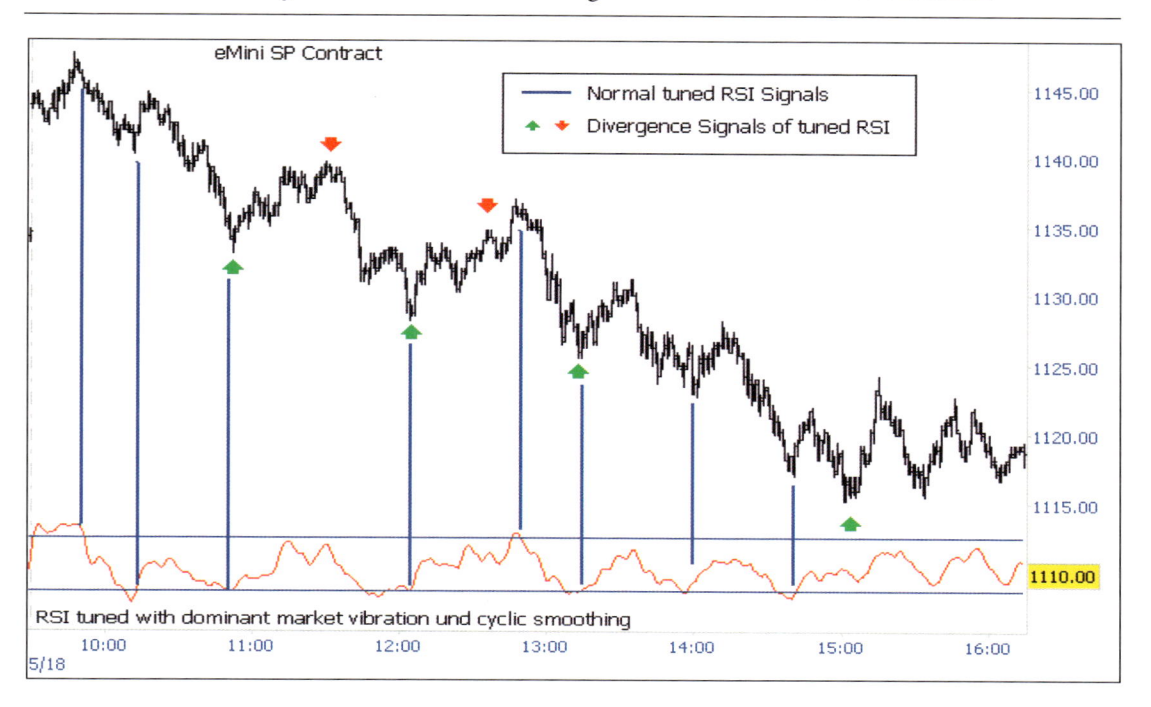

Figure 4-4: Trading signals of cyclic fine-tuned RSI

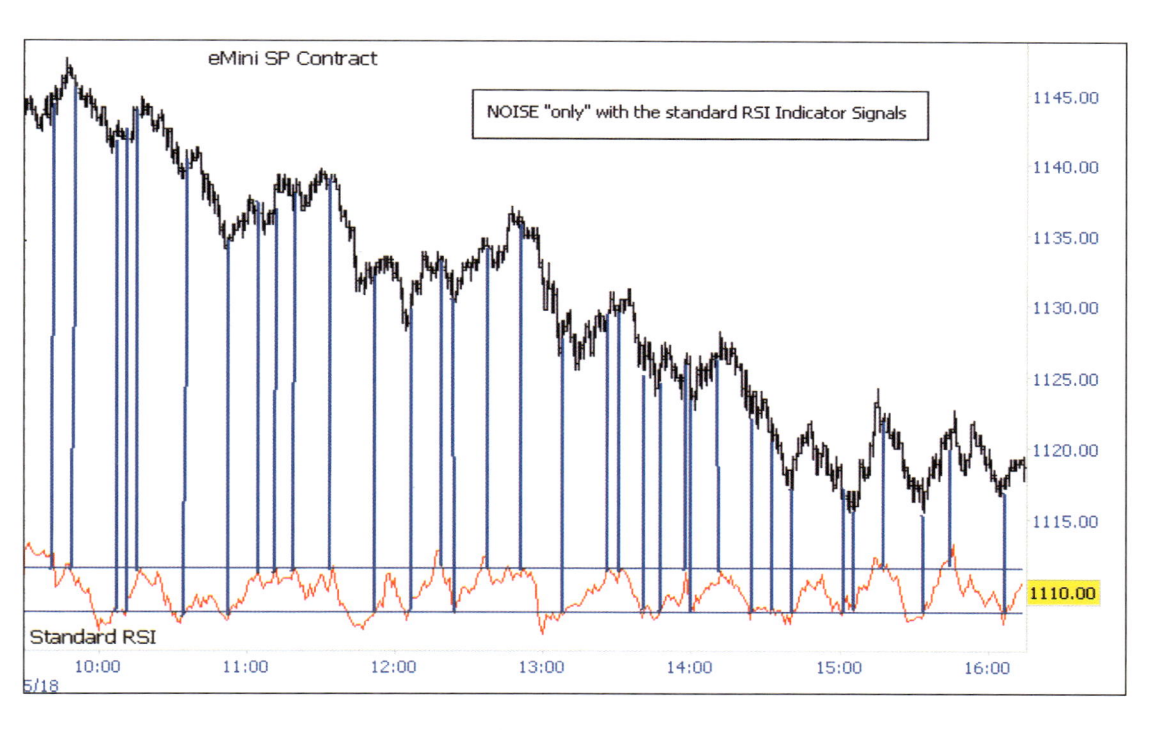

Figure 4-5: Trading signals of standard RSI

Fine-tuning technical indicators using the Dominant Market Vibration

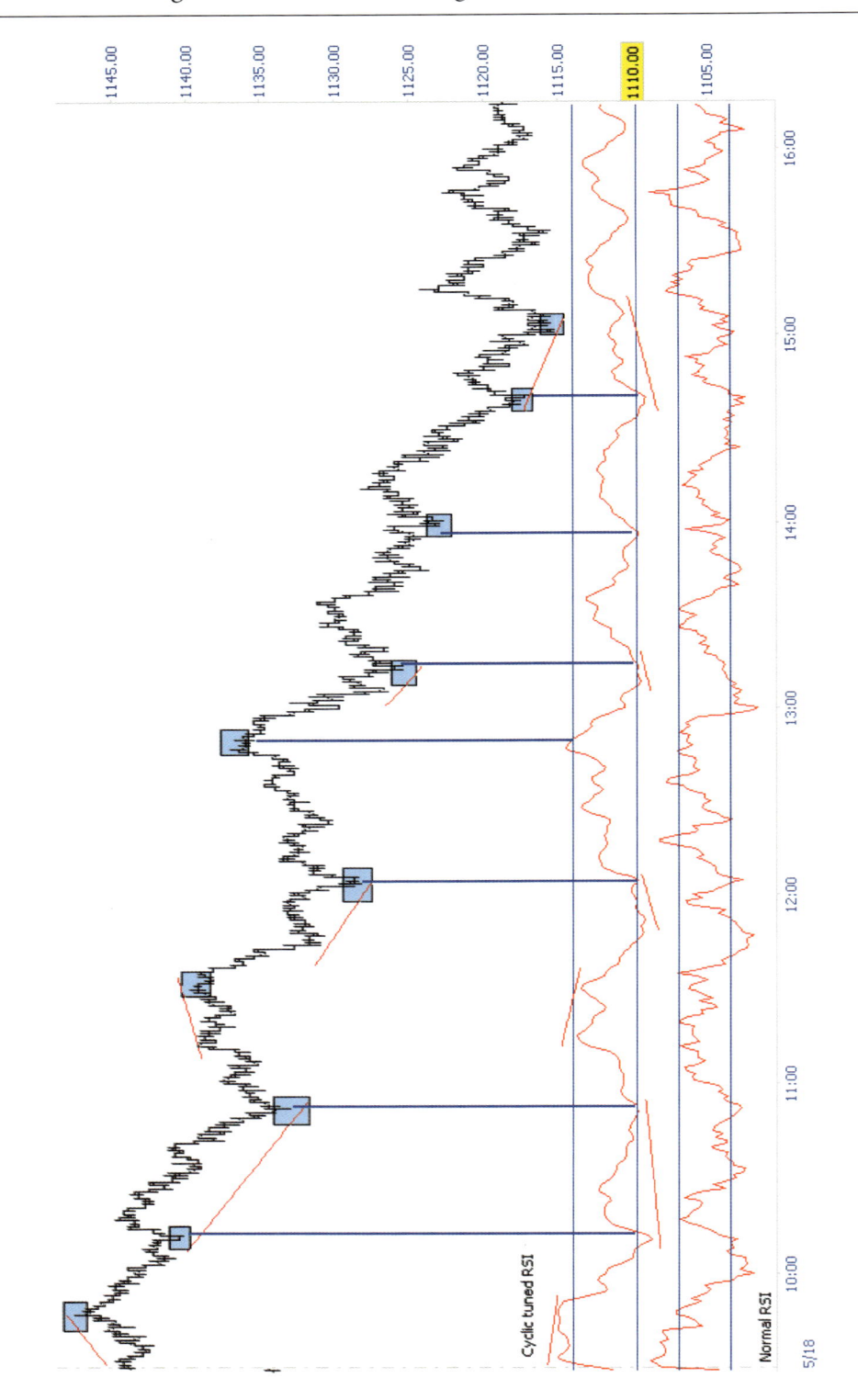

Figure 4-6: Comparison of both RSI versions / large chart

4.3 Trading S&P 500 E-mini futures contract intraday - Example 2

To demonstrate that the fact that it worked was not only "good luck", we will move on to the present as I am writing this and review whether this method would have also worked on the next trading day. To do so, we will use the standard procedure to fine-tune the technical indicators as presented in the previous chapter.

Step 1: Open chart and run cycle analyzer using (approx.) one day of data history

We will use the same chart. To demonstrate that this method works on any time frame, we will switch to a 4-minute time frame. Hence, we will simply open the 4-minute chart for May 19 before trading starts using the data history of May 18 for analysis. We used the last trading day for our analysis engine. We ran the cycle analyzer with the following settings:

Starttime: 18 May 2010 / first bar on chart at 09:34

Endtime: 18 May 2010 / last bar on chart at 16:15

Step 2: Detect the Dominant Market Vibration

After applying the cycle analyzer with the time settings to the chart, we have to open the script log to look up the detailed analysis results. The script log looks as follows:

```
Chart format: 1 bar = 4 minutes
Analysis Begins On  201005180934  and  Ends On: 201005181615
Datapoints: 100 -> Bartels Test reliable for cycle length up to: 20
Bartels Limit >= 49 %
Sorted by: Cycle Strength
Cycle length - Range Min: 10  / Max: 299
-----------------------------------------------------------------
Cycle Length // Amplitude // Date Cycle Low // Cycle Strength // %
'Real' Cycle Percent (Bartels Value)

"11  /  1.0101  /  18.5.2010.934.T   /  0.0918  /  76.02 % (0.2398)"
"21  /  1.7655  /  18.5.2010.1046.T  /  0.0841  /  97.32 % (0.0268)"
"45  /  1.4753  /  18.5.2010.1142.T  /  0.0328  /  80.49 % (0.1951)"
-----------------------------------------------------------------
```

Figure 4-7: Cyclic analysis results for May 19

The Dominant Market Vibration has a length of 11 bars here. We will obtain this value *before* the trading starts on May 19. That is, we have crucial information ahead of time to fine-tune our indicators for the next trading day.

Step 3: Use the market vibration to fine-tune indicators

The setting for the cyclic fine-tuned indicator for the next day would be half the Dominant Market Vibration:

11 / 2 = 5.5 -> 5

All we have to do is set up the RSI with a length setting of 5. Open the RSI and set the length to 5 and switch on the cyclic smoothing.

Performance review of the cyclic fine-tuned RSI indicator:

The following chart shows the trading day of May 19 including both indicators (i.e., the standard RSI and the RSI with a length of 5 and the switched-on cyclic smoothing). The trading signals for the break of the lower/upper indicator line are presented by small arrows. The additional divergence signals are denoted by large arrows.

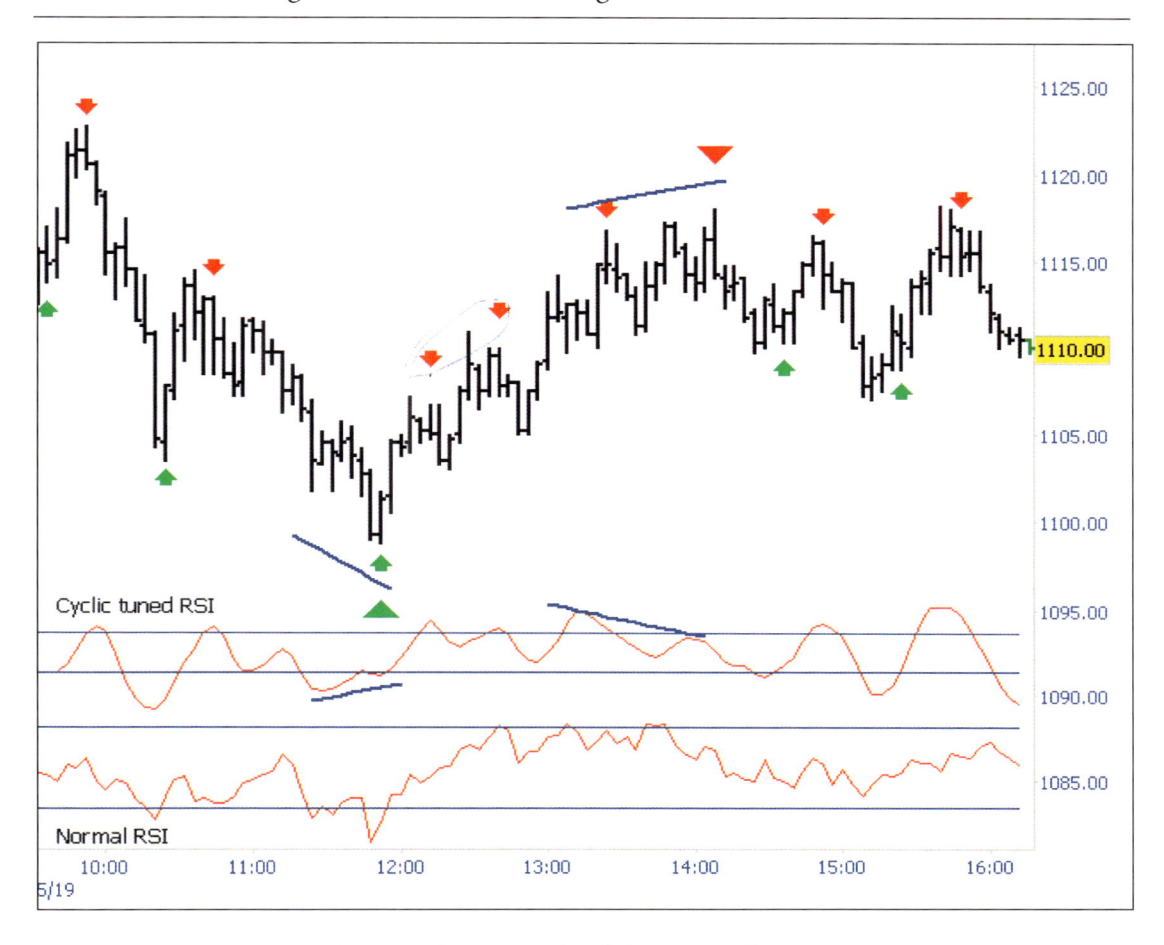

Figure 4-8: Trading signals of the cyclic fine-tuned RSI

The cyclic fine-tuned RSI identified 14 trading signals for May 19. Two of these 14 signals would not have been tradable, the sell signal around 12:15 p.m. and the sell signal around 12:40 p.m. But all other signals would have been tradable. We thus arrive at a profitability score of 85% for these signals.

You can compare these numbers to the signals from the standard RSI presented in the next chart. The standard RSI identified 8 trade signals (4 long, 4 short). But only two of them would have been tradable. The other signals would have produced losses and – more importantly – our confidence in this indicator would have vanished. I think that you would not take the fourth buy signal after having three "failed" buy signals. But let's stick to the numbers: 2 out of 8 signals implies a profitability of 25%.

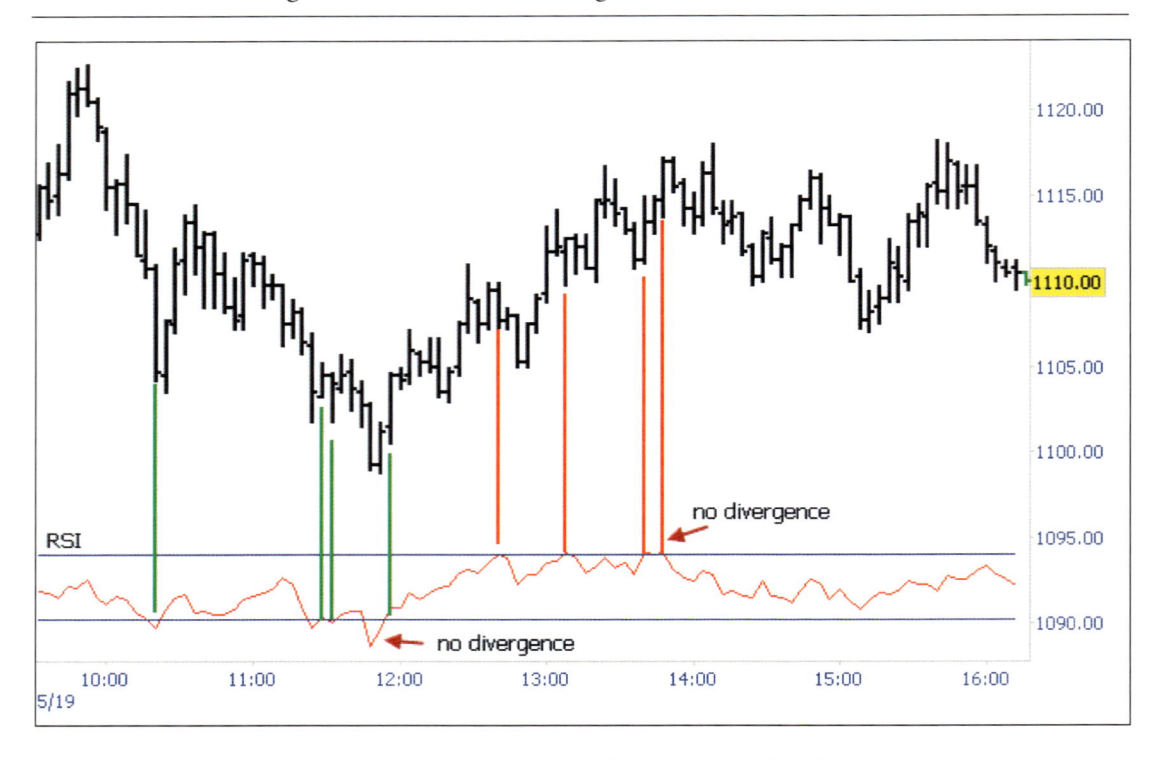

Figure 4-9: Trading signals of the standard RSI

This is the second day the cyclic fine-tuned indicator was able to deliver tradable signals. And let's not forget – the standard RSI was not able to deliver any reliable trading signals at all. This is the standard situation which may apply every day, every week, and every month. You will have an edge on trading in the markets with the cyclic fine-tuned standard indicators!

Indicator	Buy Signals	Sell Signals	Profitable Signals	Profitability
Standard RSI	4	4	2	25 %
Cyclic fine-tuned RSI	6	8	12	85 %

Figure 4-10: Profitability comparison of RSI and cyclic fine-tuned RSI

I chose the RSI for demonstration purposes only. But it works the same with all length parameter settings for the technical indicators. You can also fine-tune the stochastic or

MACD with this information as well. Simply use half the value of the Dominant Market Vibration score.

4.4 Summary

The idea of fine-tuning technical indicators with the dominant cycle length is not new. As the new and reliable engine, the Cycle Scanner, can detect the Dominant Market Vibration, you are now able to apply this method to any chart and time frame. I recommend using approximately 1-3 days of intraday data history when using intraday charts. The method also works on daily charts. It is best to use around 1-2 years of data history to identify the best parameters for daily charts.

I have also included the RSI indicator with the cyclic smoothing engine in the Cycles Main menu section.

You are now able to a) fine-tune your indicator(s) and b) smooth the signal even further. This method works with every technical indicator. But my research reveals that it works best with the RSI.

To fine-tune the RSI indicator, I recommend using half of the Dominant Market Vibration score (first score listed in the Cycle Scanner when sorted by cycle strength). You can also use the full number, but half of the Dominant Market Vibration score works best. Furthermore, you have to look at the output and the second dominant vibration may also occasionally come into play. Just familiarize yourself with this method by replaying the examples shown here on your own.

Ideas and opportunities for further research using this method include:

- Cyclic fine-tuned channel indicators (Bollinger band, Keltner channel)
- Auto-adjust the length period at each new bar (not just every day)
- Breakout-system with cyclic length / speed adjustments.

5. Cycles Are Not Static: The Dynamic Nature of Cycles

The assumption that cycles are static over time is misleading for trading purposes. Dominant Cycles morph over time because of the nature of inner parameters of length and phase. Active Dominant Cycles do not abruptly jump from one length (e.g., 50) to another (e.g., 120). Typically, one dominant cycle will remain active for a longer period and vary around the core parameters. The "genes" of the cycle in terms of length, phase, and amplitude are not fixed and will morph around the dominant parameters.

These periodic motions abound both in nature and the man-made world. Examples include a heartbeat or the cyclic movements of planets. Although many real motions are intrinsically repeated, few are perfectly periodic. For example, a walker's stride frequency may vary, and a heart may beat slower or faster.

Once an individual is in a dominant state (such as sitting to write a book), the heartbeat cycle will stabilize at an approximate rate of 85 bpm. However, the exact cycle will not stay static at 85 bpm but will vary +/- 10%. The variance is not considered a new heartbeat cycle at 87 bpm or 83 bpm, but is considered the same dominant, active vibration.

This pattern can be observed in the environment in addition to mathematical equations. Real cyclic motions are not perfectly even; the period varies slightly from one cycle to the next because of changing physical environmental factors.

This dynamic behavior is also valid for financial market cycles.

However, anticipating current values for length and cycle offset in real time is crucial to identifying the next turn. It requires an awareness of the active dominant cycle parameter and requires the ability to verify and track the real current status and dynamic variations that facilitate projection of the next significant event.

Figures 1 to 3 provide a step-by-step illustration of these effects. The illustrations show a grey static cycle. The variation dynamic in the cycle is represented by the red one with parameters that morph slightly over time. The marked points A to D represent the deviation between the ideal static and the dynamic cycle.

5.1 Effect A: Shifts in Cycle Length

The first effect is contraction and extraction of cycles, or the "cycle breath." Possible cycles are detected from the available data on the left side of the chart. Points A and B show an acceptable fit between both cycles. However, the red dynamic cycle has a greater parameter length. The past data reveal that this is not significant, and there is a good fit for the theoretical static and the dynamic cycle at point A and B. Unfortunately, the future projection area on the right side of the chart where trading takes place reflects an increasing deviation between the static and dynamic cycle. The difference between the static and dynamic cycle at points C and D is now relatively high.

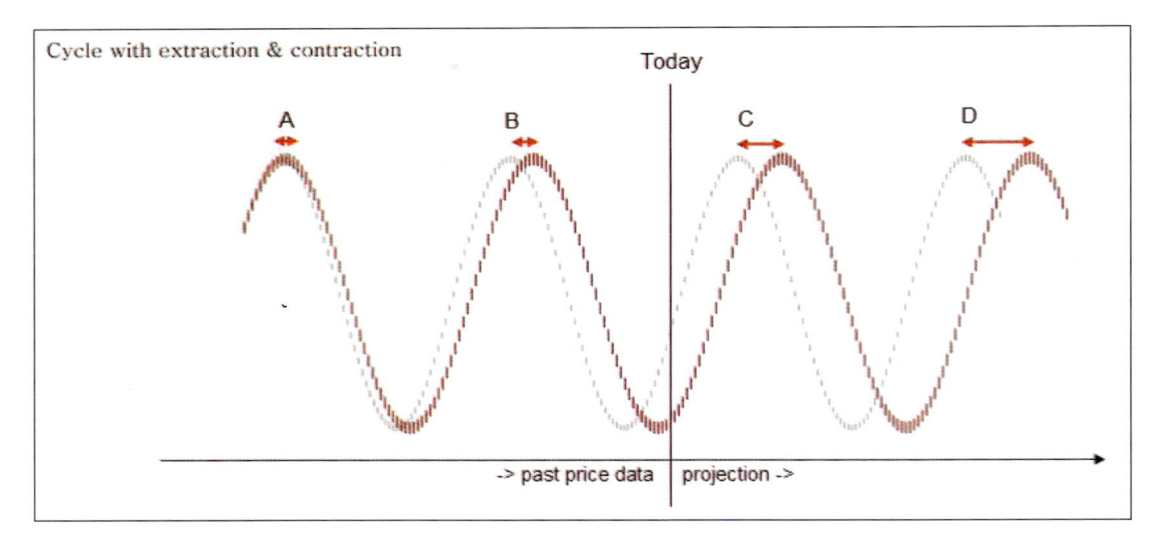

Figure 1: Effect 1 – Length Shifts

The real "dynamic" cycle has a parameter with a slightly greater length. The consequence is that future deviations increase even when the deviations between the theoretical and real cycle are not visible in the area of analysis. These differences are crucial for trading. As trading occurs on the right side of the chart, the core parameters now and for the next expected cycle turn must be detected. A perfect fit of past data or a two-year projection is not a concern. The priority is the here and now, not a mathematical fit with the past. Current market turns must be in sync with the dynamic cycle to detect the next turn. Therefore, just as an individual heartbeat cycle approximates a core number, the cycle length will vary around the dominant parameter +/- 5%. Following only the theoretical static cycle will not provide information concerning the next anticipated turning points. However, this is not the only effect.

5.2 Effect B: Shifts in Cycle Phase

The next effect is "offset shifts." In this case, the cycle length parameter is the same between the static theoretical and the dynamic cycle. The dynamic cycle at point A presents a slight offset shift at the top. In mathematical terms, the phase parameter has morphed. This effect remains fixed into the future. A static deviation is observed between the highs and the lows.

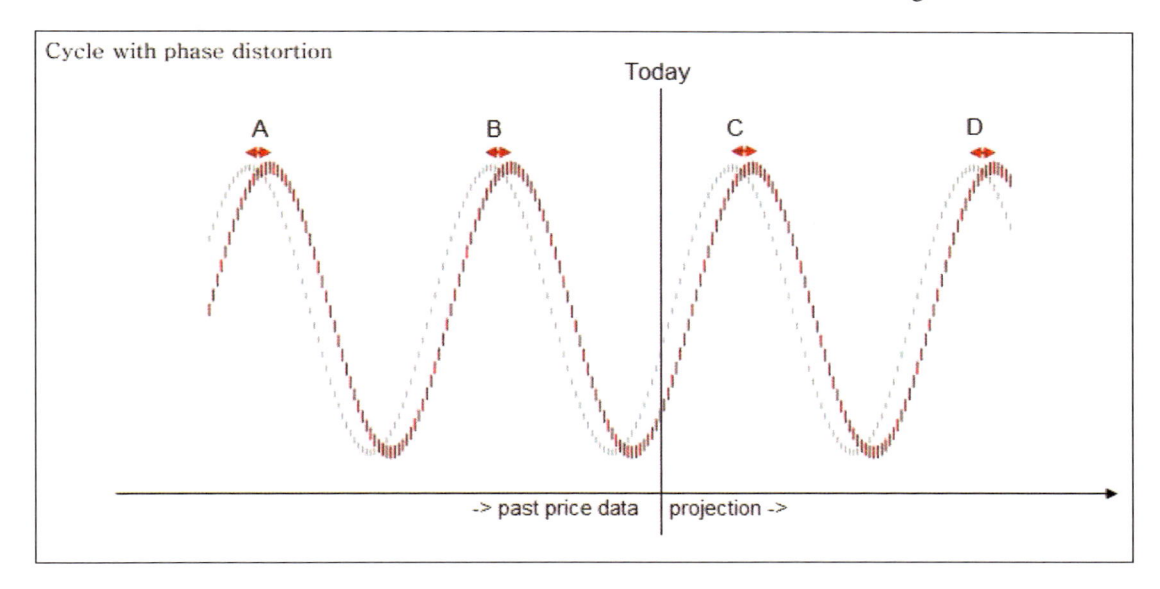

Figure 2: Effect 2 – Phase Shifts

Although this is not a one-time effect, the phase of the dominant cycle will also change continuously by +/- 5% around the core dominant parameters.

5.3 The Combined Effects

In practice, both effects occur in parallel and change continuously around the core dominant parameters. Figure 3 presents a snapshot of both effects with the theoretical and the dynamic cycle. The deviation in the projection area at points C and D shows that just following the static theoretical cycle will rapidly become worthless.

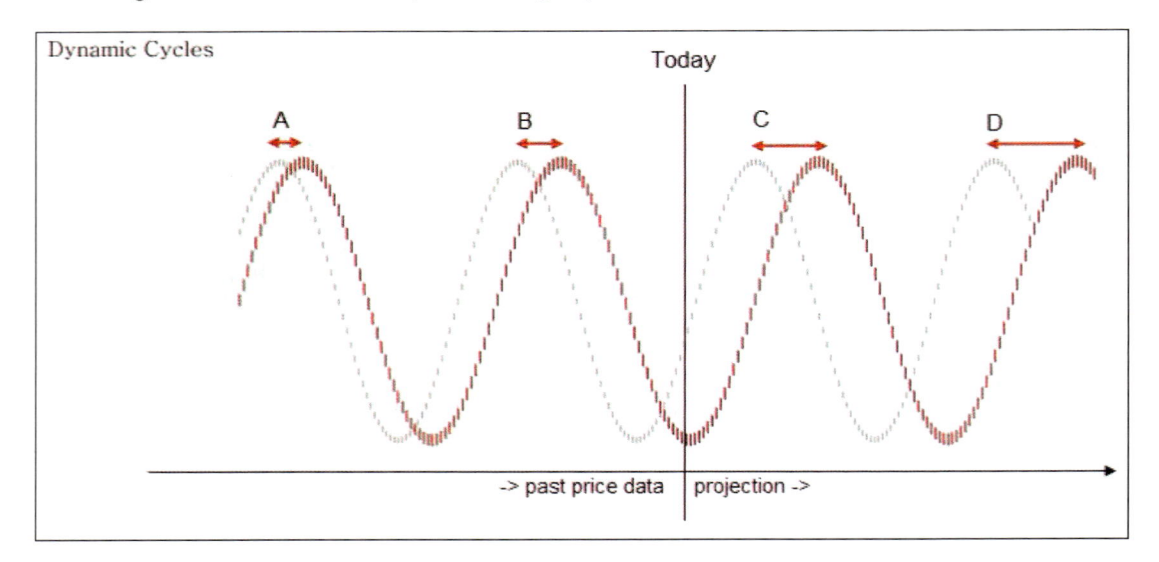

Figure 3: The Effects Combined (Grey: Static Cycle/Red: Dynamic Cycle)

The deviation is to the extent that, at point D, a cycle high is expected for the theoretical static cycle (grey) while the real dynamic cycle (red) remains low at point D.

These two effects occur in a continuous manner. Although the alignment in the past (points A and B) appear acceptable between the static and dynamic cycle, the deviation in the projection area (points C and D) is so high that trading the static cycle will lead to failure.

A cycle forecasting example incorporating these effects explains the consequences on the right side of the chart.

We check the following two examples named "A" and "B". The price chart is the same for both examples and is represented by a black line on the chart. In both examples, a dominant cycle is detected (red cycle plot) and the price is plotted.

Cycles Are Not Static: The Dynamic Nature of Cycles

In both examples, two variations of the same dominant cycle are detected. The tops and lows show alignment with the price data and two cycle tops and two cycle lows align. This implies that the same dominant cycle is active in both charts. There is one core dominant cycle and the two detected cycles are variations of this same dominant cycle.

Therefore, from an analytical perspective view, both cycles could be considered valid from observations of the available dataset.

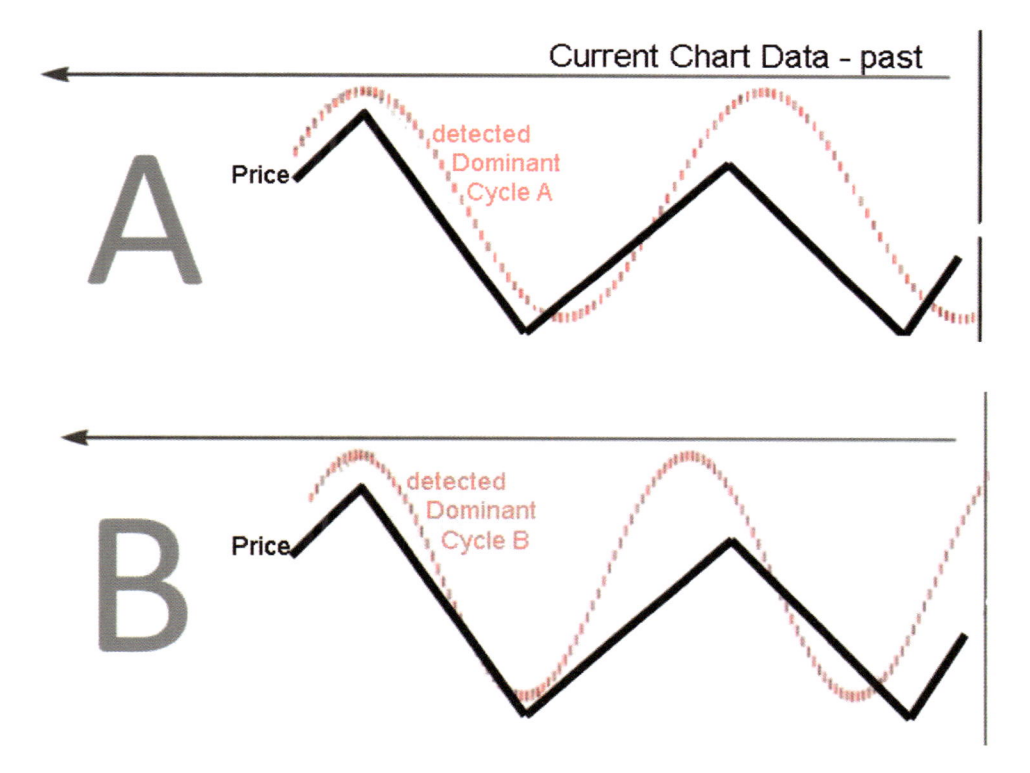

Figure 4: Same Price Chart – Two Detected Cycles

The effects reveal that although past data deviation is convincing, it can significantly impact the projection area. We examine the projection of both cycles.

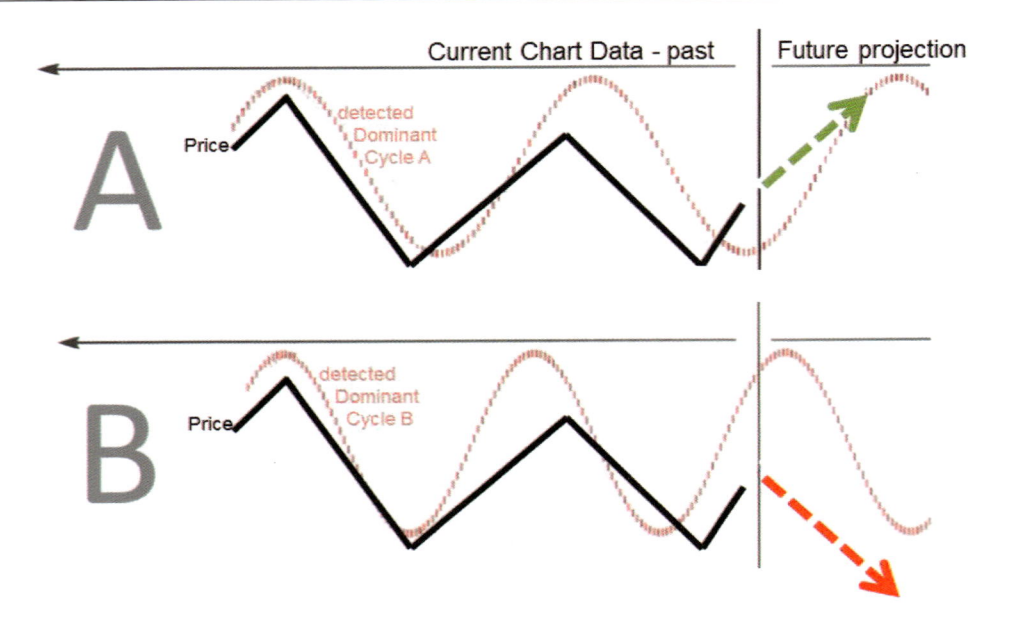

Figure 5: Cycle Projection of Both Examples

We observe two contrasting projections. Example A shows a bottoming cycle with a projected upturn to a future top. Example B shows the opposite, a topping out cycle with an expected future downturn.

While we can detect a dominant cycle on the left area of the chart, the detailed dynamic parameters are the significant differentiators and are crucial to a valid and credible projection.

Classic static cycle projections often fail for this reason. Detecting the active dominant cycle represents one part of the process. The second part is to consider the current dynamic parameters with respect to the length and phase of the second part. Although the perfect fit of a cycle within the distant past between price and a static cycle might appear convincing from a mathematical perspective, it is misleading because it ignores the dynamic cycle components. Doing so simplifies the math, but is of no value for trading on the right side of the chart. The examination of past perfect fit static cycles is not necessary. The observance of two to five significant correlations of tops and lows, AND the consideration of current dynamic component updates will yield valid trading cycle projections.

This example underpins the significance of an approach that combines a dominant cycle detection engine with a dynamic component update.

5.4 Video Lesson – Dynamic Cycles Explained

The following video illustrates the two effects in action.

Video Lesson

Dynamic Cycles Explained

http://www.whentotrade.com/wtt-dynamic-cycles-explained/

6. Forecasting the next important market turn – Time, direction & polarity

Let's move on to look at other ways of using the cyclic information we have for trading on the markets. In the previous chapter, I showed you how to fine-tune indicators by means of the Dominant Market Vibration score. However, the Dominant Market Vibration score can be used in different ways. One approach is to determine what the actual dominant cycle is at each new bar. When we know the wavelength of the given cycle, we can apply specific techniques to determine the actual phase of this cycle. The phase provides information on when to expect the next important high/low in the market.

I consider this a dynamic approach because it is characteristic of cycles for their phases and wavelengths to change continuously over time. That's also the reason why static cycle frameworks often fail when they are applied to financial markets. You can, of course, detect cycles based on past data, but when you apply this static information to the wavelength, amplitude, and phase of a cycle to build forecasts for a future time period, you do not take into account that the phase, amplitude, and wavelength of the identified cycle will vary over time (this effect is commonly paraphrased as: "Cycles appear and disappear").

6.1 Introducing a new forecasting method based on the Dominant Market Vibration

I will now introduce a dynamic approach for building tradable forecasts. Every time a new bar appears, we will reassess the dominant cycle in terms of wavelength, amplitude, and phase offset. We will then plot this cycle in the future. However, we will only focus on the next expected turning point – that's what we are interested in. We can call this turning point – ETA – Expected Time of Arrival.

Then, as we move forward in time, every bar signifies an update on the next expected turning point. This dynamic forecast based on the Dominant Market Vibration provides information about the next turning point with regard to TIME and DIRECTION. We will get real-time information on when to expect the next major turning point in the market. This information can be updated every time a new bar appears. That is, the ETA information is updated at every new bar.

Now the difference between many cycle researchers' approach and mine should be evident. I do not apply a framework with static cycles and try to make the market fit into it. Often, you read about the significance of the 4-year cycle, the 50-week cycle, and the 7-year cycle and how these "static" cycles can be applied to the actual market situation. That's not my approach here. I do not offer you a "static" cycle framework. I offer a dynamic model that determines which cycles are active at a given time.

I use this method in order to be "prepared" for important turning points in the market. I do not blindly trade these ETA points. But when used in combination with other tools or Fibonacci levels, you will have very powerful set-ups to trade the market.

Charts can speak more than a thousand words. However, before we move on to review some real examples, let me introduce a few new indicators and tools.

6.2 Introduction of the Dynamic Cycle Explorer method

So far, we have arrived at a new method for detecting cycles in financial instruments. When we apply cycles to trading, we also need visual information about the presence of cycles in the given data. It does not suffice to focus on theoretical cycles alone. We need to isolate the current cycles with a detected wavelength from the available financial data. These cycles will not look like sine waves. The markets are not as clean as sine wave-like cycles. Cycles' amplitudes, phases, and wavelengths change continuously over time. Hence, the detected cycle will look different from a theoretical sine wave structure. But we need visual information of the past to verify our "theoretical" cycle and the actual cyclic behavior of the financial instrument with this particular wavelength. We have to eliminate all cycles from the data that have higher and lower wavelengths than our cycle length. Ultimately, we only want to look at the behavior of the financial data in relation to our selected cycle length.

Now, we can plot the relevant information we have on the detected cycle length on top of each other:

- The isolated cyclic behavior of the price based on our wavelength;
- The theoretical cycle (sine wave plot) based on the detected phase and amplitude.

This information is very useful to analyze past price behavior. We now have the possibility to see the past phases and amplitude shifts of the cycle. We can build a "visual correlation" between the theoretical cycle and the cyclic price behavior.

6.2.1 Plotting price cycles in financial markets – Visualization of price cycles

We first need a method to isolate individual cycles from the price data. That is, we need to find a way to plot the cyclic behavior of the price data, not the theoretical cycle. A way to filter out all the longer and shorter cycles.

A lot has been written about these techniques. I will not repeat all of the algorithms here. One very effective way of filtering out the longer and shorter cycles is to use a special subset of two centered moving averages. This method was first introduced by Brian J. Millard in his book "Channels & Cycles: A Tribute to J.M. Hurst". It is called "Average Minus Average" or "cycle highlighter". His method of isolating cycles is far more superior to other techniques because it only requires one value to be specified, namely, the wavelength of the cycle that we want to isolate.

To apply this technique, a centered moving average with a length equal to the wavelength of the cycle to be isolated is set. A second centered moving average is then calculated with a length that is half of the first average. In the final step, the difference between these two averages is determined. If you are interested in more detailed information on how to use centered moving averages to extract cyclic information, I recommend reading Millard's book.

Millard's technique is very useful for us because our new engine for cycle detection introduced in the previous chapter provided us with the value we need – the wavelength of the cycle.

We can use the given value for the detected Dominant Market Vibration as input for the cycle highlighter. We can now discern the cyclic behavior of the price for past data.

As is the case with centered averages, the difference between the two averages will expose a loss of points at the beginning and at the end of the plot. This technique thus does not help us build forecasts. But it does help us gain a visual understanding of the cycle and compare the detected cycle with the cyclic behavior of past data. Therefore, I will expand the cycle highlighter method and take the basic idea further. I will call this new approach "Dynamic Cycle Explorer". This technique has a "built-in" cycle highlighter.

An important factor when using dominant cycles for forecasting is to compare the wavelength-isolated, past cyclic movement of price with the theoretical dominant cycle based on the information on the actual phase and amplitude.

When we build an overlay of all the information derived, we obtain a visual tool to detect past phase and amplitude shifts. This provides us information on how "reliable" or "stable" this cycle was in the past. We will also use this information to fine-tune our offset points (last low or high) for the cyclic analysis.

The following figure illustrates all elements of the Cycle Explorer technique. For demonstration purposes, I have used the example data from the first chapter. We know that the data included a cycle with a length of 30 calendar days. The date chosen for the actual analysis using this dataset was 1 April 2007.

This is what the Cycle Explorer will show you:

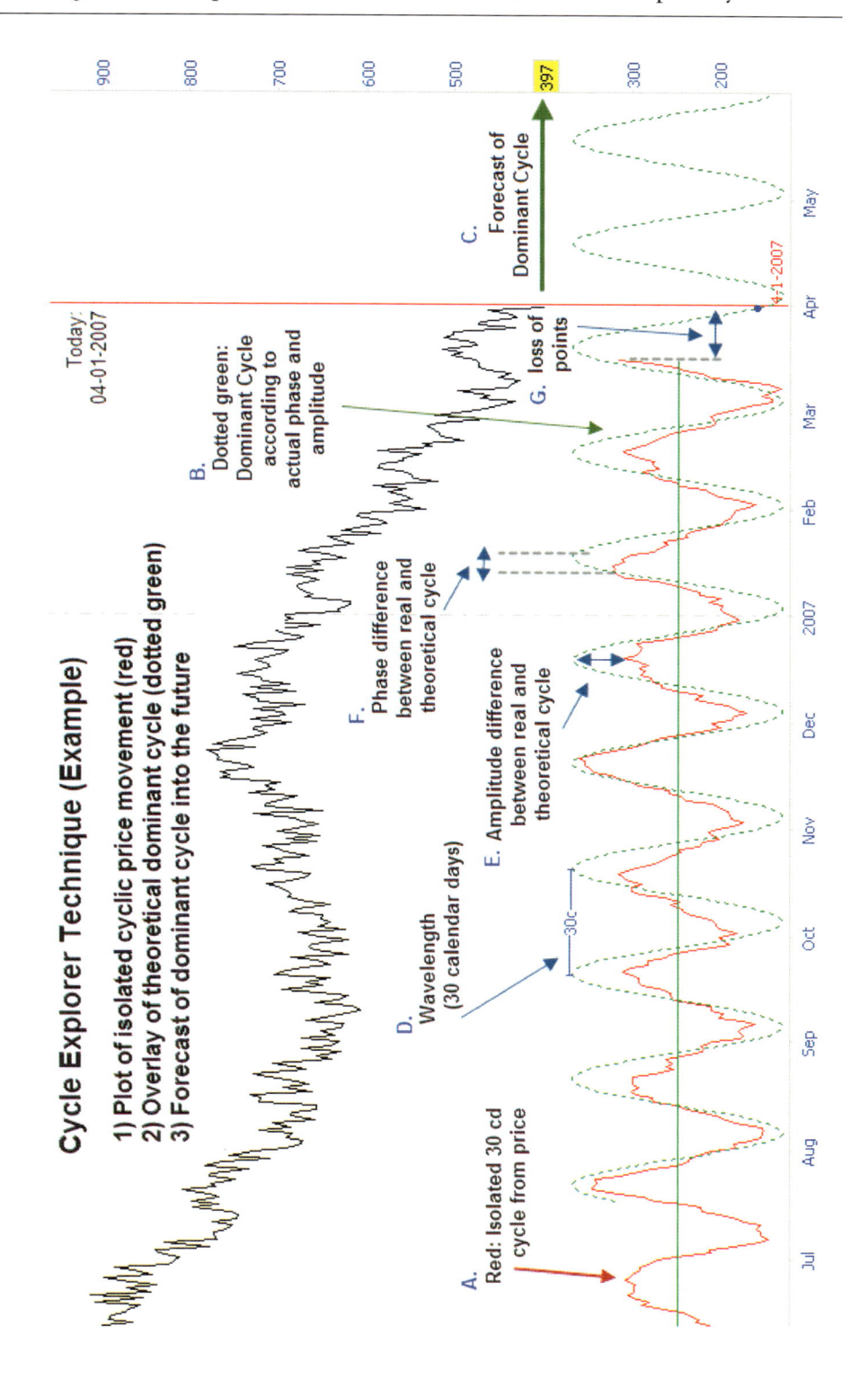

Forecasting the next important market turn – Time, direction & polarity

Figure 6-1: Elements of the Cycle Explorer tool

Cycle Explorer - Interesting factors:

A. Isolated price cycle (red line)

The red line is the extracted cyclic price behavior with a length of 30 calendar days. All other elements have been filtered out of the price data. The method used in this case is Brian J. Millard's cycle highlighter.

B. Dominant cycle plot (dotted green line)

This includes a built-in mechanism to detect the actual offset and amplitude of the given 30 calendar day cycle. This offset is calculated on the basis of the last price information obtained. In this case the low offset is on 4 January 2007. We therefore know where the actual offset of the cycle is today. Using this information, the theoretical (sine wave like) cycle is plotted backwards as on overlay. We can now discern the relevant information: The real cyclic price behavior and the ideal cyclic movement for the given length of 30 calendar days.

C. Forecasted cycle

According to the determined phase status of the 30 CD cycle, the cycle is projected and plotted in the future. Hence, you can spot future turning points of this ideal cycle.

D. Actual (detected dominant) cycle length

The length of the detected cycle is marked on the chart. You can see that it is the 30 CD cycle. This length was automatically detected by the Cycle Explorer tool.

E. Difference of price and cycle amplitude

This is an important element that is visible: At each given cycle's trough and crest, we can compare the ideal with the real amplitude of both plots. The difference in the amplitudes reveals whether this cycle length was present at the given time or not. You can thus observe the dynamic flow when cycles disappear (the amplitude falls to zero of the cyclic price movement) and when cycles are very active (the amplitude is the same as the ideal cycle amplitude).

This is the first indicator that is able to visually illustrate the points in time when a given cycle disappears or is present. This information is very useful at the current point in time (i.e., today). You can thus check whether the amplitude of the cyclic price movement today is lower than the given ideal amplitude. In that case, the cycle is losing power. But if the amplitude is near the ideal cycle, then the cycle is real and present.

F. Difference of phase (high/low)

The other information we are able to obtain now is the deviation of past high/low offsets between the cyclic price movements and the ideal cycle. We can determine whether the cyclic component based on the given wavelength is stable (i.e., in sync) or not. To do so, we have to look at the last turning points of the ideal cycle. The closer the turning points of the isolated price cycle and the ideal cycle are, i.e., the more in sync they are, the more reliable are the forecasted turning points with reference to information on time.

G. Loss of points

The algorithms used with centered moving averages for the cycle highlighter reveal a loss of points at the end of the plot. This amounts to half of the selected cycle length. We cannot see the real cyclic price movement for the last 15 calendar days on the chart in our example. For the purpose of forecasting, it is therefore very important to plot the theoretical cycle in the future with the actual phase offset. You can see that the dotted green line is a smooth continuation of the red line.

We have used our sample cyclic data to demonstrate how this indicator works. The red line is obviously very close to the ideal green line since we have used theoretical cycles to build this model. The difference is attributable to the fact that trends and random noise information were added to the test data.

When you come across such a "match" between the cyclic price movement and the ideal cycle, there is a high probability that the projection on the right side of the chart will be useful for trading.

Let's see it in the example:

This would be our "ideal" forecast based on the 30 CD projection. It provides a closer look at the chart presented above.

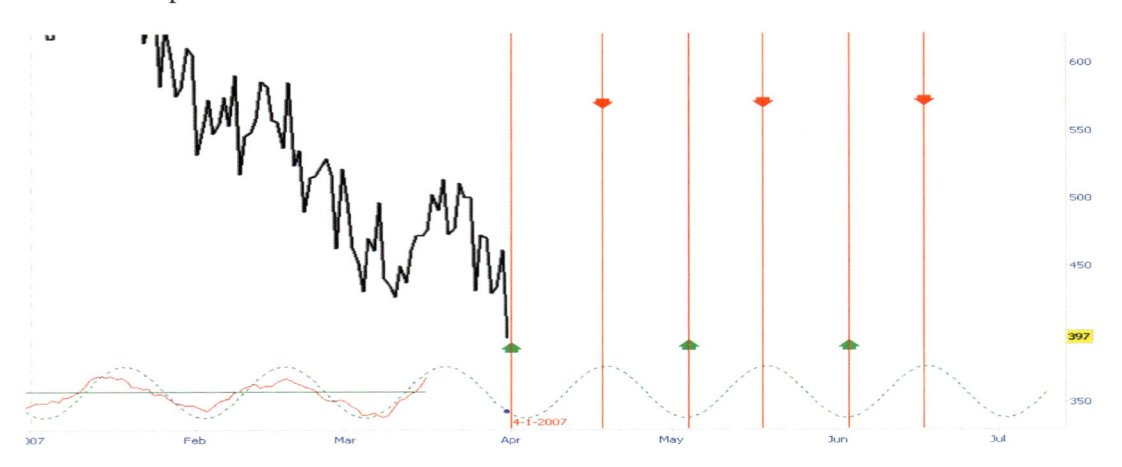

Figure 6-2: Ideal 30 CD projection (example Dataset 3)

And this would be the outcome of this sample dataset:

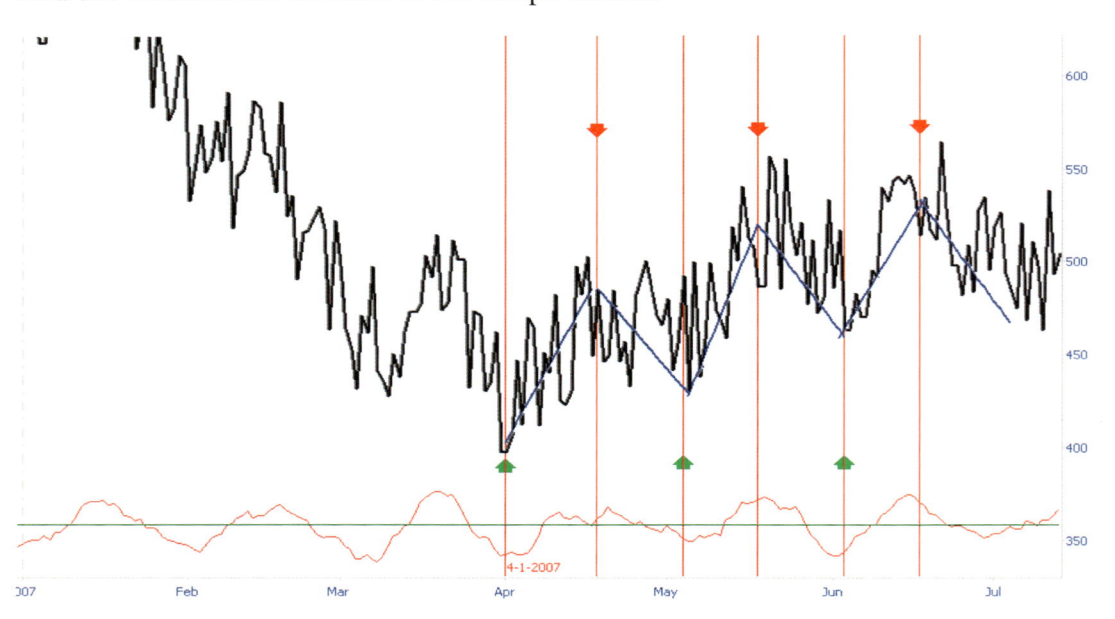

Figure 6-3: Outcome of the 30 CD projection

In other words, if you have a "good match" for the identified cycle length between the isolated cyclic movement of the price and the ideal cycle, then the cycle projection will be of much value for the right side of the chart and for trading. Cycles can only be used in a predictive sense when they are going through a regular phase. That is what this example demonstrates.

Now, let's review another example with a cycle length that is not present in the data. For this, we will use the "Manual Cycle Explorer". The difference between the Dynamic and the Manual Cycle Explorer toolkit is that the dynamic engine automatically detects the Dominant Market Vibration. In the Manual Cycle Explorer, you have to manually set the cycle length you wish to review. Our example shows you how to "check" whether a static cycle frame will work for projection purposes or not. We will thus check whether a cycle length of 46 CD is present in the market. We have to manually enter the value 46 into the Manual Cycle Explorer tool (note: This cycle is not present according to the sample dataset introduced in the first chapter).

The Manual Cycle Explorer delivers the following figure:

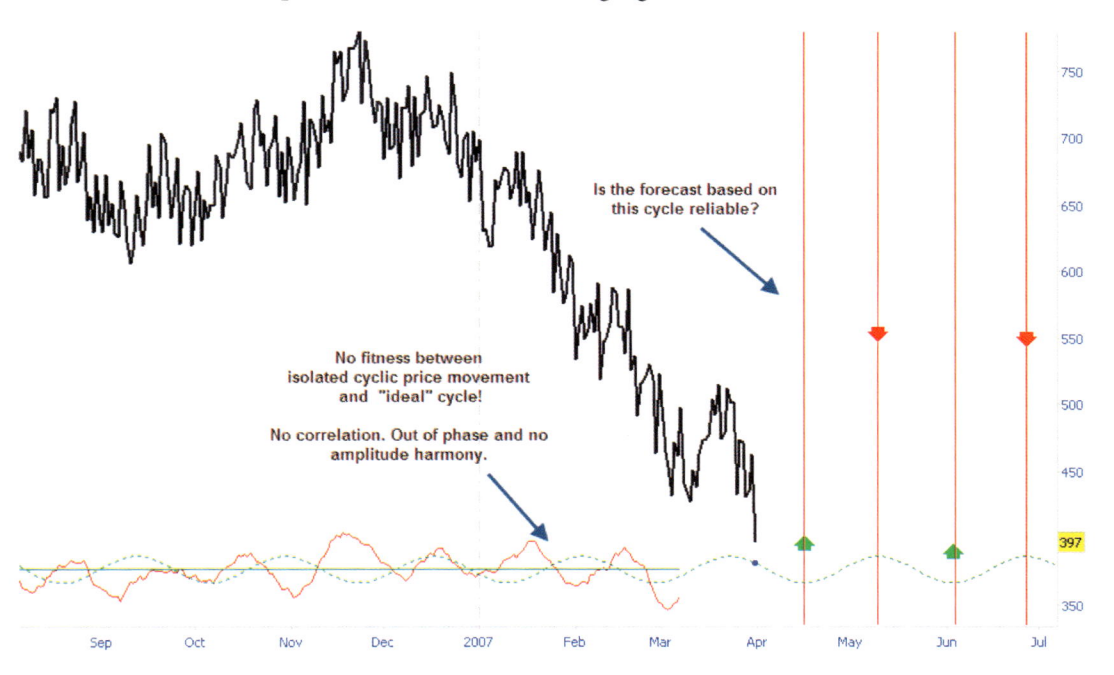

Figure 6-4: Manual Cycle Explorer example

The important information is indicated in the chart. It is clearly visible that the ideal 46 CD cycle and the isolated cyclic price movement of the same length are not in sync. Neither the phase (high/low of both lines), nor the amplitude have a high correlation. As already mentioned above, these results indicate that we should not use this type of cycle for forecasting! However, if you do not have the possibility to review past data for a given cycle up to the present, you cannot check whether a cycle is actually valid or not. You can only blindly "rely" on newsletters and pray that they are right. Yet now you have a powerful tool that will help you analyze predictive information on different current cycles.

In our example, we knew by a visual check alone that we would not use this cycle length for trading. But let's review the complete example. The forecasted market turning points based on this cycle are marked with arrows in the charts.

The next chart displays the result if we had used this cycle for trading:

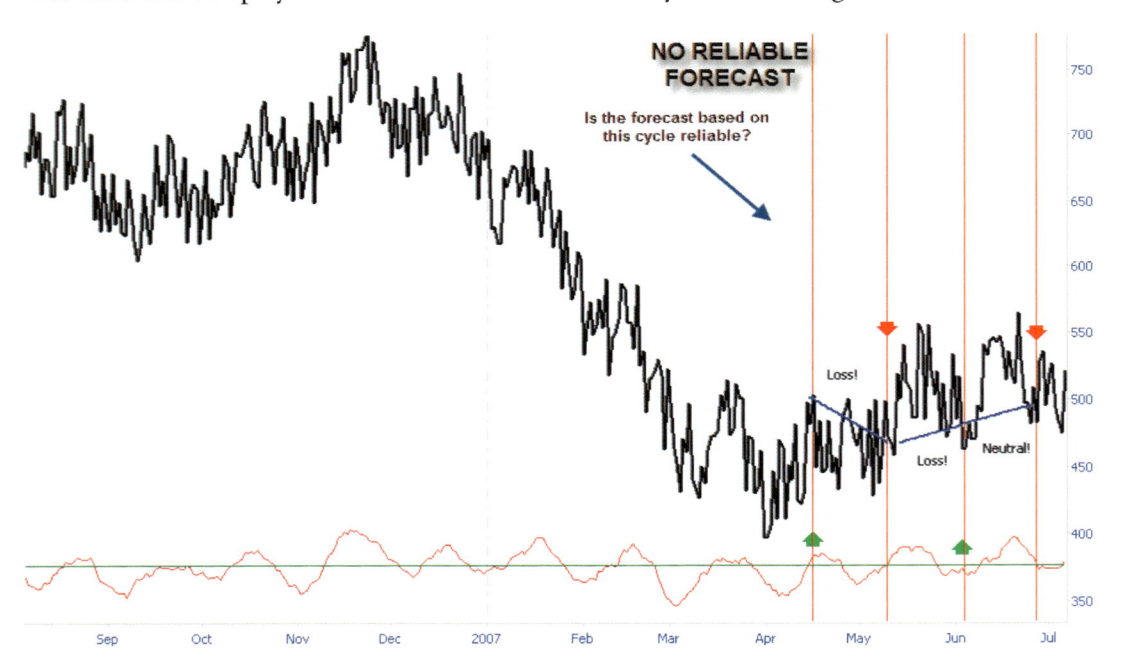

Figure 6-5: Review of 46 CD cycle

No information of this cycle would have been tradable at all. Now you can clearly see it: If you do not have a match in the past data, do not use the projection of the given cycle!

These examples serve to show how important information on the status of various cycles can be determined using market data. Through this means we can determine whether a particular cycle is going through a regular phase, namely, when its contribution to the overall movement can be estimated. We are also able to identify those cycles that go through a disordered phase based on price movement. You can now sort out the cycles that can be used for forecasting and those that should not.

The "dynamic" component of the Cycle Explorer:

The Cycle Explorer is a combination of three crucial tools:

1. The plot of the isolated cyclic price movement.

2. The plot of the "ideal" cycle according to the actual phase and amplitude in the past.

3. The projection of the "ideal" cycle according to the actual phase and amplitude in the future.

But this new tool has an additional built-in feature:

The automatic detection engine for the actual dominant cycle. This implies that you do not have to enter the wavelength that you want to examine using the Cycle Explorer. The wavelength is automatically detected through our powerful new algorithm introduced in the previous chapters. Simply select an important turning point in the past as the starting point for the automatic cycle analysis. Subsequently, the tool will appear on the chart automatically presenting all relevant information mentioned above.

And the best is that a new calculation is done at every new bar. In other words, no "static" cycle is being used here. The actual dominant cycle is ascertained at every new bar. The Cycle Explorer Indicator is updated every time a new bar appears. You can apply this technique to any time frame.

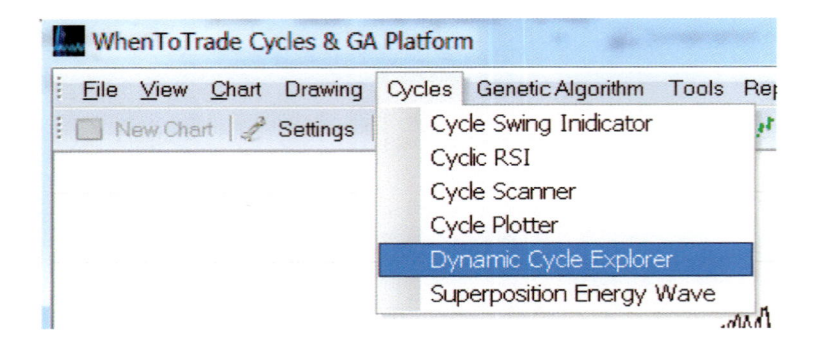

You now have the new Dynamic Cycle Explorer toolkit at your fingertips. It is ready to be applied to your favorite financial instrument. If you want to check static cycles, you can also use the manual version of the indicator. Simply enter the cycle length you want to explore and its suitability will appear on the chart.

I will demonstrate how to build tradable forecasts built solely on this powerful new indicator in the next chapter.

6.3 Using the Cycle Explorer as a quality check for static cycle frameworks

Even if you do not plan to use this method, the Cycle Explorer is of much value when dealing with static cycle frameworks. Hence, if you read in the cycle newsletter that "the 50-week cycle is about to bottom now", enter a weekly chart, set up the Manual Cycle Explorer with a length of 50 weeks and compare the actual cyclic price data for this length with the "ideal" cycle.

Now you have acquired the knowledge of how to "check" whether this information is reliable for usage on the right side of the chart where your trading takes place. You can perform a quality check for any given static cycle on your own. The Cycle Explorer will display the past phase and amplitude shifts of this cycle. You can review on your own whether any given cycle is active, whether it is in sync with the market or whether it has disappeared.

You now have a technical indicator to check the amount of actual cycle expansions or contractions at every new bar. Cycles continuously expand and contract from their original wavelength. This is what often causes "static" cycles approaches to fail. However, now you can measure the "flow" of the cycle. It was Walter Bressert who first proposed that trying to trade based on the idea that something must happen in a fixed interval of time (static cycle) was unrealistic. The Cycle Explorer builds on this idea and has developed it into a visual indicator for the first time to be put into 'trading practice'.

This tool can also be used to check the information included in many cycle newsletters on static cycle frameworks of a given length.

6.4 The Cycle Explorer as a visual confirmation tool

Perhaps the following question comes to mind:

"Why do we need the Dynamic Cycle Explorer when the algorithm presented in the first chapters is already able to detect the most dominant cycle?"

You have a point. If the algorithm is superior to others, we do not need this visual tool. But even I do not trust my own engine that delivers me information on the current Dominant Market Vibration. I know that the algorithm works. But putting money on the line is also a "brain game". I need some visual confirmation that I can see with my own two eyes! The Cycle Scanner engine is thus a "left brain" tool. It involves proprietary digital signal processing. The visual plotting engine of the Cycle Explorer is a "right brain" tool. If I can actually see the correlation of the cyclic price movement and the ideal cycle of the given dominant cycle, my brain sends me a "green light" to put my money on the line.

That's very important. Most cycle research only presents ideas on how to build forecasts. I wanted a visual confirmation tool that reveals the suitability of the cycles by simply looking at them.

When the Cycle Explorer picture on the left side of the chart presents a well-matched cycle, I can use the given projection on the right side of the chart to trade real money.

6.5 Building a forecast based on the Dynamic Cycle Explorer

I will now provide some examples on how to use this concept that has guided me over the last year. Again, my approach does not involve cherry picking or curve fitting. These examples have been posted in real-time to a small trusted cycles' group. If any reader is still skeptical after reading my book, I will gladly prove that these examples were posted in real-time.

This book will, for the first time, present the technique I have applied to produce these charts and forecasts. After reading this book, you will also be able to use this technique. I am disclosing all relevant information and introducing all necessary tools in this book and am handing them over to you. Treat this newly acquired knowledge with the appropriate respect – if inappropriately used, this tool/script could be ineffectual. If dealt with appropriately, it will be crucial for unlocking the power of cycles for financial markets.

As we have seen in the introductory chapter on the cycle detection engine, there is always more than one cycle active in the market. I will now introduce a forecasting method for building forecasts with two dominant cycles. This model incorporates the idea that we have to watch long-term and short-term cycles, which have to be jointly considered. Consequently, we will monitor the dominant cycle for a short-term time frame as well as that for a long-term time frame.

All we need to do is set up our Dynamic Cycle Explorer which extracts the dominant cycle for a given window. We will use these two sets of windows to determine our dominant cycles:

- Window for short-term dominant cycle:
  Wavelength range between 20 – 100 bars

- Window for long-term dominant cycle:
  Wavelength range between 100 – 200 bars.

If you are working with daily charts, I recommend using calendar days for the cyclic analysis of daily charts, not trading days. The primary influence on daily charts originates from external forces (such as astrological cycles) and these forces don't stop on weekends when no trading takes place.

6.6 A step-by-step guide to building a tradable forecast model / Daily S&P Index

We will start with this example, which occurred shortly before the major market low in February 2009. Let's see whether we would have been able to forecast the major low in March 2009 with our forecasting technique.

Actual Date: 25 February 2009.

Step 1: Detect and project the dominant short-term cycle

Use the Dynamic Cycle Explorer tool to determine the dominant short-term cycle. It can be found in the WTT Main Menu.

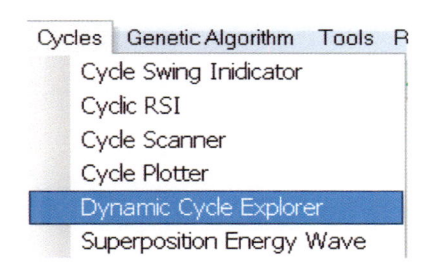

<u>A. Set the Dynamic Cycle Range Filter (Min. / Max.)</u>

Set the cycle length range you would like to monitor when opening the script in the input parameter. For example, on a daily chart monitor the dominant short-term cycle using a range of 20 to 100.

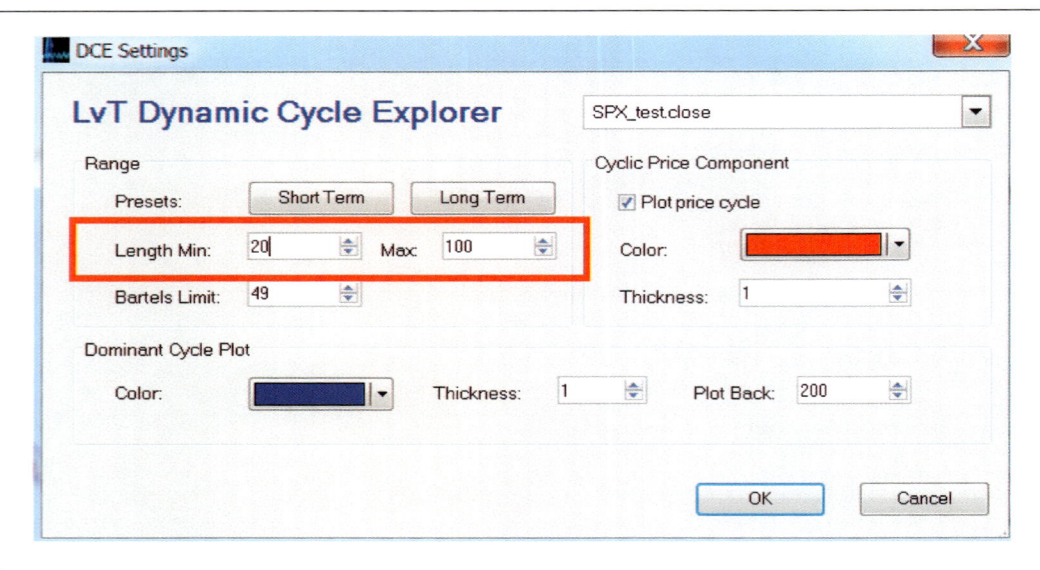

After you have set the parameter, set the look-back period's starting point as a hot spot on the chart using the mouse. The range is needed because the embedded Cycle Scanner engine will automatically identify the most active cycle within this particular range.

B. Enter start anchor in the chart using the mouse and click on bar

The start anchor is used to identify the dominant cycle period by means of proprietary Fourier analysis routines from the actual data point (last bar on the chart) back to the anchor point. This determines the amount of data history to be used for cycle detection. If you would like to identify longer-term cycles, you should use a longer period of data history. Accordingly, if you want to detect shorter-term cycles, you can use a shorter time frame.

Dominant cycle detection works better if you use major markets' lows or highs as the anchor point.

Take a look at the correlation between the red and green-dotted plot. If you have a good match between both, then you can rest assured that the dominant cycle identified (dotted sine wave cycle) is in sync with the actual cyclic market behavior (red line).

We will use the major low of 15 July 2008 as our starting point here. This is the fixed point for our look-back period for the cycle analysis: 15 July 2008 to 25 February 2009. It is acceptable to use 7-8 months of data for cycles up to a length of 80/100 days. We thus have an important low and sufficient data for the detection of algorithms.

Below is the example for the selected period of 20-100 calendar days on the daily S&P 500 with the anchor point set to 15 July 2008. The algorithm automatically identifies the most active cycle length between 20 and 100 days. The algorithm also checks the actual phase and amplitude settings. The identified cycle will be plotted on the chart as an indicator with a dotted line. The given cycle length is also extracted based on the current price and plotted as a solid line. We are thus able to compare the cyclic price behavior of the given length with the theoretical cycle.

Figure 6-6: Short-term dominant cycle

C: Check suitability of detected dominant cycle regarding the cyclic price movement

You can only follow the dominant cycle if there is a good match between the cyclic behavior of the price data (solid red indicator) and the sine wave cycle (dotted green line). Therefore, we have to visually check the final turning points of the theoretical cycle (dotted green line) and the real price behavior aligned with the detected wavelength (red line).

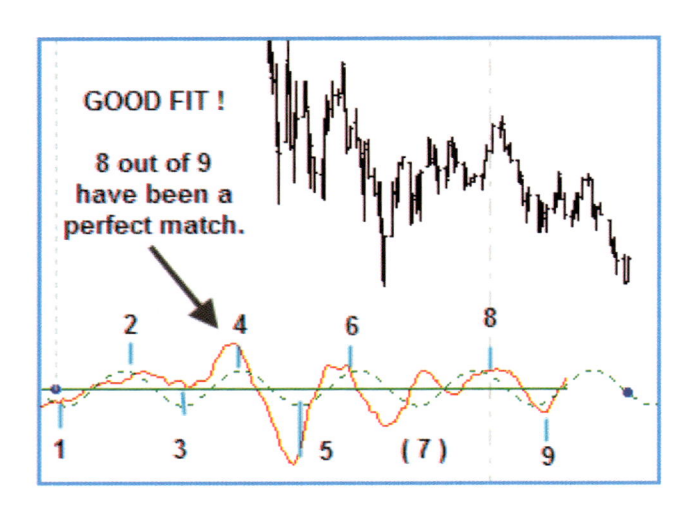

Figure 6-7: Check suitability of detected cycle and price behavior

This anchor point of a market low used here has identified a dominant cycle that has eight perfect turning points in the last four cycles. Only point 7 was off. This example demonstrates that this cycle was truly active in the past on the price movement.

E. Check indicator headline plot for additional information

Any information on the identified dominant cycle will be printed in the indicator headline. In our case, we have a dominant short-term cycle with a wavelength of 32 bars (trading days) or approx. 46 bars (calendar days). We do not need this information for our trading forecast here. This number is for information purposes only.

Within Wave59, you won't be able to see the cycle length on the chart directly. Instead, you have to open the script log to see the current detected cycle length.

F. Use cycle for projection

You can now use the cycle information to project future market behavior based on the short-term dominant cycle. It projects an upcoming low at the beginning of March.

1. Initial Projection

2. Update & verification at the expected time of arrival

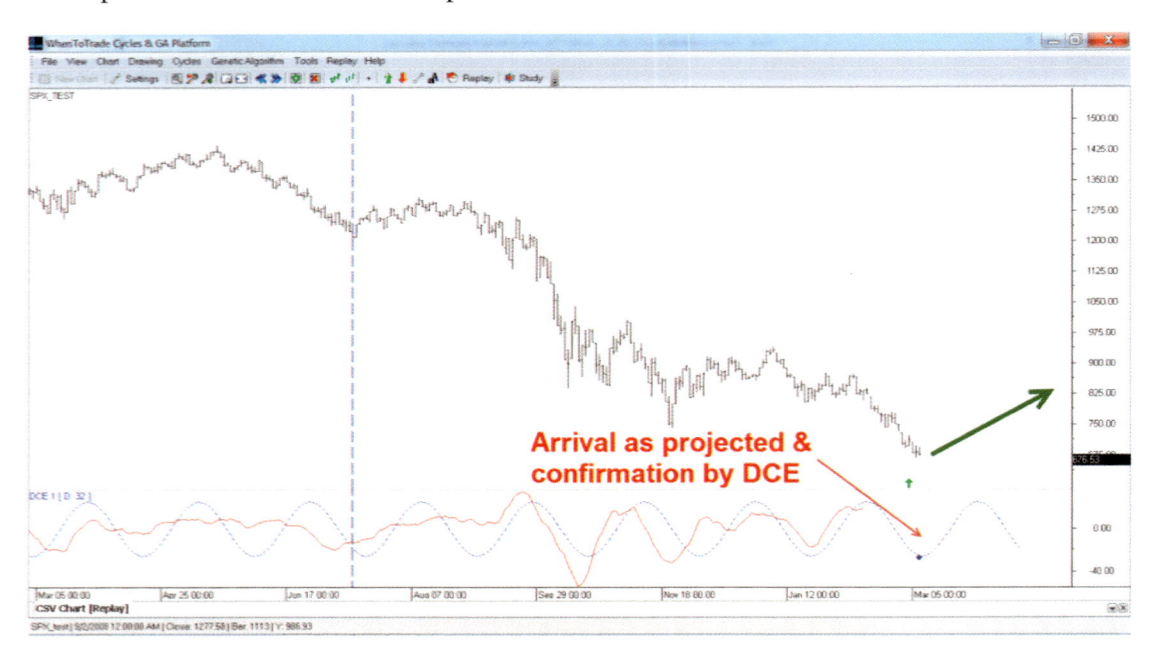

Arrival as projected & confirmation by DCE

3. After the fact outcome & result of initial projection

Upswing as projected by the DCE

Sidenote: However, I do not recommend only using short-term dominant cycles for forecasting. The best forecasts – according to my research – are based on one dominant long-term cycle and one short-term cycle to better fine-tune the important turning points. Let's therefore add the projection of the dominant long-term cycle to our model as well.

Step 2: Identify and project the dominant long-term cycle

G. Set up additional Cycle Explorer

In this example, an additional Cycle Explorer has been added to monitor a long-term dominant cycle of 100 to 200 cycle length (input parameter).

Figure: Input parameter Range for long-term dominant cycle detection

Repeat the same steps from A to D as described above.

The hotspot will be set further in the past, because a longer cycle requires more data history for the routines to be able to detect the given cycle. Therefore, a major market high in 2007 was used (11 October 2007).

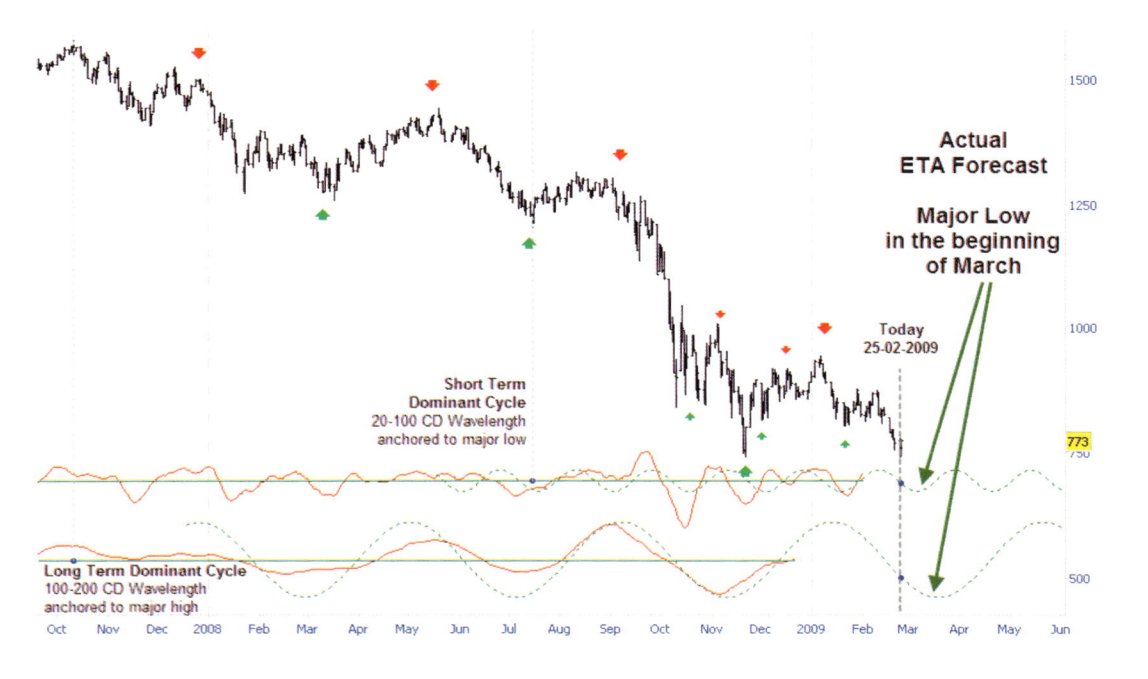

Figure 6-8: ETA forecast for the next major turning point

Now we can see both dominant cycles on one chart. Again, the visual check of the longer-term dominant cycle reveals that we have a good match between the ideal cycle and the cyclic price movement (red and green dotted lines). We can see that this will be achieved around the beginning of March. Both cycles project a future low at this point in time. These cycles are plotted separately, but are both included and added together in the price data. You can expect major turning points in the market when both dominant cycles forecast a low/high on the same date.

I call these situations "Estimated Time of Arrival" (ETA). It's similar to the navigation system in your car. The system provides you information on what time you can expect to arrive at a given point. Likewise, this technique gives us information about when (with reference to time and direction – not price) we will arrive at the next important market turn.

We would be alarmed about a market low at the beginning of March 2009 when looking at this picture. But bear in mind: We did not select a fixed cycle framework with known cycle lengths. We only selected important highs/lows and entered a random range to look for dominant cycles. The detection of the dominant cycles was conducted completely automatic. On top of that, the same forecasted low in March is projected if trading days are used in the analysis.

If you see the same projection on calendar days and trading days chart, the signal will even be more trustworthy. I recommend to check both timeline options.

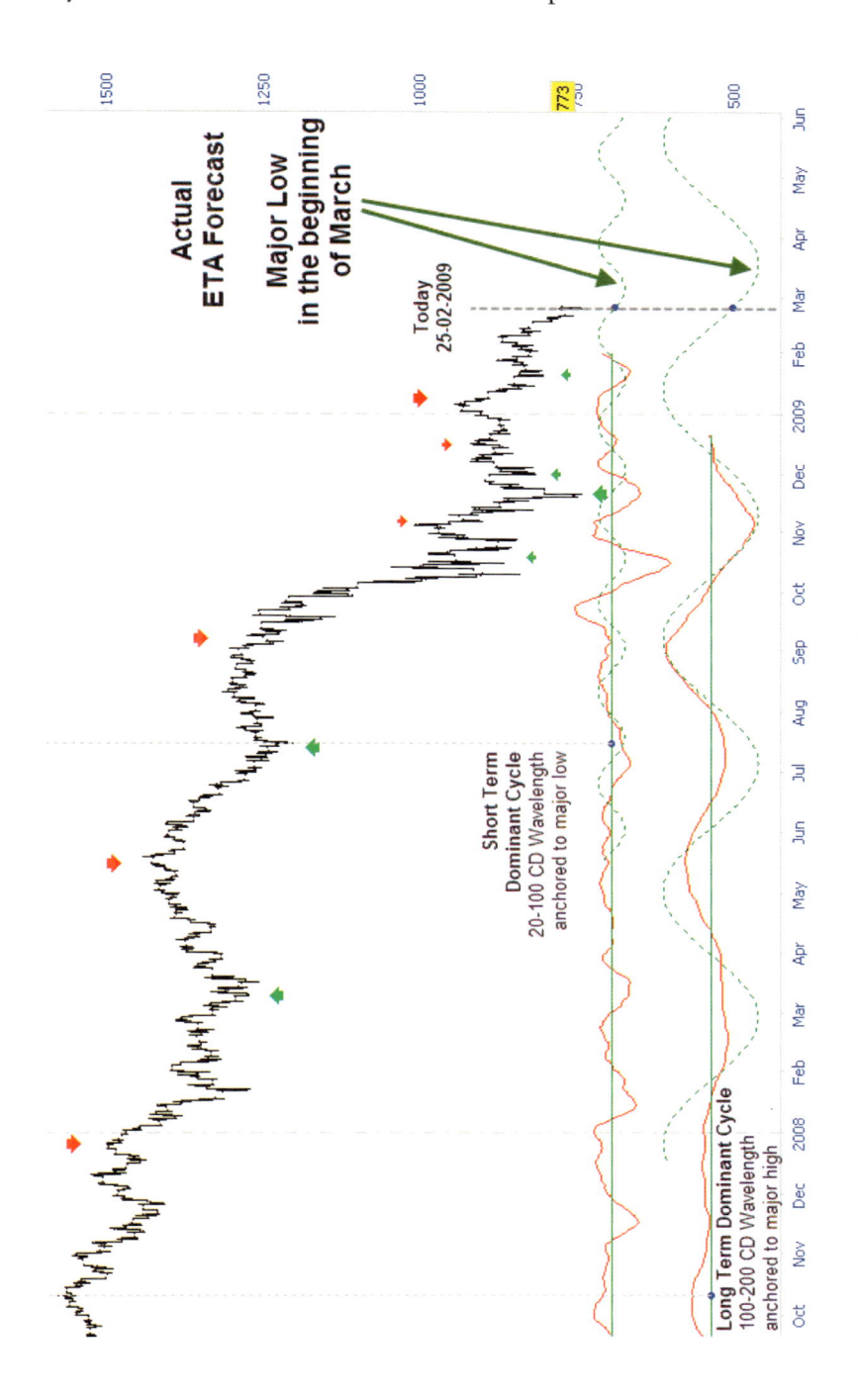

Figure 6-9: Full chart view of ETA projection based on cycles

You can see that we also have six good fitting turning points between the sine wave cycle and the market price behavior for this long-term length.

The turning points according to the detected cycles are marked in the chart with red and green arrows. We can thus see that these cycles have a high correlation with all major turning points over the last year.

Step 3: Project the next major turning point

Now we will apply the cyclic information derived from the dominant long- and short-term cycles to build our own projections. Both cycles point toward a low at the beginning of March. And both cycles will climb until the end of March. Crucial turning points will arise when the short and long-term dominant projections are in alignment, i.e., when both cycles reach a low at the same point in time, there is a high probability that the market will also hit a low.

So, we will be notified on February 25 with the S&P 500 at 773 that the long downtrend will possibly come to an end at the beginning of March. We should take a close look at other indicators during the next weeks to fine-tune the close of short positions and to get ready to go long in the market.

Now we have built our first projection for the next Estimated Time of Arrival (ETA), the next major turning point based on two dominant cycles. The main point here is that the tools used have been able to identify the dominant cycles completely automatically – there is no need to apply a static framework to cycles on the chart. There is no need to pore over the chart for hours to detect these cycles. It's all done for you if you enter the cycle range and select the last important high/low.

One of my main goals was to code all these cycle factors with a high usability for trading purposes. From the viewpoint of a trader, this can be accomplished in minutes.

Ok, let's go ahead and see what happened at the beginning of March 2009.

6.7 Updating the forecast after the projected turning point / Polarity forecast

We will move forward in time to March 26. We will use the same chart with the same indicators, i.e., we will not change any parameter of the indicators. This particular date is interesting, because we are now able to see that we had a solid low – as projected – at the beginning of March. The next question is how the market will develop.

We will apply the same method. And I will introduce another forecasting method based on the two dominant cycles: A polarity forecast.

First, we will check when both cycles will reach the next alignment of their highs/lows. This is the case at the beginning of May. Our next important ETA point will thus be May 10. This event is marked on the chart with a red arrow.

However, there is much more information we are able to use for predictive trading purposes. We do not only want to forecast important dates/times. We also want to forecast periods with a high probability in terms of trend. Will the market move up, down or sideways? I refer to this predictive information as the cycle's polarity forecast. With this information, we can forecast periods of uptrends, downtrends, and sideways markets. This information will also be of much value for trading.

It is quite easy to build a polarity forecast when you have two active dominant cycles on the chart:

Cycles Movement	Expected Trend	Polarity
Both cycles are moving in alignment UP	Uptrend	POSITIVE GREEN
Both cycles are moving in alignment DOWN	Downtrend	NEGATIVE RED
One cycle is moving up / the other is moving down	No trend sideways	NEUTRAL YELLOW

The following chart displays both types of information. The forecasted periods are highlighted with the polarity value in accordance with the introduced method. And the next ETA is also displayed on the chart.

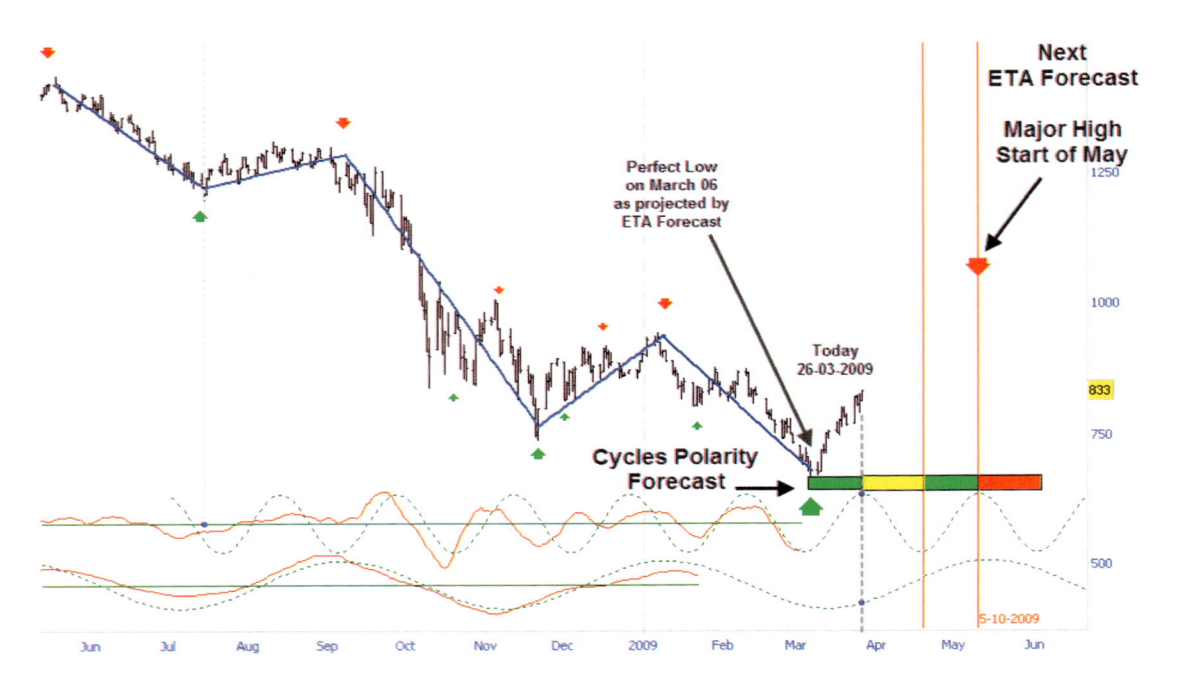

Figure 6-10: ETA & polarity forecast on March 26

This forecast provides us with the following information for trading:

- Expect a sideways/neutral market from now until mid-April;

- Expect an uptrend thereafter from mid-April until the beginning of May (around May 10);

- After May 10, expect the market to decline.

As the next forecasted turning point would be May 10, let's move forward in time. The next chart presents the result of this trading forecast.

Figure 6-11: Polarity review on May 10

Let's review our polarity forecast:

We had a solid sideways to slightly upward-moving market until mid-April. Precisely as projected. After this period, the market moved toward its next important turning point, the projected ETA – May 10. Will the market enter a downtrend now? That's the central question. Our polarity forecast was on the money and provided us with solid information on position and intraday-trading (you can use the daily polarity projection as a filter to only allow trading signals on intraday charts with reference to the daily polarity.) The updated cycle projection with both indicators on the chart is in alignment with our forecast performed on March 26: Both cycles reveal that the high has been reached at this point in time.

Our polarity forecast proved accurate – now let's close our long position and open a short one (as shown by the ETA projection). And let's build/update our next polarity forecast based on the actual state of the dominant cycles.

6.8 Updating the polarity forecast and the next ETA CIT projection

The next chart displays upcoming expectations:

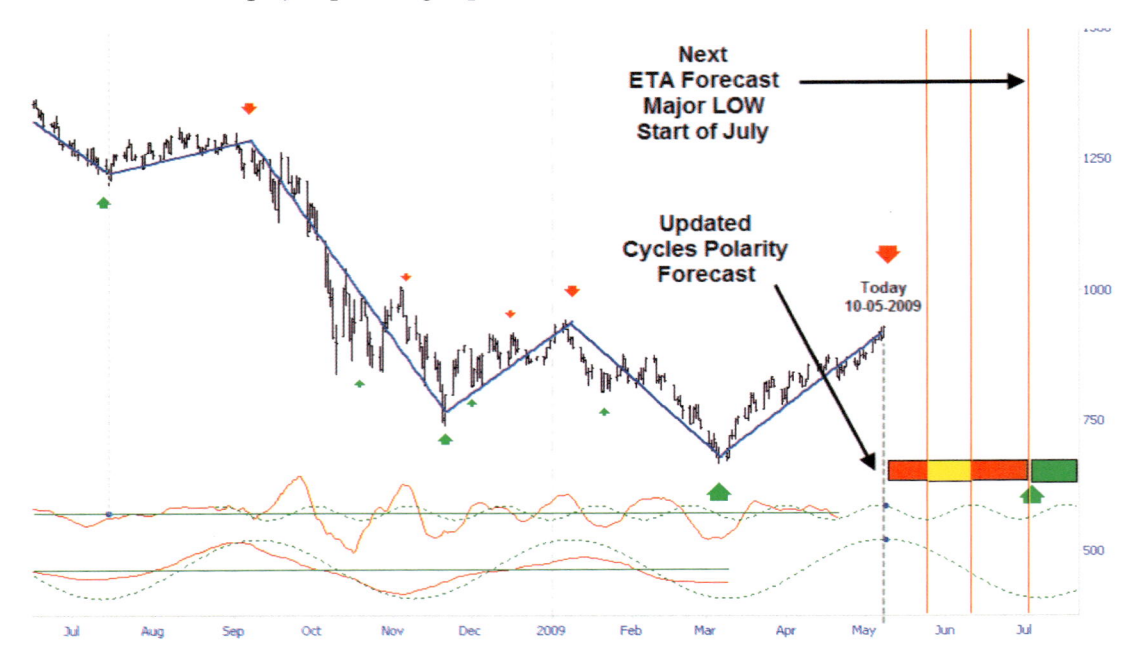

Figure 6-12: ETA & polarity forecast on May 10

We expect a down trending market with a sideways time window around the beginning of June. The downtrend should come to an end at the beginning of July. The polarity areas are again marked on the chart based on the method presented above.

Let's quickly move on in time to the beginning of July.

6.9 Review of polarity and ETA and updating the next forecast

First, let's start with a review. Again, the polarity forecast guided us accurately from our last forecast built on May 10 up to now, July 8 (see Figure 6-13, page 121). We have moved down to our projected Estimated Time of Arrival (ETA) during the next important market low. The next ETA forecast reveals a market high somewhere in October. Hence, we are prepared now to look for an expected long upward trend in the market. I would recommend using technical indicators based on price to move into the market for a long trade. Trade the price – not the forecast.

Figure 6-13: Polarity review and ETA forecast on July 8

6.10 Complete review of all forecasted CIT dates and polarity windows

These examples have shown us the estimated position of the dominant cycles in the past and present. The underlying purpose of this example in terms of extracting dominant cycles is to predict how the combined data will develop in the near future. I have introduced a simple forecasting method on how to project the expected point in time for the next major market high or low. In addition, I have shown you how to predict trending phases of the market.

This is a real example based on my trading last year. And this is the first time I am opening up my "books" to explain my approach in detail. This is the first time I will hand over the complete indicator set required for you to do this on your own.

The next chart presents all projections in one chart. The predicted polarity areas are highlighted in their respective color. The predicted ETA points are marked with arrows on the chart. Keep in mind that all CIT dates and color coded areas have been projected in advance.

Why don't you review this trading method on your own. You will quickly understand the significance of identifying the dominant cycles.

Now we can start to connect the dots between the different chapters. Because the forecasted neutral polarity areas are the time-windows during which standard technical indicators work best on intraday charts! Hence, you will know in advance when to use technical indicators for trading intraday charts. The yellow areas are the times when I would recommend using the method presented in Chapter 4 (fine-tuning of indicators). Now you can see how it all comes together to represent a complete trading approach.

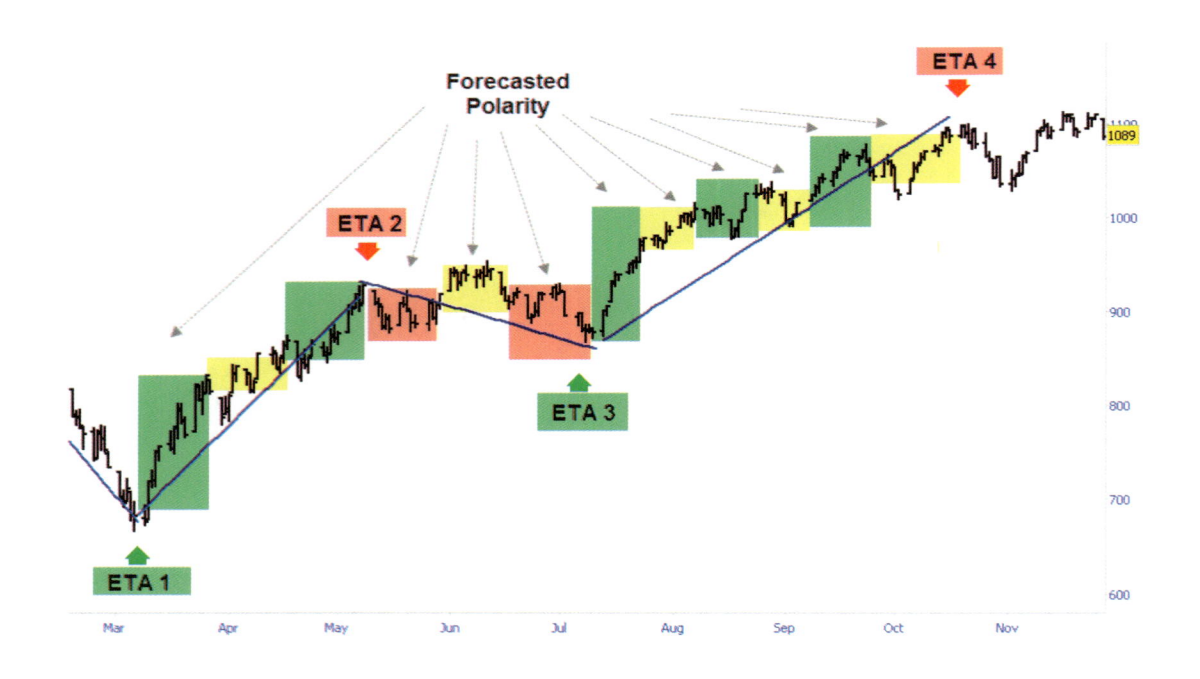

Figure 6-14: Complete Review of all ETA and polarity forecasts

6.11 Combining a semi-static and purely dynamic forecasting model for trading

The previous chapter has introduced a quasi semi-static forecasting technique based on two dominant cycles. I call it 'semi-static' because it involves the building of a forecast that will be static over the next month(s) until the next important ETA point arises. We will update the forecast when the predicted ETA point arises. Accordingly, the forecast is static from ETA to ETA. It is semi-static because we update the projection at each ETA point with a new current cycle evaluation in terms of phase and wavelength.

The next method combines the presented semi-static technique with a purely dynamic model. The dynamic model is again quite simple. Instead of waiting until the projected ETA arises, we will update the forecast at every new bar. We can do this because the calculations will be performed automatically.

There is a beneficial advantage to combining both methods. First, we will obtain a projection of the next ETA from the static projection. We will mark this ETA in the chart with a fixed line at the ideal cycle's next given high/low. We will also gain an understanding of the timeline ahead.

Next, we will update this cycle projection at each new bar. The Dynamic Cycle Explorer will adjust the projection in accordance with the dominant cycle's actual phase status. We also take into account that a cycle will not be static over time and that the phase and wavelength will vary. We accept this fact not only by following the static projection, we will identify the dominant cycle's actual phase and wavelength shifts and arrive at a new projection at the dominant cycle's next important turning point. We can then compare the last static projection (red line in the chart) with the actual updated projection including the ideal cycle's revised plot. We can now "see" the cycle's phase and wavelength shifts. And instead of following a static cycle framework, we can follow the dynamic flow of the cycle. In other words, our semi-static method gives us an Estimated Time of Arrival. And in addition, thanks to our Dynamic Cycle Explorer, we receive an update of the ETA at every new bar.

This is the method that was used in the preview video on the web page. I called this preview "The Magic Time Cycle". It is the Dynamic Cycle Explorer in action. In this example, I have removed the isolation of the cyclic price behavior represented by the red line. In the video, the Dynamic Cycle Explorer only plots the green ideal cycle. You have probably realized now that this indicator has even more capabilities. But I did not want to reveal it all in the preview videos. You can rebuild the video example with the Dynamic Cycle Explorer.

Using this combined technique, we have been able to identify the following turning points in the market ahead of time.

Please watch the included video when you have read this example (Link: http://www.whentotrade.com/dynamiccycles1/). If you want to rebuild this example for training purposes, use the following settings:

1. Open a daily chart of the S&P 500 Index (X.SPX) set to calendar days;

2. Switch to Replay Mode and set the start bar to October 7, 2008.

    a. Attach the Dynamic Cycle Explorer to the chart with the following settings: Min Length = 75 (or 100 calendar days)
    b. Max Length = 150 (or 200 for calendar days)

3. Anchor the starting point for analysis to the October high of 2007.

To reconstruct the approach, follow the steps as shown in the video:

1. Mark the next ideal cycle high/low with a red line on a chart (fixed ETA forecast).

2. Move ahead in time by pressing "space".

3. Follow the updated cycle projection of the Dynamic Cycle Explorer. The Cycle Explorer checks the actual wavelength, phase, and amplitude at each new bar and updates the plot.

4. Pay close attention to incidents when the updated or static forecast arrives at the forecasted high or low. Whatever comes first.

5. Please use additional technical indicators to time your trade entries and exits when using this technique for trading. Do not trade the forecast – trade the price!

6.12 The combined semi-static and dynamic trading approach in action on the S&P 500

The following example illustrates the usage of the Dominant Cycle Explorer in real trading. I will review the last two years of trading and will show you how the Cycle Explorer was able to predict every major turning point ahead of time.

We begin with our analysis on October 7, 2008. There has been a severe plunge in the market over the last few days. It is an interesting point in time to "turn" on our Cycle Explorer and check whether we can get an idea of when this downturn will come to an end. We will use the long-term market high of October 12, 2007 as the Cycle Explorer's anchor/starting point, as well as a calendar day chart.

This is the situation on October 7, 2008:

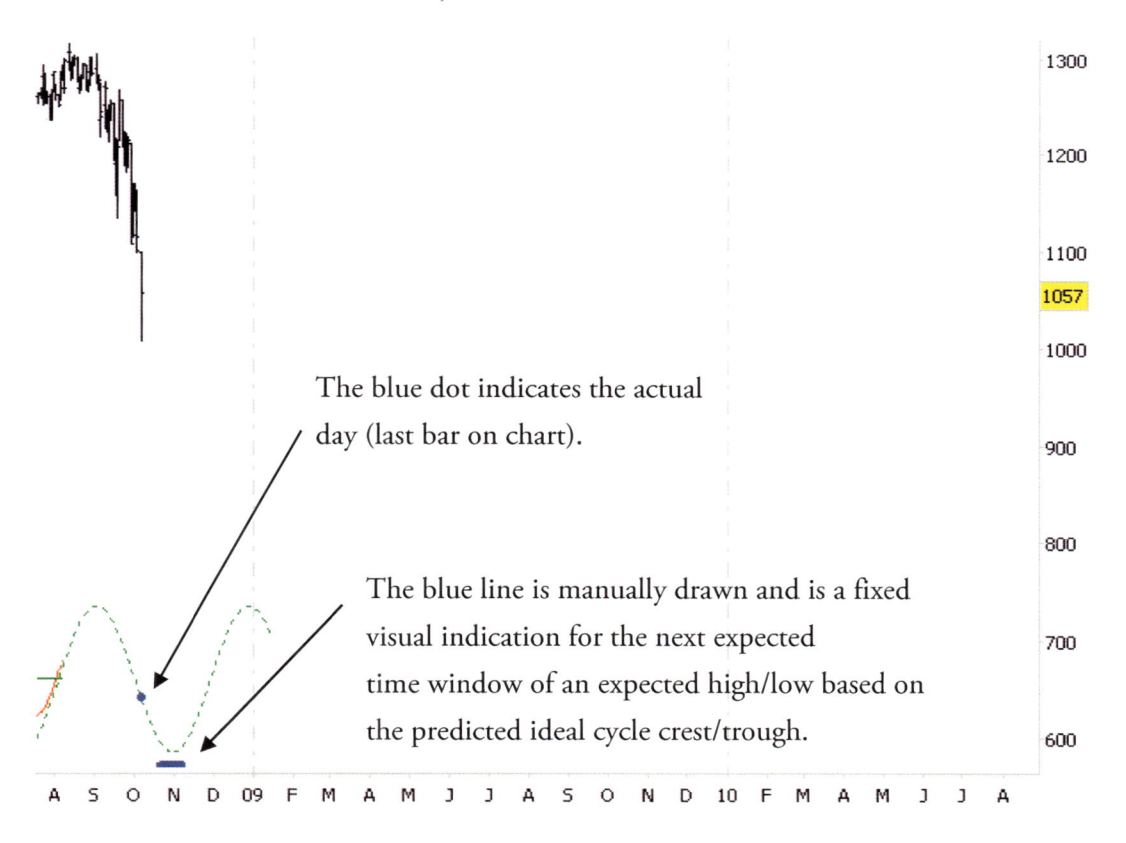

Figure 6-15: October 2008: Next low around the end of October

The Cycle Explorer reveals that there still is room for the market to move even lower throughout the next week. The next market low is expected around the end of October.

Let's fast forward to the end of October now:

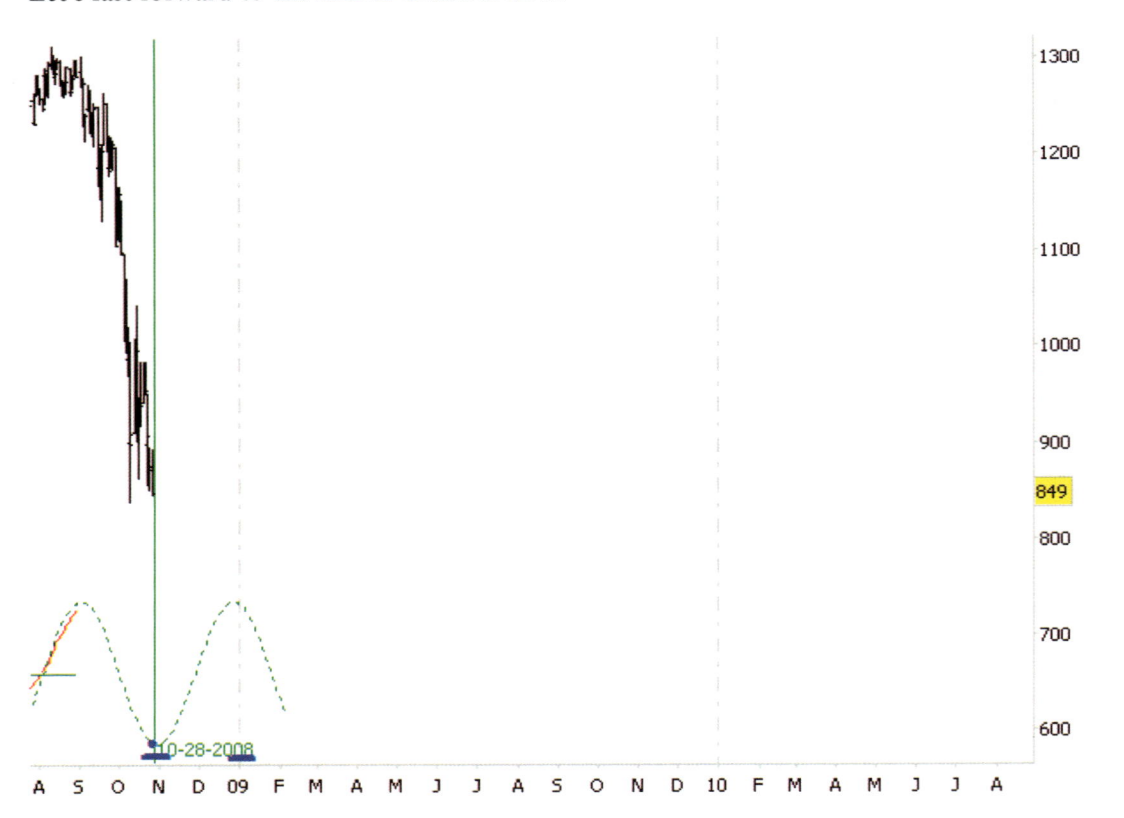

Figure 6-16: October 28 -> Next high around the end of 2008/beginning of 2009

From October 7 to October 28, the market dropped another 200 index points as predicted be the Dominant Cycle Explorer. We can now see the low on the dominant cycle precisely within the time window forecasted on October 7. So this is a good time to close the short and enter a long trade. The next market high is expected around the end of 2008 or the beginning of 2009, as indicated by the actual dominant cycle plot.

Again, let's see what happened around that time window.

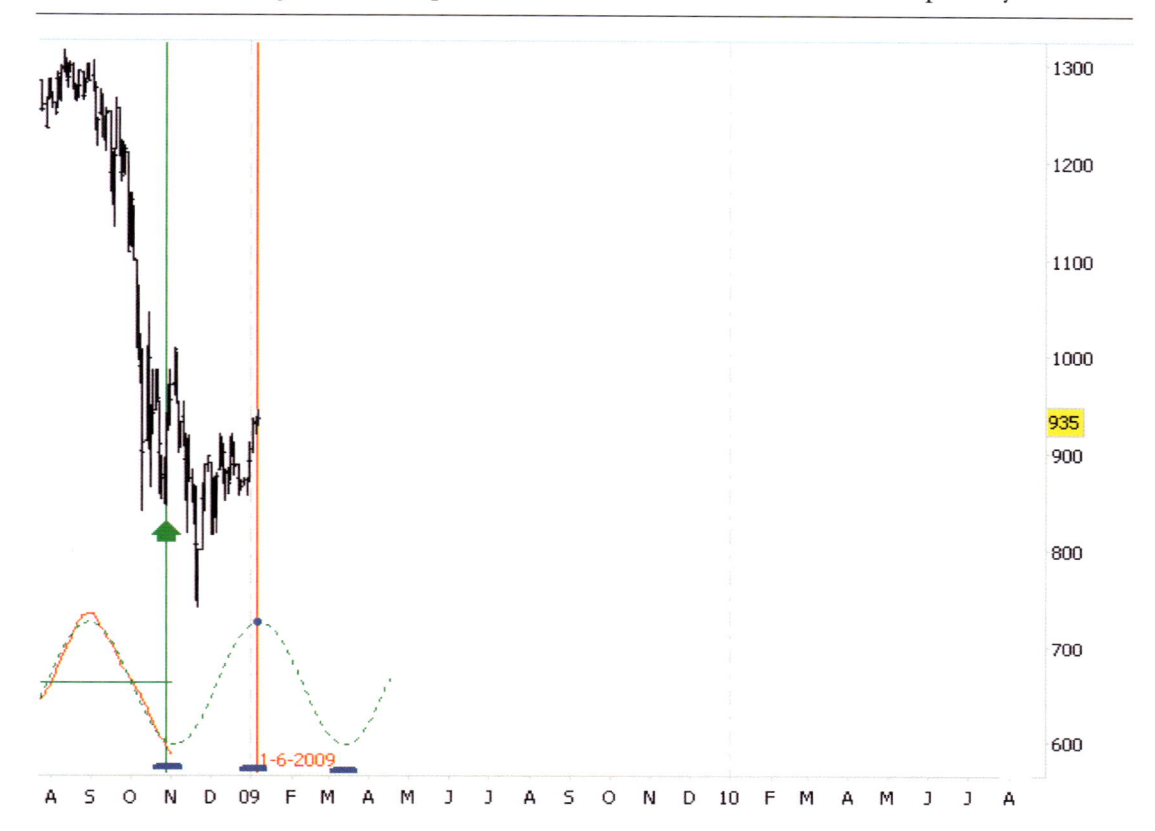

Figure 6-17: January 6, 2009 -> Next low around the beginning of March

We moved forward to the point at which the Dynamic Cycle Explorer reached the cycle high. The updated cycle high arrived precisely within the predicted time frame around the beginning of 2009 – on January 6, 2009.

The market climbed from 849 to 935 points, a jump of around +10%. We can now book the long profit, close the long trade and open a short position.

The next market low is expected around the beginning of March. This is indicated on January 6 by the next ideal dominant cycle low plotted at the beginning of March. Please keep in mind that the indicator setting was not touched or changed at all.

Consequently, we will go short and move forward in time until the Dynamic Cycle Explorer arrives at the cycle low in real-time.

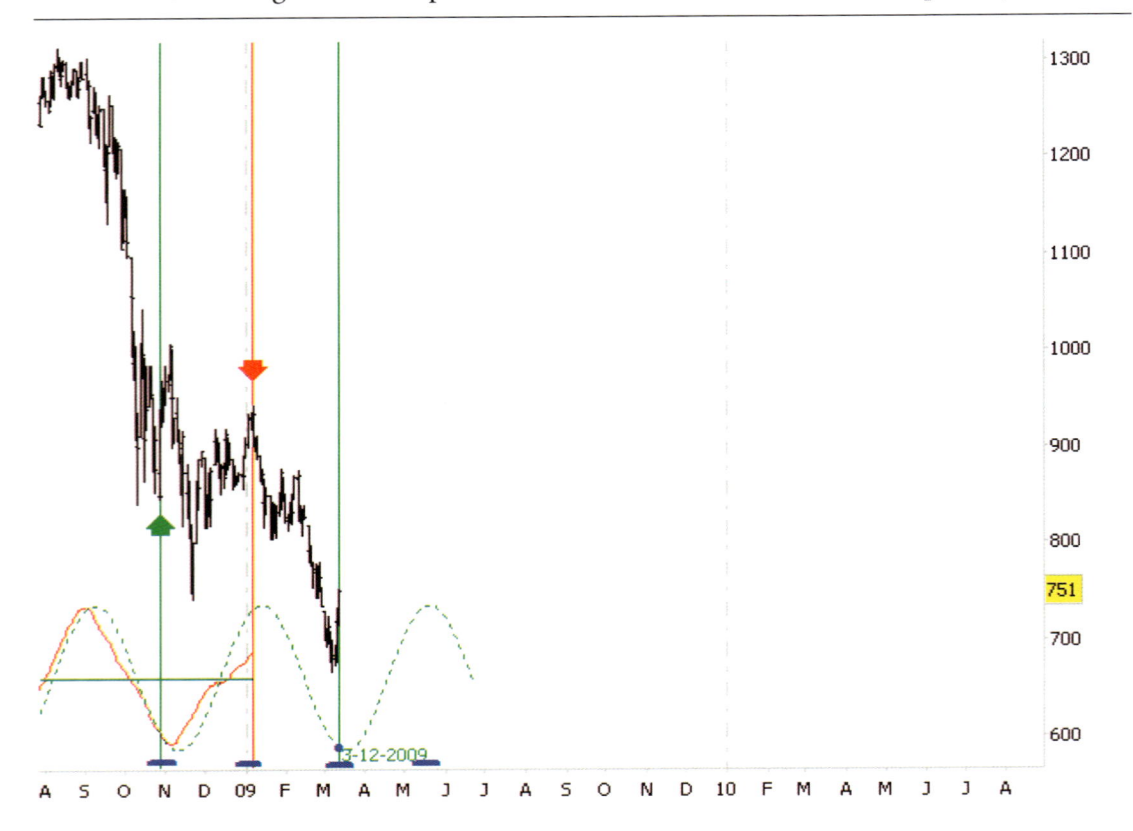

Figure 6-18: March 12 -> Next high around the beginning of May

This is where we are on March 12, with the actual cycle low illustrated by the blue dot of the updated dominant cycle. Again, precisely as expected within the time window that was predicted on January 6 - indicated by the blue line.

The market moved down 184 points (from 935 to 751 points). With a down move of around 19%, we are now able to close the short trade with a gainful profit according to the dominant cycle prediction. We will now establish a long position.

The next expected market high is expected around the beginning of May. This time window is indicated on the chart by the blue line. This is our time window of interest.

Again, the indicator settings are still the same. The algorithm adapts itself to the Dominant Market Vibration at each new bar. That's what makes it so special. You don't have to bother with cycle analysis and a lot of tools. It's all done by the Dominant Cycle Explorer. This is where cycle trading really becomes straightforward.

Let's move to the next dominant cycle high on the indicator.

Figure 6-19: May 8 -> Next low expected around mid-July

The Cycle Explorer detected the dominant cycle high on May 8 at the beginning of the forecasted time window (keep in mind: The blue line was fixed on the chart after the forecast was done to indicate the expected time window for the next turn. The ideal cycle plot - indicated by the dotted green line - can change after each new bar to specify where we are in the actual ideal dominant cycle).

The market gained 156 points during this time which again corresponds with a profit of 20%. The dominant cycle delivered yet another profitable trade and suggests closing the long position here and establishing a short one.

The next expected market low is projected for the beginning of July. We have to watch the market closely when we reach this point in time. We will move forward in time until the Dynamic Cycle Explorer arrives at the next dominant cycle low.

Figure 6-20: July 15 -> Next high expected around the end of September

On July 15, we arrived at the cycle low within the expected time window. The market moved down, but we have not been able to determine the precise high and low using the dominant cycle. That's a common situation. Don't expect the dominant cycle to detect the exact turns. The dominant cycle offers high probability in terms of depicting the time window of the next important change in trend.

The market moved up from 907 on May 8 to 933 points on July 15. So we have to cover our short trade here with a loss of 26 points.

As the Dominant Cycle Explorer shows, the next market high is expected around the end of September. We will therefore establish a long position now and move forward until we arrive at the next dominant cycle high.

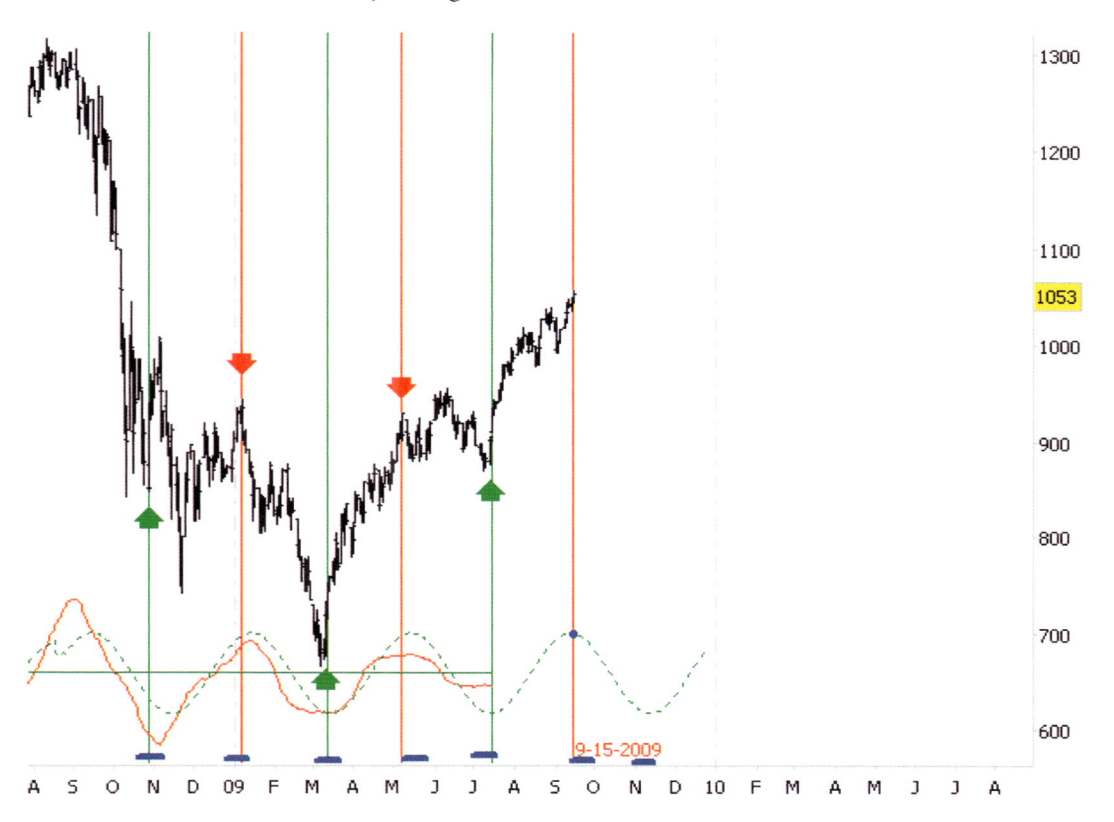

Figure 6-21: September 15 -> Next market low around the beginning of November

We reach the actual dominant cycle high on September 15 as indicated by the blue dot on the updated dominant cycle indicator plot. The high lies within the expected fixed time frame forecasted two months ago.

The market moved up from 933 to 1051 points – a gain of 118 points or 12%. Hence, we close or long trade with a profit here and switch to a short position.

The time window for the next expected low is forecasted for the beginning of November, indicated by the dominant cycle low during this time. The occurrence is again marked on the chart by a fixed blue line.

That is, the next two months are still ahead of us and we will move forward until the Dominant Cycle Explorer signals a cycle low.

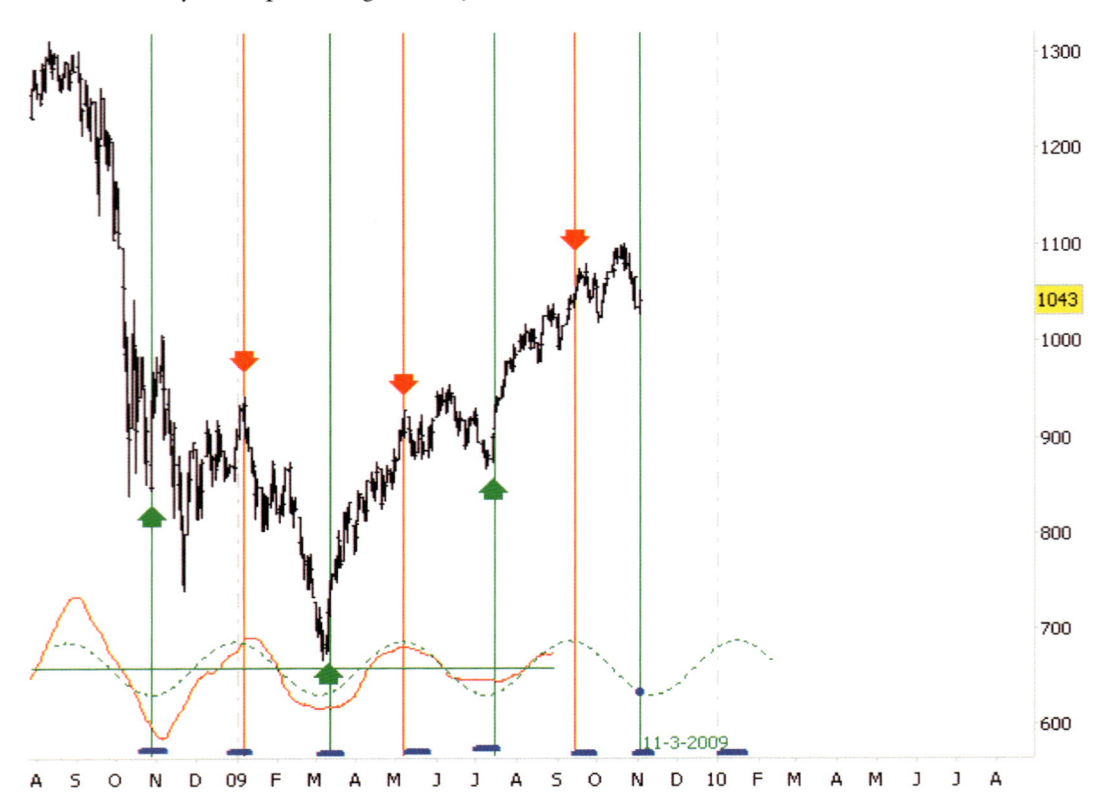

Figure 6-22: November 3 -> Next high at the beginning of January 2010

The Cycle Explorer denotes a cyclic low on November 3 as illustrated by the actual blue dot and cycle projection. This again lies precisely within the predicted time window of the September 15 forecast.

The market primarily moved sideways from 1053 to 1043 points during this period. As we have been short selling the market, we can book a profit of 10 points here.

The next move should be an upward trend until the beginning of January 2010. This is the next anticipated time window within which we expect the next important market top.

We will switch our short to a long position now and move forward until the Cycle Explorer reaches the next dominant cycle high.

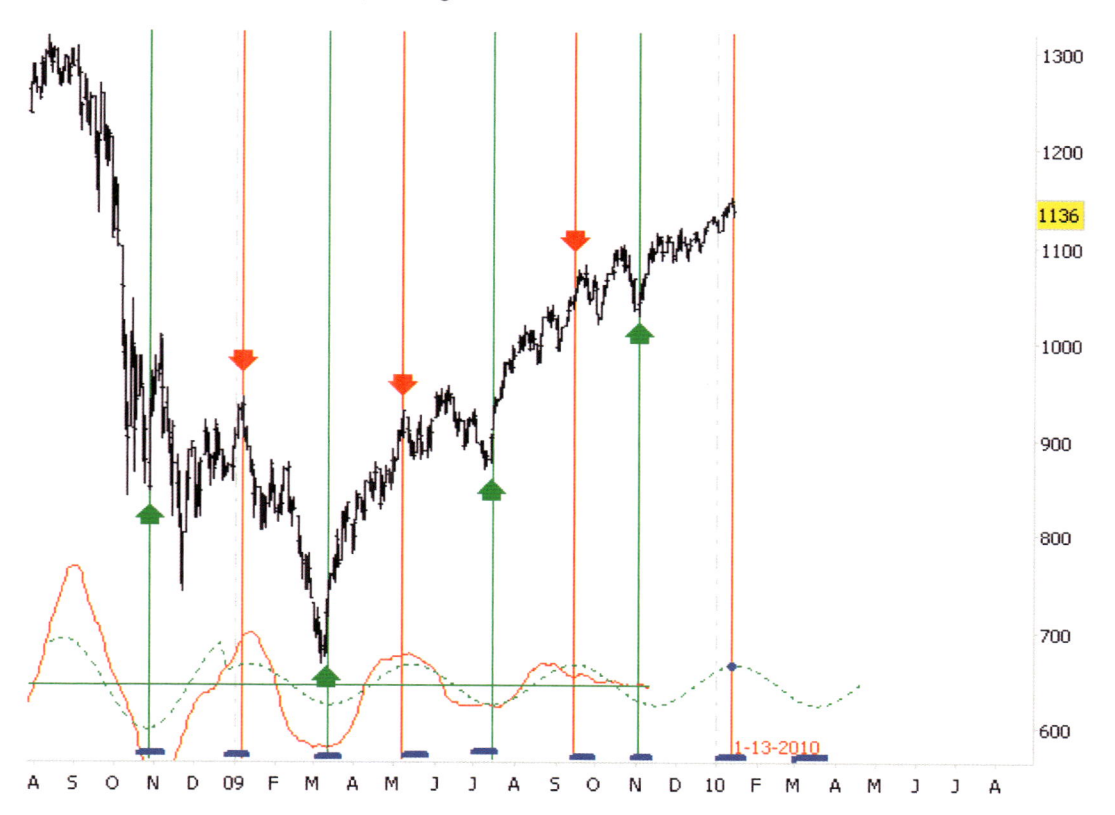

Figure 6-23: January 13 -> Next low around the beginning of March

The Cycle Explorer reaches the next cycle high on January 13 within the predicted time frame resulting from the analysis of November 3.

The S&P 500 index moved up from 1043 to 1136 points with a profit of 93 points or 9%. We would close our long trade here and expect the next move to drive the S&P down with the dominant cycle pointing downward at the beginning of March.

To reiterate, the indicator settings have not been changed at all. The anchor point is still the high of October 2007 and the range is still between 100 and 200 days for the Cycle Explorer to detect the dominant cycle.

In other words, you don't have to spend hours analyzing different cycles and you don't have to try to squeeze the market into a static cycle framework. The Cycle Explorer does this for you at every new bar. You only have to enter important points – the anchor date and the range to look for.

We will move forward to see where our Cycle Explorer will specify the next dominant cycle low.

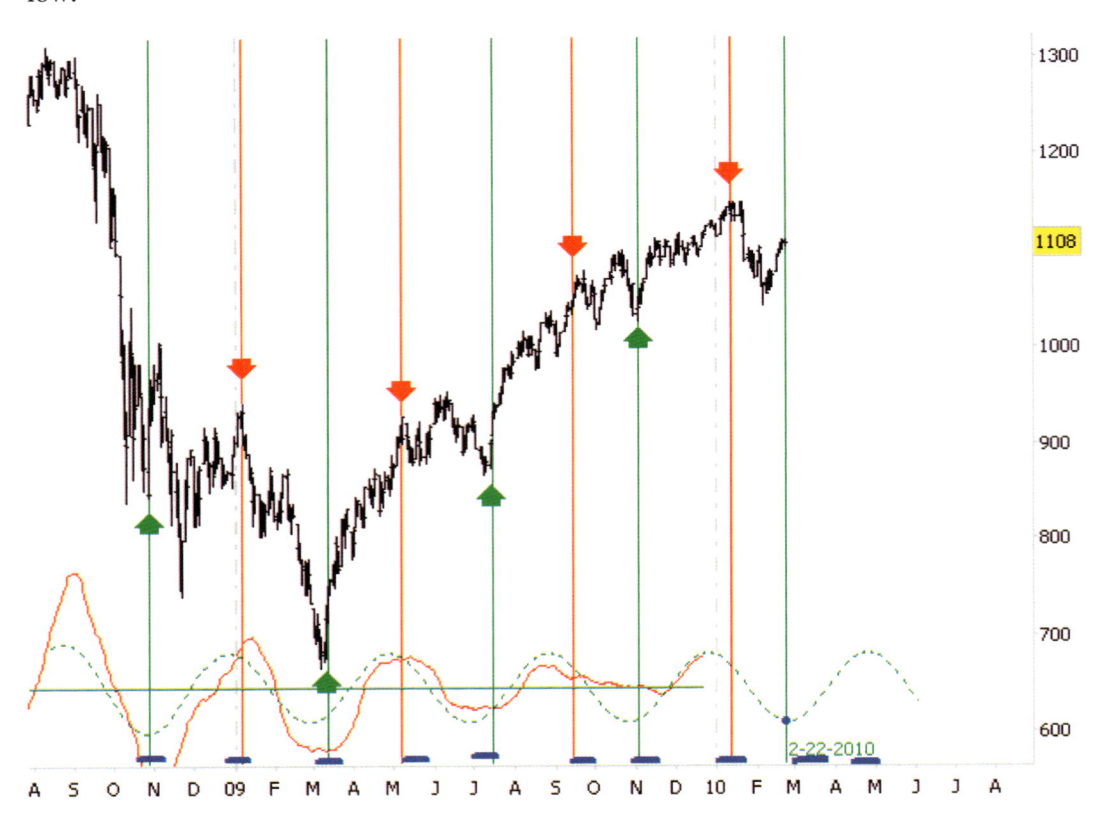

Figure 6-24: February 22 - Next high around the end of April

Now the dynamic phase adjustment of the indicator is visible. We have an interesting situation here because the wavelength of the dominant cycle shifted. On February 22, the Dynamic Cycle Explorer indicated the actual cycle low as demonstrated by the blue dot on the cycle projection.

In this particular case, the low comes before our expected time window which starts at the beginning of March. The Cycle Explorer signifies that it has detected a bigger shift in the dominant cycle. The dynamic phase adjustment also took place earlier – but it can now be clearly seen on the chart. The price has already moved up, which confirms that the cycle low has been reached.

We will follow the current updated cycle forecast. This means that we will close our short trade here. The S&P 500 lost 28 points, down from 1136 to 1108 points, implying that we booked a small profit of 28 points during this period.

We will now switch to a long position and expect the next important market top at the end of April. This time window is again marked with the blue line on the chart.

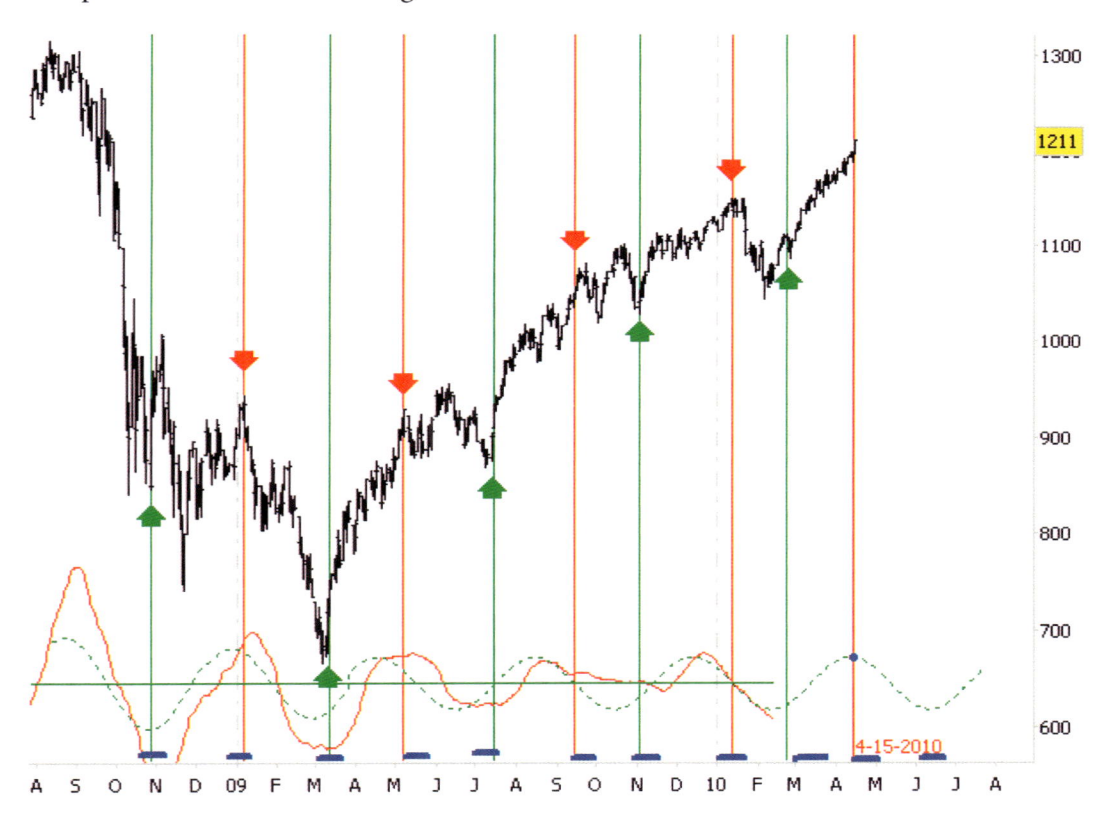

Figure 6-25: April 15 -> Next low around the beginning of June

The Cycle Explorer points to April 15 as the next dominant cycle high. As indicated by the blue line on the chart, again within the predicted time window from our analysis on February 22. You have two indications here – the projection and the actual situation –

which are in alignment with the cycle high. The prediction gave a time window – the Cycle Explorer's actual updates present the exact same situation on April 15.

The S&P Index moved up from 1108 to 1211 points, a gain of 103 points or +9%. According to our rules, we will close our long position here with a profit of over 100 index points and switch to a short position.

The next expected time window for the market to bottom is the first half of June. So we will move forward to see what the Dominant Cycle Explorer will tell us.

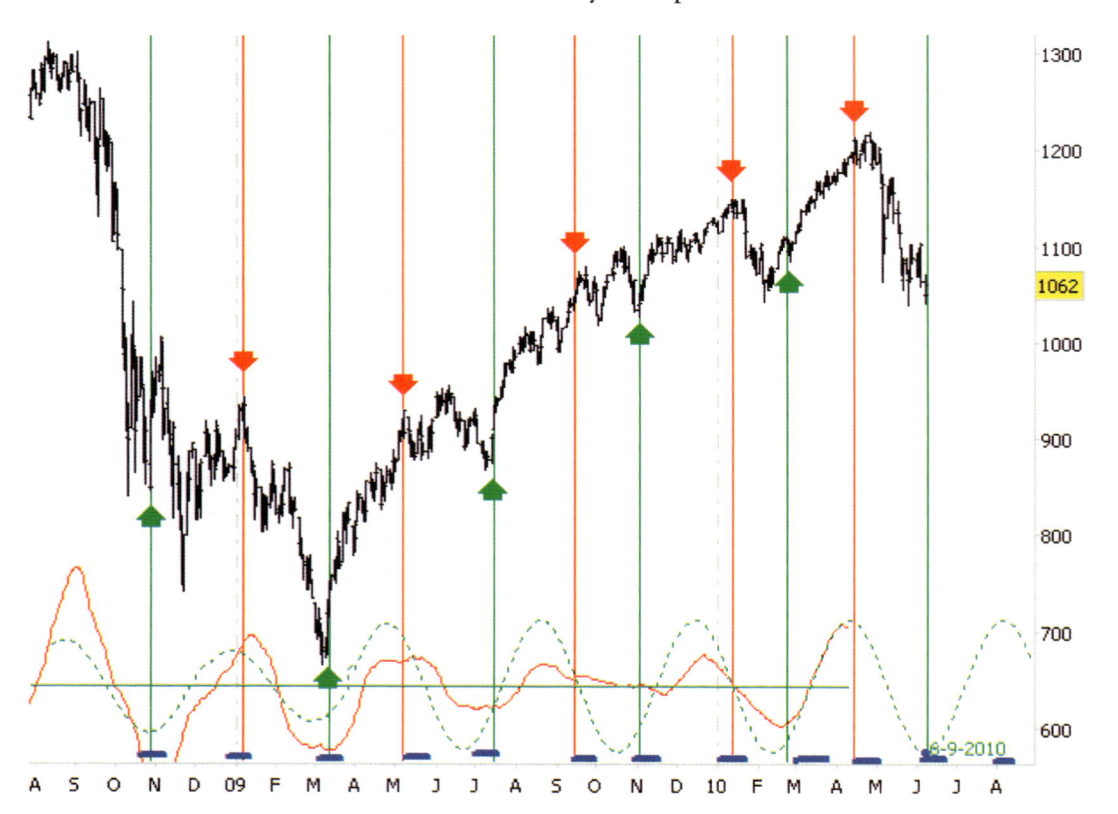

Figure 6-26: June 9 -> Next high at the beginning of August

The indicator shows the next dominant cycle low on June 9 as represented by the blue dot on the ideal cycle trough. Again this occurs as expected within the time window forecasted in April.

The index lost 149 index points from 1211 to 1062 points, which equals a loss of 12%. However, as we have been short during this period, we can book the profit now. As the updated Dominant Cycle Explorer indicates, we would expect an upturn from now until the beginning of August. That means that we will now enter a long position.

The next important time window is again marked on the chart with the blue line. We will be watching the market closely during this period.

As usual, let's move forward bar-by-bar until the Cycle Explorer arrives at the updated ideal cycle top in real-time.

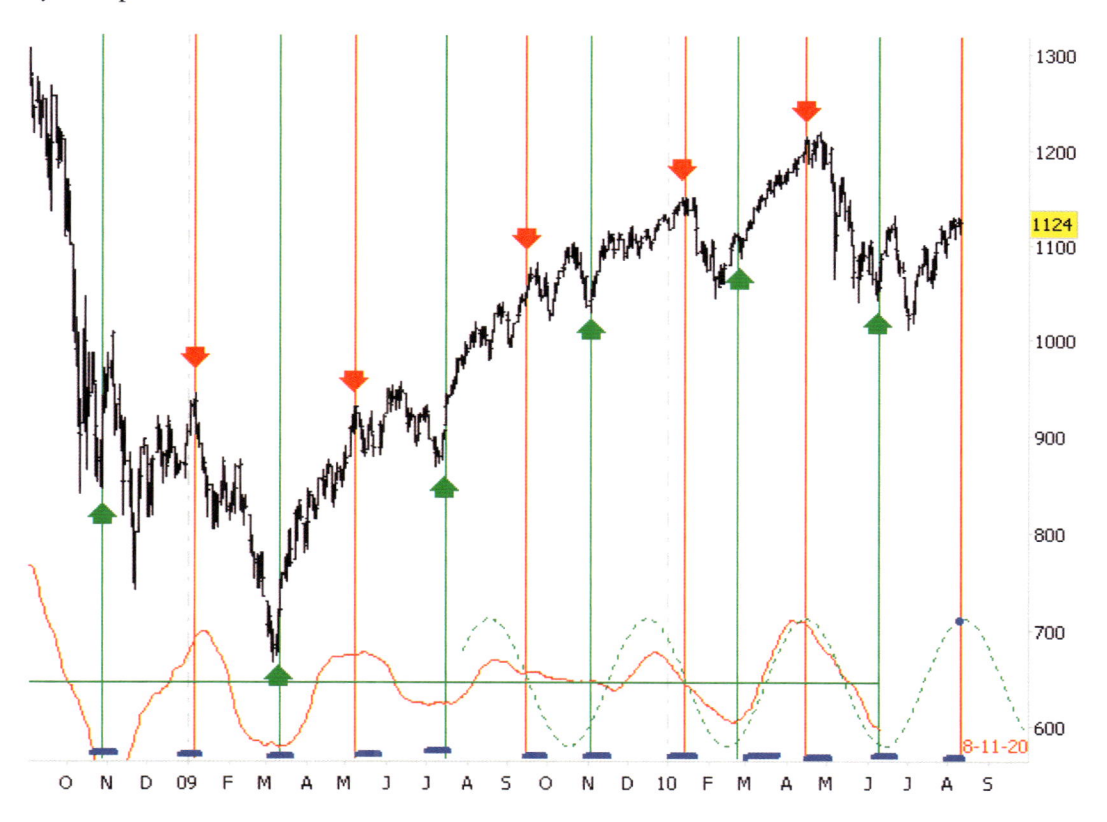

Figure 6-27: August 11 -> Actual market high

The next occurrence arrives on August 11. The Dominant Cycle Indicator shows the arrival at the dominant cycle crest illustrated by the blue dot on the ideal cycle plot. Again, it is not surprising that this occurs within the predicted time window.

The market moved up from 1062 to 1124 points with a gain of 62 points. We can close our last long position with this profit and switch to a short position. We will follow the path of the dominant cycle with a short position now. The next expected move is a down move.

This chart was inserted after I finished the book to prove that these methods still work today. I don't have to search for a situation back in time where this tool worked. And I don't have to choose a specific time frame within which it worked. I showed you that this tool worked without any interruption over a period of two complete years.

Today is August 20 and the S&P Index is 1072. The high indicated was again correct with an actual profit of 52 points.

The final chart displays the indicated market turns. These signals have come in ahead of time via the ideal cycle top/bottom prediction and have been confirmed in real-time by the updated dominant cycle plot at each new bar. And throughout the entire period, the indicator setting was not modified. The anchor point was fixed on the market high in October 2007 and the setting was the detection of the dominant cycle between a range of 75 and 150 bars/trading days (100 and 200 bars/calendar days).

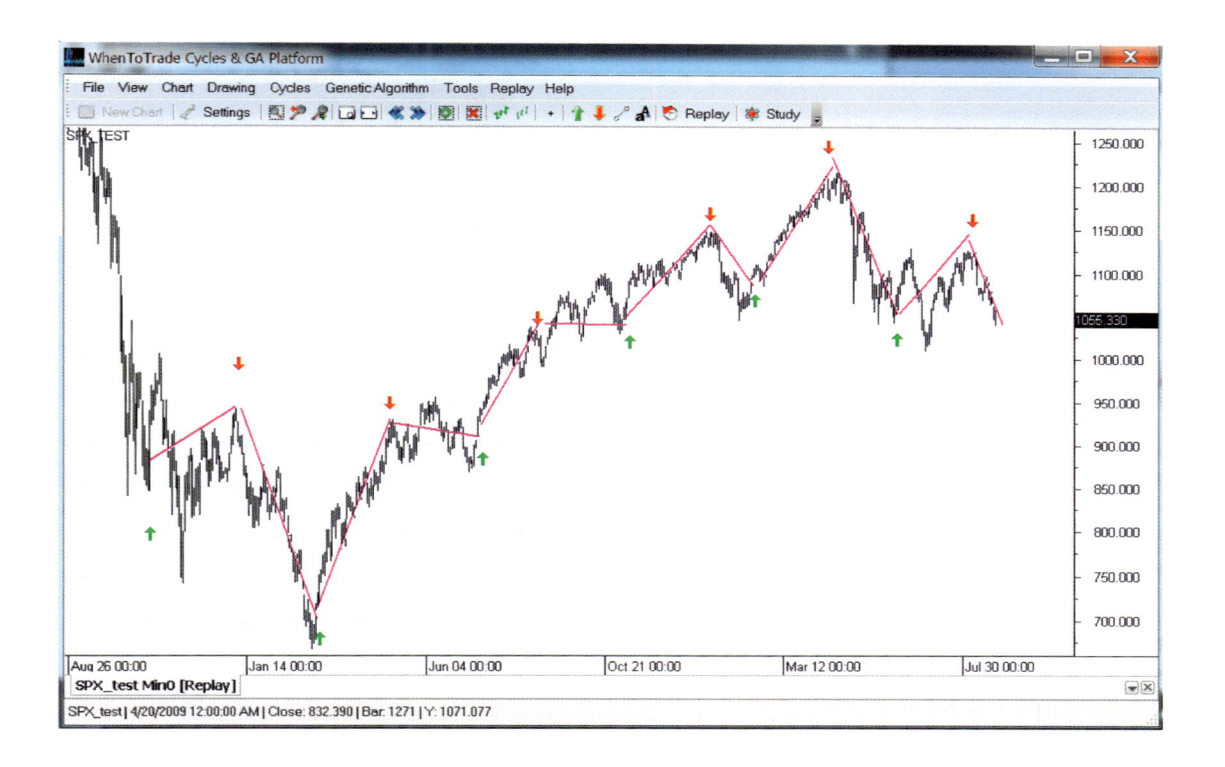

Figure 6-28: Signals over the last two years

As you can see, it was not a static cycle or cycle framework that delivered this outcome. It was the adaptive characteristic of the Cycle Explorer that was able to detect and adapt to the actual market vibration. The result was a highly accurate forecast of the next market turn in terms of time and direction. The dynamic update of the next important cycle crest or trough at each new bar indicated the precise position.

You would have been able to follow this path alone by looking at the chart based on this cyclic approach. It is fitted and coded into an easy-to-use technical indicator.

The following table summarizes the last two years of using this indicator as described in this chapter.

Date	Cycle Indicator	S&P 500 Index	Profit / Loss	Total Profit Cycle Swing
10/7/2008	-- start	1057	-	-
10/28/2008	LOW	849	208	208
1/6/2009	HIGH	935	86	294
3/12/2009	LOW	751	184	478
5/8/2009	HIGH	907	156	634
7/15/2009	LOW	933	-26	608
9/15/2009	HIGH	1053	120	728
11/3/2009	LOW	1043	10	738
1/13/2010	HIGH	1136	93	831
2/22/2010	LOW	1108	28	859
4/15/2010	HIGH	1211	103	962
6/9/2010	LOW	1062	149	1111
8/11/2010	HIGH	1124	62	1173
8/20/2010	-- end / TODAY	1072	52	1225
Total absolute profit		15		1225

Figure 6-29: Summary of Cycle Explorer signals

The table presents the impressive results in absolute numbers as illustrated in the charts. There have been 13 trades in total. Only one of these 13 trades was a loss. This gives us an accuracy rate of 92% over the last two years. This simple study gained a total of 1225 index points, which equals a profit of over 100% compared to the index start at 1057 points. The simple buy and hold strategy for the respective index would have resulted in a profit of 15 points (1.4%).

The numbers speak for themselves. Bear in mind that all this cycle analysis was carried out by the indicator itself. You could have read thousands of cycle newsletters during this two-year period which would have driven you crazy with all the possible outcomes.

You have probably realized by now that this indicator is a straightforward tool for trading. The mathematics and digital signal processing behind it is not. But that's of no relevance for usage in the trading arena.

This method works on all time frames and data series. You can use it on intraday as well as on weekly charts. All you have to do is carefully select the anchor point, the range, and the sensitivity of the statistical test that has to be passed (Bartels score). Play around a little with this new weapon to familiarize yourself with it and treat it with respect.

6.13 Video Lesson – Dynamic Cycles: S&P500 bar-by-bar review

Please review the step by step example in a non-interrupted bar-by-bar video. Click video or link below.

Review the non-interrupted bar-by-bar video of the last 2 years:

http://www.whentotrade.com/dynamiccycles1/

7. Measuring and trading Dominant Sentiment Cycles

A popular measure of the market sentiment for the S&P 500 Index is the Chicago Board Options Exchange Volatility Index (Ticker Symbol: VIX). It is often referred to as the *fear index*.

The VIX measures volatility and has an inverse relationship to the stock market. The more the VIX increases in value, the more panic there is in the market. The more VIX decreases in value, the more complacency there is in the market.

As a measure of complacency and panic, the VIX index is often used as a contrarian indicator. Extremely low VIX readings indicate a high degree of complacency and are generally regarded as bearish. Conversely, extremely high VIX readings indicate a high degree or anxiety or even panic and are regarded as bullish.

It would be useful to detect the cycles of trader sentiment. Because emotions swing from panic selling to over-confident buying in the form of cycles, sentiment indicators are a useful vehicle to transfer our cycle's toolkit to. If we are able to predict the expected sentiment highs or lows with our cycle analysis approach, we can use this leading information for trading purposes.

Let's use the conditions on February 20, 2009 for our example.

[S&P 500 Index chart showing decline from mid-2008 through early 2009, with annotation "February 20th 2009 Where is the bottom?" and value highlighted at 770]

Figure 7-1: S&P 590 on February 20 - Where is the low?

The market fell hard at the beginning of the year 2009. This would be an interesting point in time to see what the sentiment cycles would tell us here. Will the market decline further or is this perhaps already the low? This was a hot question around this time. So let's see what the sentiment cycles would have shown us.

We will use two dynamic cycle explorer indicators to monitor the situation of the actual long- and short-term dominant cycles. We will use the standard setting of the Dynamic Cycle Explorer. So nothing special here with reference to the indicator settings. This case is presented next.

7.1 The long-term Dynamic Cycle Explorer

The long-term range is set to: 100 – 200 calendar days or 75 – 150 trading days.

The long-term version is anchored to the October 10, 2007 low of the volatility index. This corresponds to the market all-time high of the S&P Index in 2007. The situation is one of extreme comfort buying sentiment in alignment with a major market high.

7.2 The short-term Dynamic Cycle Explorer

The short-term range for the next indicator is set to 30 – 100 calendar or approx. 20 – 75 trading days.

The short-term version is anchored to the July 15 high of the volatility index which is linked to the market low in the S&P 500. It's another extreme market panic which is in alignment with a sentiment top.

The next chart shows the setting on the VIX index on February 20. You can see the raw VIX data and the two Dynamic Cycle Explorer indicators applied to the chart. The anchor dates are highlighted on the chart.

Figure 7-2: Volatility cycles set-up on 20 February

Perhaps you are asking yourself why the last extreme highs around October/November 2008 have not been used here. There is a particular reason for this: The data history from February 2009 to November 2008 does not give us sufficient data points to perform our cycle analysis. That's the reason we have used the sentiment extreme crest (market low) in July 2008 and the sentiment extreme trough (market high) in October 2007. These two VIX market turns correspond to market turns. So we have two points where market sentiment and price behavior are in alignment. Two good points in time to start our cycle analysis for the sentiment cycles.

The detected long-term dominant cycle has a length of 128 calendar days and the short-term dominant cycle a length of 48 calendar days. This can be seen in the indicator log or by measuring the cycle high-to-high length bar by bar. Keep in mind that these cycle lengths were not derived from a static cycle framework – these cycles were completely automatically detected by our cycle analysis engine introduced in the second chapter.

But before we can use this analysis for forecasting, we have to review whether this setting would be reliable in accordance with our rules.

a) Fitness check of cycles between ideal and theoretical cycles

The first quality review involves a visual check of the correlation of the ideal detected (dotted green line) and the real sentiment cycle (red line). Especially the highs and lows of the ideal and real cycle should be in close alignment.

The next chart is a close-up view of the two indicator plots on the VIX chart. For better reading, the raw VIX data is not shown because we are only interested in the state of the cycles here. We do not need the raw data because the red line is the cyclic movement of the raw data for the cycle length of the detected cycle and the dotted green line represents the plotted ideal cycle. All other cycle lengths have been filtered out of the original raw data.

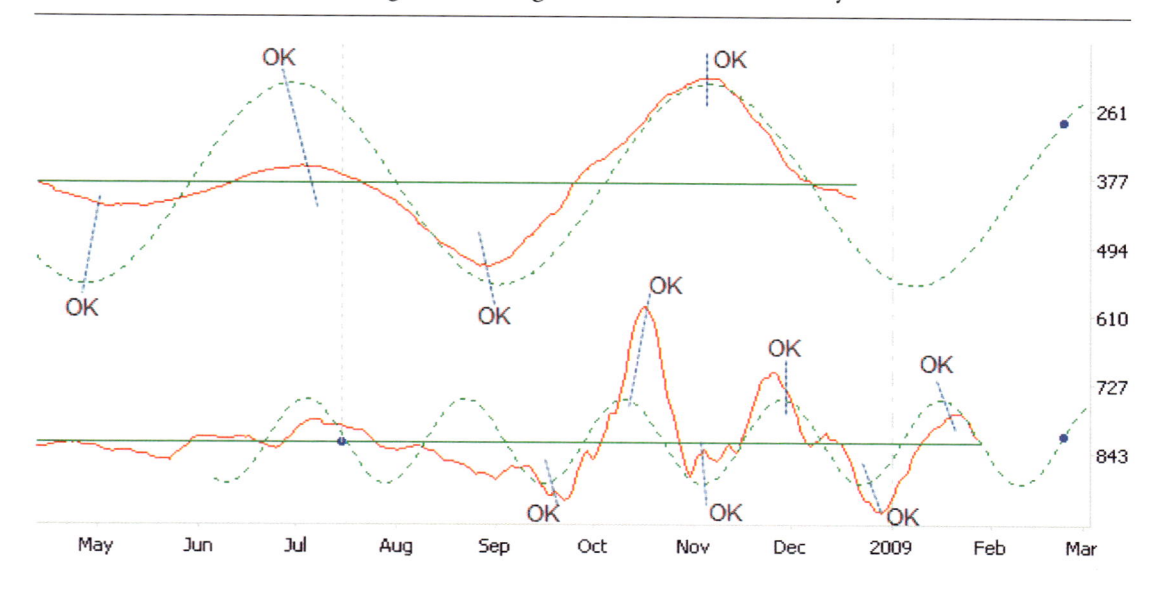

Figure 7-3: Zoom-in on dominant volatility cycles plot (visual check)

The figure reveals that we have a good fit between the ideal (green) and real (red) cycles on both of the automatically detected dominant cycles. The incidences are marked with a small line and the text "OK".

This analysis has passed our first quality check. The next quality review will cross-check the sentiment cycles with the behavior of the market index. Even if we have a nice fit of the sentiment cycles, we need confirmation that these sentiment cycles also represent important turning points in the stock markets.

b) Alignment check between dominant volatility cycle syncs and major market lows/highs

The next chart shows the VIX cycles in the lower windows and the S&P 500 Index in the upper windows. The time axis between both charts is in sync. We are able to track the important turns of the sentiment cycles on the market.

The arrows in the lower chart show incidences where the long- and short-term cycles are both at their lows/highs. When two cycles of different length are in sync with reference to their highs/lows, it is important to monitor these incidences. Because the additive force will come into play in these incidences.

The incidences where we have an alignment of the long- and short-term dominant cycle in the past are also highlighted with green and red arrows and the price chart of the S&P 500 can be seen in the upper half.

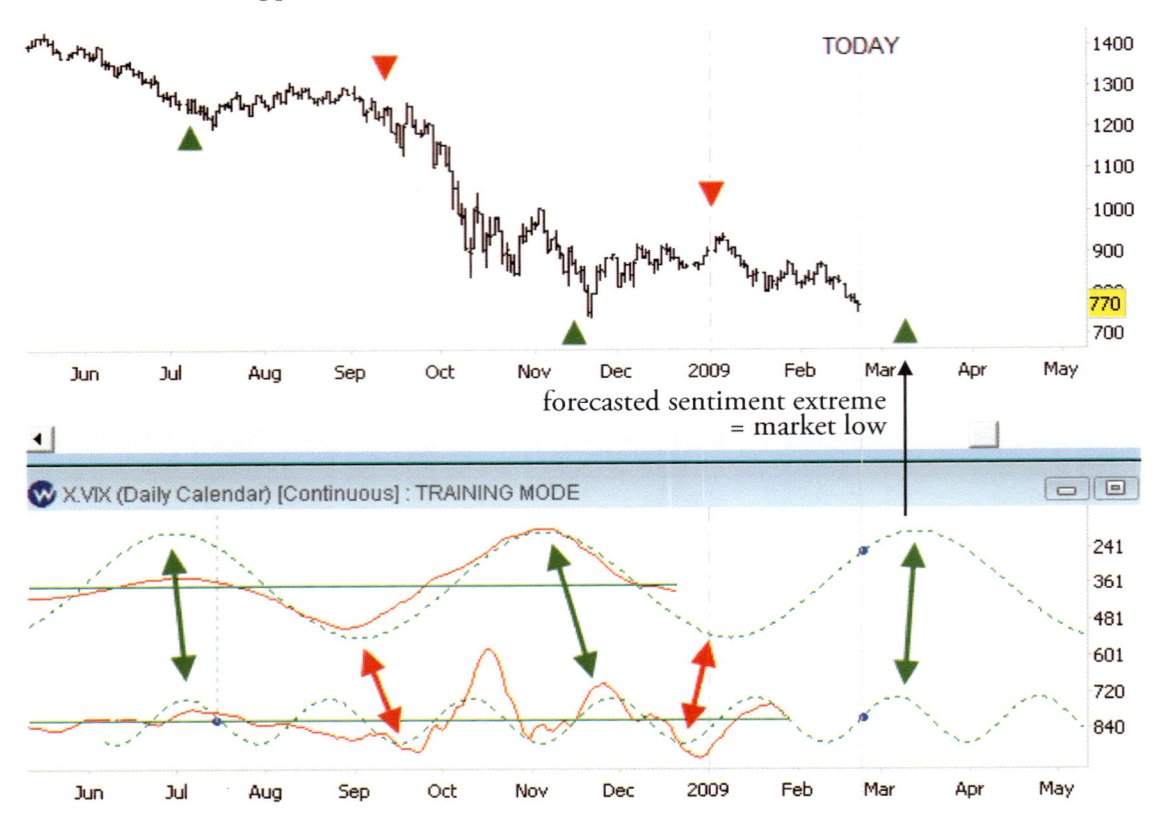

Figure 7-4: S&P 500 Index and dominant volatility cycle alignments

As we can see, we have a good alignment between the major dominant sentiment cycle syncs and major market turning points. We have passed our second test. Now, we can use this analysis for forecasting. And as the chart shows, the next incidence at which we expect the next sentiment cycle alignment between the long- and short-term dominant cycle in the first half of March 2009.

So this is the important information we want. We do not forecast months or years ahead. But the information we generated on February 20 would have signaled a high alert for the first half of March 2009. With regard to trading, this tells us that we would expect the selling to continue into March and to then hit a major bottom in the first half of March.

148

We can use other indicators to fine-tune our market entry. So we are looking for closing our short positions at the beginning of March and establishing a long-term bullish position in the first half of March. The next chart shows how the forecast done on February 20 would have played out with the progressed price chart.

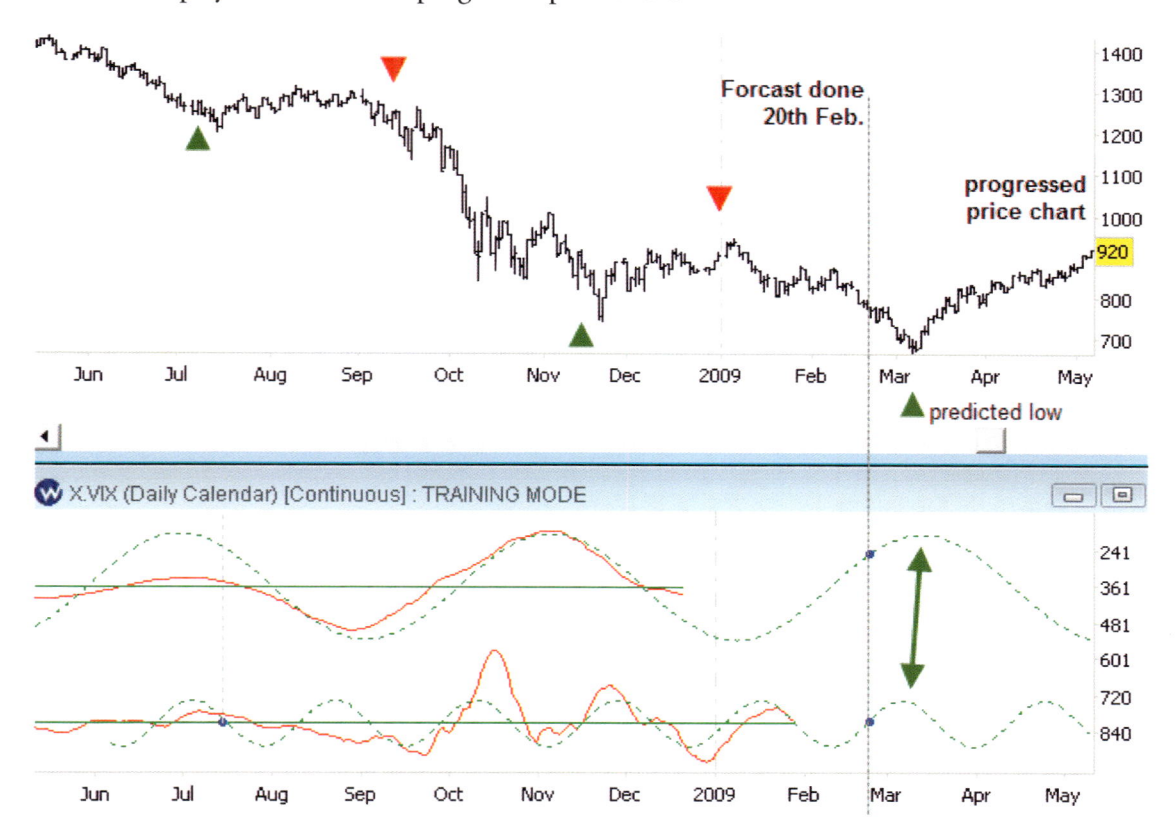

Figure 7-5: Volatility cycles forecast from February 20 and a progressed price chart

The dominant cycle technique - applied to sentiment indicators - warned us in February with clear precision that the selling climax would end in the first half of March 2009. And it was spot on.

7.3 Sentiment Cycles Follow-up progressions

Here are just some short follow-up progressions on the sentiment cycles.

The projection showed a possible sentiment extreme at the beginning of March. Here is the update when the dynamic-updating indicators reached their precise cycle high on March 13.

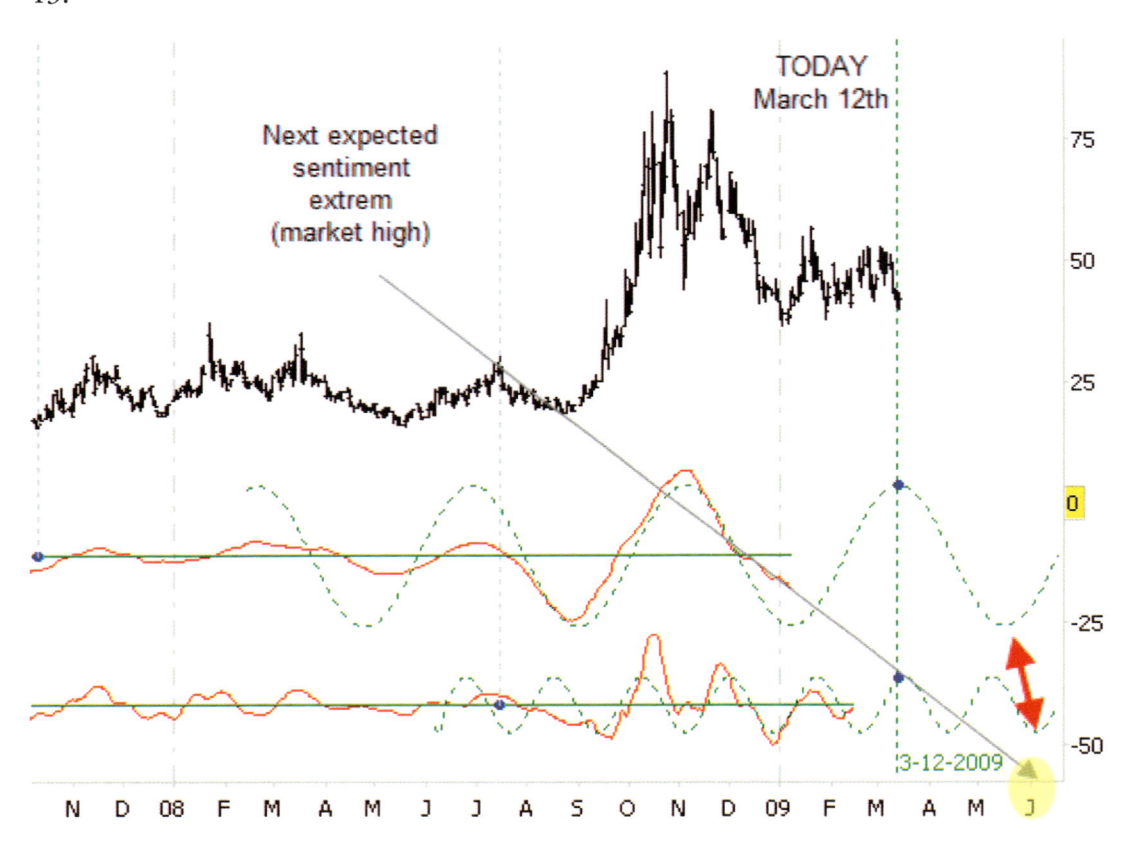

Figure 7-6: Status of sentiment cycles on March 12

You can see in Figure 7-7 that there was a perfect prediction of the market bottom in March and an accurate forecast of the next expected market high at the beginning of June 2009. What makes it so special is that these forecasts are based on dominant cycles derived from sentiment measurements, not price.

The following chart highlights the outcome of the two projected sentiment extremes in the first half of March and the beginning of June 2009 based on our sentiment cycle analysis from February and March 2009.

Again, please keep in mind that the detected dominant cycle length did not stay constant. The indicator detected the active market vibration and automatically adjusted the dominant cycle length. Even if the settings of the indicator have not changed (range and anchor), the indicator automatically adjusted the phase and wavelength at each new bar according to the actual market vibration. Just like the automatic navigation system in your car. It automatically updates your estimated time of arrival in accordance with the actual driving conditions, like traffic and speed. This is exactly what the dynamic Dominant Cycle Explorer will do on the financial time series.

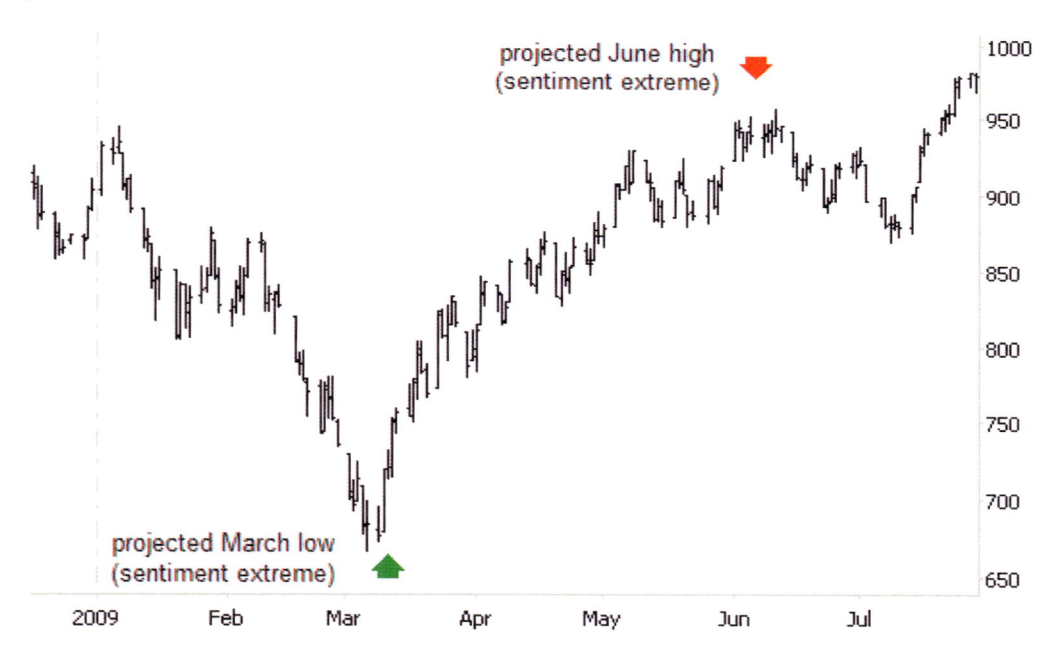

Figure 7-7: Outcome of dominant sentiment cycle projection from February/March 2009

The next chart is a "fast forward" to show you that each major market high/low is accompanied by a correct alignment of forecasted sentiment cycle extremes. The chart shows the actual analysis at the end of March 2010. Again, the anchor point and range settings have not been touched. The settings of both indicators are still the same as at the beginning of this example!

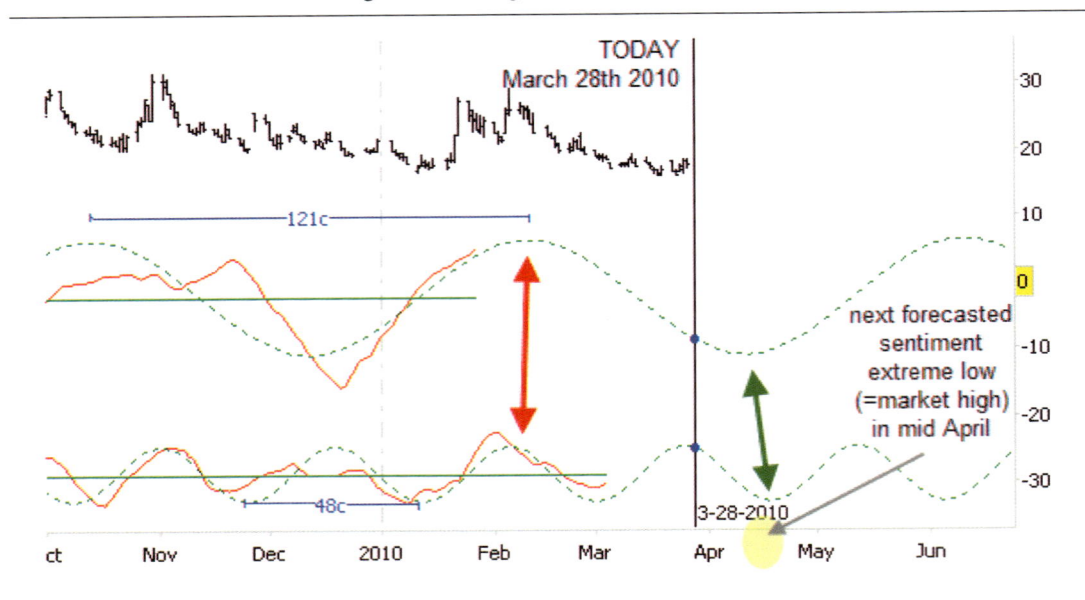

Figure 7-8: Sentiment extreme projection on March 28, 2010

You can see that both dominant cycles had their last extreme alignment in February 2010 which corresponded to the major bottom in 2010. Now, at the end of March 2010 the entire technical analysis community is discussing when the upturn will come to an end. Our dominant sentiment cycles approach gives us a clear picture. We would expect the next sentiment extreme in mid-April. The following chart displays this situation and how it would have played out.

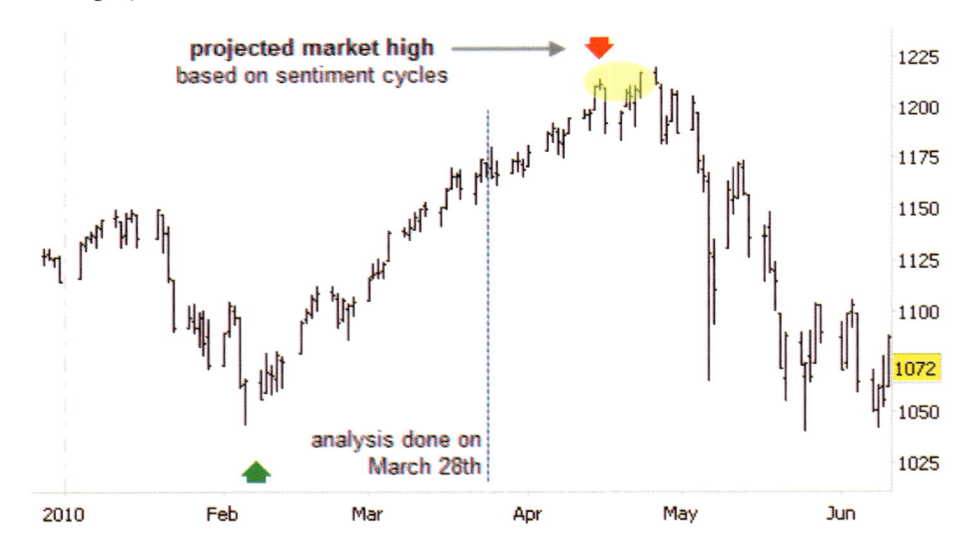

Figure 7-9: Forecasted market high in mid-April

8. Cycles within Cycles: Combining price and sentiment cycles

Traditional cycle approaches must take two crucial success factors into consideration: First, which cycle detection algorithm is used plays a decisive role. Which dominant cycle should be used to forecast or adjust technical indicators? If the wrong cycle is detected on the "left side" of the chart, every trading and forecasting approach will fail on the more important "right side" of the chart. However, current "cycle" detection engines are not developed to adequately deal with the features of financial time series. The algorithms currently being used to detect cycles in financial markets derive from the domain of frequency analysis toolsets like Fourier, DFT, Wavelets or MESA. All of these algorithms have shortcomings in the detection of financial market cycles.

Secondly, even if the right cycles are detected, financial market cycles are not "static". Despite the dynamic nature of the cycles that drive markets, traditional approaches project cycles as theoretically static single or composite waves into the future. Dominant cycles continuously vary over time in terms of length, amplitude and phase offset based on their inner core parameter. This means that the length component of a dominant cycle with a length of 80 days may easily vary between 76 and 84 days – but it remains a dominant cycle of "80" days nonetheless. However, you will not know whether a cycle has contracted or expanded if you only follow a simplistic static projection.

Most cycle approaches will fail

Hence, most of the current cycle systems will fail in the long term due to one of the two issues discussed above. If you want to trade cycles successfully, you have to accept the fact that there is no cycle detection algorithm out there that can adequately deal with the characteristics of financial data. What is even more relevant for every trading approach is the fact that cycles have a dynamic nature and will not stay static over time.

These facts are not new. However, I have not found any tool or approach that is able to deal with these two key problems. Traditional approaches to financial market cycles have not advanced much since Hurst and the mathematics of Digital Signal Processing – variations have certainly been introduced, but no real progress has been made in this field for quite some time.

A new cycle approach

With that said, I introduced my "own approach" to cycles in the previous chapter to overcome these key issues. The presented detection algorithm outperforms most existing "traditional" tools on cycle analysis. Furthermore, I developed a trading approach that can deal with the fact that dominant cycles "morph" over time and have to be continuously monitored in terms of their current phase and length. The research work has resulted in a dynamic cycle toolset which was introduced in the previous chapter and is now, by and large able to automatically track dominant cycles. The following example explains and illustrates this dynamic approach to trade cycles in financial markets.

8.1 The Dynamic Cycles Approach

This chapter introduces a dynamic approach for building tradable forecasts. This is only one of different possible techniques – complex in the backyard – but simple, beautiful and powerful on the price chart. Every time a new bar appears on the chart, we will reassess the state of the current dominant cycle – as our carrier wave for price movements – in terms of wavelength, amplitude and phase offset. The integrated cycle's detection algorithm will perform this completely automatically. Subsequently, we will update this cycle by plotting it into the future. However, we will only focus on the next expected turning point – that's what we are interested in. I refer to this turning point as ETA – Expected Time of Arrival. We are not interested in projecting the complete static cycle into the future. We are interested in monitoring the next ETA point based on the detected dominant carrier wave.

As we move forward in time, every bar signifies an update on the next expected turning point. This dynamic forecast based on the actual state of the dominant cycle provides information about the next turning point in terms of time and direction. We will obtain real-time information about when to expect the next major turning point in the market while we continuously reassess the parameter of the dominant carrier wave. This information is updated every time a new bar appears. It is difficult to do this manually, so I automated all tasks required to perform this operation. The outcome is the "Dynamic Cycle Explorer" which was introduced in Chapter 5. This tool automatically performs all of these steps. We can therefore fully focus on trade evaluation instead of manual cycle research.

The difference between many cycle researchers' approach and mine should be evident by now. I do not apply a framework with static cycles and try to make the market fit into it. One often reads about the significance of the 4-year or 28-day cycle and how these "static" cycles can be applied to the actual market situation. This is no longer a promising approach. I have seen too many "static" cycle frameworks fail on the right side of the chart. I have successfully used this dynamic model that determines which cycles are active at a given point in time for over 10 years now in my own trading.

You use this method to be "prepared" for important turning points in the market. ETA points should not be traded blindly. When used in combination with other tools, you will have very powerful setups to trade in the market, which show up in advance.

Charts say more than a thousand words. Let's look at this dynamic cycles approach in action.

8.2 The dominant carrier wave on the price chart – October 2010

I will use a "dynamic intermarket cycles-within-cycles approach" example to demonstrate the power of this approach. Let's start in October 2010 with the long-term perspective on the weekly chart of the S&P 500 index. The dynamic cycle explorer is attached to the chart. The indicator detects the dominant cycle and checks possible length and phase shifts for this carrier wave at every bar. The example is based on the pure standard settings of this fully automated indicator – there is no way to back optimize or curve-fit this tool. You would have arrived at precisely the same situation if you had attached it to the chart on your own on the given day. The dominant carrier wave is plotted as a blue theoretical cycle at the bottom of the chart and automatically extended into the future. If we look at the past, we can see that the detected cycle fits nicely to the peaks and valleys of the price history.

8-1: Weekly S&P 500 with dominant cycle and ETA projection (8 October 2010)

What we are interested in is the next ETA point, represented by the dotted blue line, the word ETA and the short purple line: The next major top is expected to arrive around 29 April 2011. We are thus in an upswing that is expected to last for the next 6 months from now on. That's the picture the current cycle analysis gives us – the long-term carrier wave that will guide us to time our trades on the daily chart. We will now monitor the ETA point week by week to check whether the projection will change or not. We do not use this one-time analysis as a fixed projection that cannot be modified. Instead, we update this projection every week once we obtain the next bar. This means that we will follow the main dominant cycle and check whether the length or phase of the cycle has changed, which might lead to an adjusted ETA projection.

I compare this type of analysis with the Garmin navigation in your car. It provides you with the current estimated time of arrival at your destination. This arrival time is continuously updated in real time based on the given traffic conditions. This is precisely what we will do with the dominant cycle: We will check its current status at every bar and adjust our ETA projection if needed. So, if we move forward in time, our ETA point will become more and more accurate from bar to bar.

8.3 The peak is detected in advance - May 2011

As we move forward in time, the next chart illustrates the state of the cycle in mid-May. The blue ETA projection and the dotted line marked with "29. April" have not moved since October 2010. As the updated current dominant cycle projection indicates, the length and phase has slightly shifted as we progress toward 29 April 2011. The peak is now projected for mid-May as denoted by the updated dominant cycle and the blue dot for the current bar. The core cycle is still the same as in October 2010 – only the phase and length have slightly shifted and the dynamic explorer was able to detect and has followed the "inner" vibration of this dominant cycle. The indicator setup has not changed at all throughout the entire time.

8-2: Updated cycle projection in May 2011 with shifted cycle peak

In general it seems that the market already peaked in the original projection for 29 April. The updated dominant cycle is now also at the current peak projection. The highlighted box on the chart with the red arrow confirms this based on the original projection from October and the current state of the dominant cycle in mid-May. This is a high valid signal that the dominant cycle remained stable and that we can determine the peak of the carrier wave which we have been following now since October 2010. The uptrend has evidently come to an end. And we can see this before the price moves.

Now, since we have reached the peak, we want to find out when the next estimated time of arrival (ETA) for the expected low will be. This point is again highlighted by the blue dotted line - dated 27 January 2012. If you compare this projection to that of October, you will see that the projected low has shifted from 20 to 27 January. This is our approach – we are only interested in the next ETA, not the full static cycle projection. Finally, we can see it: The peak occurs in mid-May 2011 and we expect a downward trend until the beginning of 2012. At this point in the cycle analysis, we again move forward bar by bar and follow the carrier wave to detect shifts in the length or phase of the dominant cycle.

8.4 Following the vibration of the dominant cycle – September 2011

For the period from the peak in May until October 2011, we are able to follow the transformation of the active dominant cycle using the dynamic cycle explorer: As we progress bar by bar from October on, we see that the cycle contracts and that the phase slightly shifts, with the result that the projected ETA moves closer and closer to the current day.

Please watch a short video to review the non-interrupted dynamic behavior bar by bar at: http://www.whentotrade.com/dynamiccycles2/

The next chart presents the state of the cycle on 2 September 2011. We observe that the next ETA was updated based on the current state of the dominant cycle. The next ETA on the long-term chart is now expected to be 7 October 2011 instead of January 2012. Compare the last two cycle projections from May and September – you can see that it is still the same general dominant carrier wave: Three peaks and two valleys aligned to price behavior – and the next valley is expected to occur in October instead of January. This is the power of the dynamic approach – it analyzes the active dominant cycle with reference to current price behavior and vibration – it does not "curve-fit" the static cycle to the past! If we only considered our static projection from May, we would still be expecting a low in January 2012. As we are continuously monitoring the dominant cycle, we now know that this dominant cycle's dip is expected to arrive earlier.

Cycles within Cycles: Combining price and sentiment cycles

8-3: Dynamic shift of the expected dip projection with updated ETA (2 September 2011)

If we look at the actual analysis of 2 September more closely we can see that we have already entered the cyclical trough period, which will last until mid-October. If you are familiar with cycle analysis, you know that an expected turning point will never occur precisely on the day/week of a sine wave peak or low. We should therefore be prepared for a possible upswing from this point on since we have moved into the bottom of the cycle. This juncture is interesting because the price already dropped 3 weeks ago. The main question at this point is: Has the cycle now perhaps reached the bottom?

8.5 Cycles within cycles – Sentiment in September 2011

To answer this question, we apply the cycles within cycles approach. To time the trade, we have to move to the next lower timeframe. To determine whether the bottom has already been reached, we have to analyze the dominant daily carrier wave. And to add an extra bonus to the cycles approach, I will use sentiment cycles on the daily timeframe instead of the daily S&P 500 to analyze our position in the market. Markets are driven by emotions. Therefore, if we are able to analyze the current sentiment cycle, we have the source and leading information for price behavior. The Volatility Index (VIX) is a useful measurement for the sentiment of the market.

Hence, to determine whether we are approaching or are already in a major low on 2 September 2011, we apply our cyclic work to the VIX on 2 September 2011.

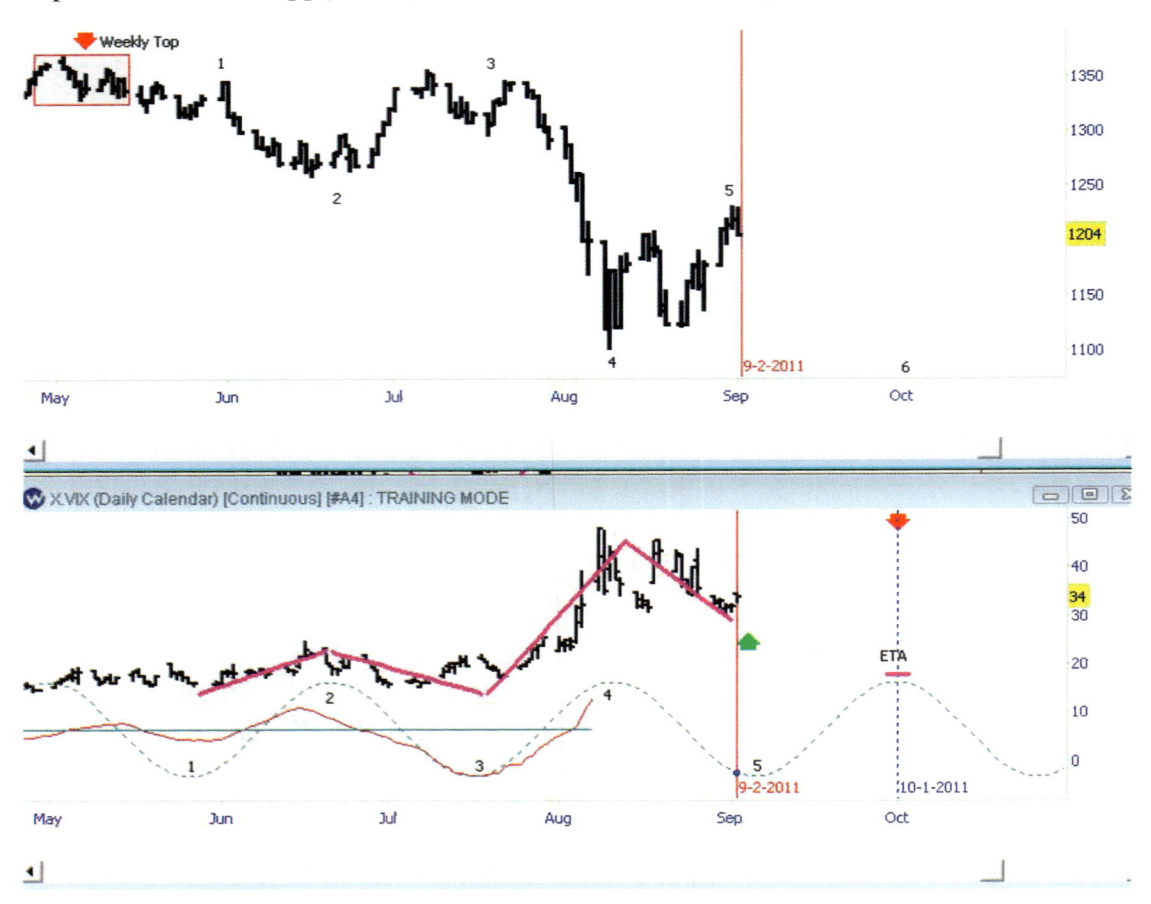

8-4: Daily S&P 500 with VIX and actual dominant sentiment cycle (2 September 2011)

The major market peak which we identified correctly using the weekly cycle analysis is represented by the small box on the upper S&P chart. We are short since May. We now attach the same indicator to the daily chart of the VIX (bottom chart). We apply the same standard settings, i.e., nothing special again. Simply drag the dynamic cycle explorer onto the chart. The algorithm detects and plots the current dominant carrier wave right onto the chart. The main swings of the detected cycle are marked with the numbers 1 to 5 on the

VIX and S&P chart. You can see that we have a vice-versa correlation of the sentiment cycle: A sentiment cycle's peak corresponds to a market low and vice-versa. This confirms that the automatically detected dominant cycle in the VIX is valid with regard to the market's major turning points. On 2 September 2011 – the date we shifted our attention away from the long-term cycle projection to determine whether the dip had already occurred – we clearly see that the actual turning point No. 5 occurs with an expected low in the sentiment index taking shape now (=market high). The next ETA projection is expected to occur during a period of high sentiment reading, topping on 1 October 2011 (Point 6). What does this mean with regard to our main question: Should we establish a long trade because the long-term cycle is forming a low right now? The answer is quite simple: The daily chart reveals that price has increased since the major low in August (Point 4). However, we know based on this current low sentiment cycle that the market has reached a daily peak at Point 5! Not a good time to place a long trade, because we expect the market to move down into the projected Point 6 as shown by the sentiment cycle ETA for 1 October 2011.

In addition, we can get a clear message now by combining long- and short-term dominant cycle analysis: If you only looked at the daily chart, you would go short now. However, based on your knowledge about the longer-term cycle, you know that we expect a major market low to take shape during this time – not the long-term situation we would necessarily like to place short trades in (only allowed in the aggressive mode)! So, the long-term analysis protects us from placing a short trade here. On the other hand, if you only used the long-term projection, you would probably want to go long now. In this case, the short-term analysis prevents us from going long now in the current situation of the market sentiment.

Support now comes from the cycles-within-cycles approach: We know from the long-term cycle that we can expect a low to take shape over the next few weeks into the beginning of October. The current short-term cycle projects the next market low to begin forming around 1 October. Here we have it: A fit of the long- and short-term projection, an expected major low around 1 October 2011. This is the timing on the daily timeframe now. Do not go long on 2 September 2011. Wait until the beginning of October before establishing the next major long position.

8.6 Current sentiment cycle fits into the long-term wave – October 2011

Again, let's move forward in time and track the dominant carrier sentiment wave day by day from 2 September onward. The next chart illustrates the situation on 4 October. The same dominant cycle is still active as the indicator demonstrates. Again only a slight shift took place, as indicated by Points 1-5 and the ETA mark with the blue line, which have not moved since our original analysis. The current cycle peak should have been reached as the analysis of 4 October shows.

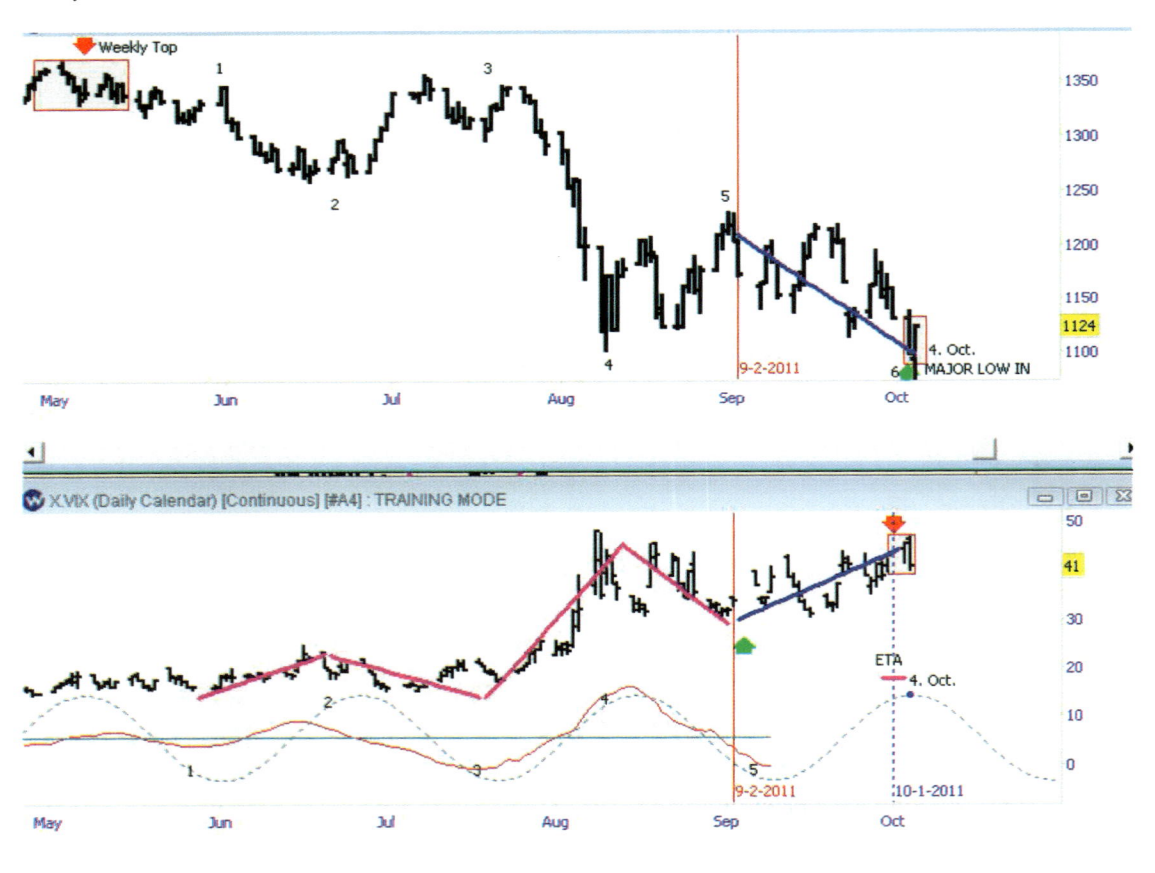

8-5: Daily S&P 500 & VIX with updated cycle (4 October 2011)

We can observe that price dropped during the time sentiment on the VIX moved up into our ETA window. Just like it was projected by the identified dominant carrier wave. And now as we approach the projected ETA, our current cycle analysis confirms that we reached

8.3 The peak is detected in advance - May 2011

As we move forward in time, the next chart illustrates the state of the cycle in mid-May. The blue ETA projection and the dotted line marked with "29. April" have not moved since October 2010. As the updated current dominant cycle projection indicates, the length and phase has slightly shifted as we progress toward 29 April 2011. The peak is now projected for mid-May as denoted by the updated dominant cycle and the blue dot for the current bar. The core cycle is still the same as in October 2010 – only the phase and length have slightly shifted and the dynamic explorer was able to detect and has followed the "inner" vibration of this dominant cycle. The indicator setup has not changed at all throughout the entire time.

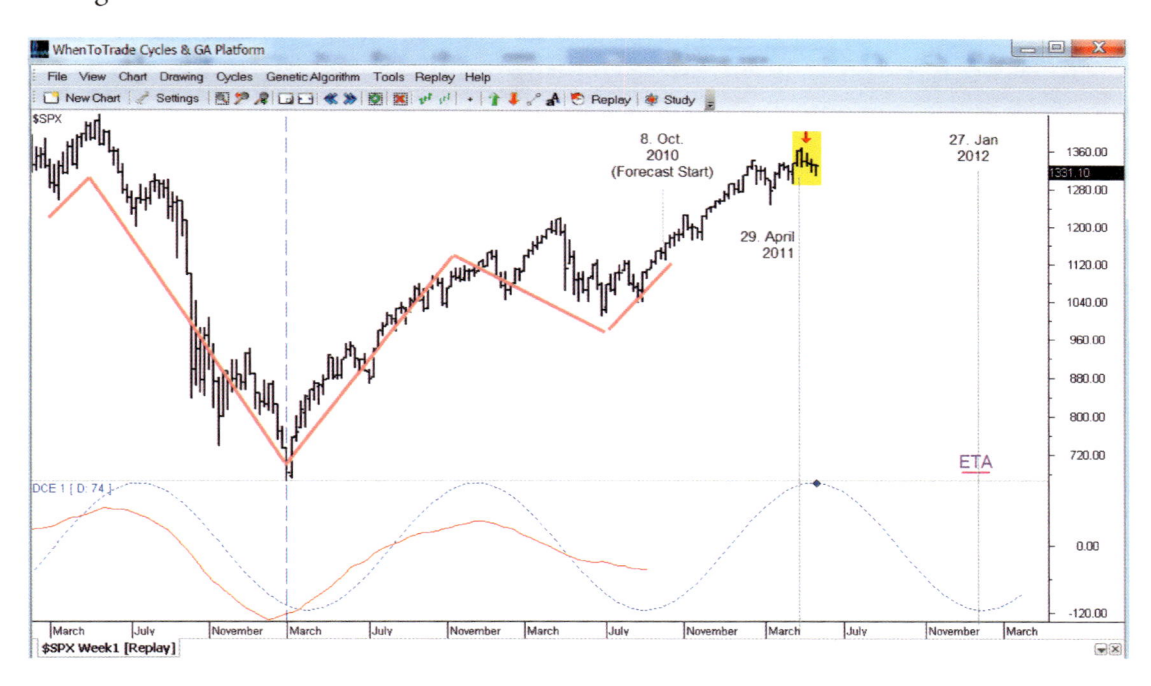

8-2: Updated cycle projection in May 2011 with shifted cycle peak

In general it seems that the market already peaked in the original projection for 29 April. The updated dominant cycle is now also at the current peak projection. The highlighted box on the chart with the red arrow confirms this based on the original projection from October and the current state of the dominant cycle in mid-May. This is a high valid signal that the dominant cycle remained stable and that we can determine the peak of the carrier wave which we have been following now since October 2010. The uptrend has evidently come to an end. And we can see this before the price moves.

Now, since we have reached the peak, we want to find out when the next estimated time of arrival (ETA) for the expected low will be. This point is again highlighted by the blue dotted line - dated 27 January 2012. If you compare this projection to that of October, you will see that the projected low has shifted from 20 to 27 January. This is our approach – we are only interested in the next ETA, not the full static cycle projection. Finally, we can see it: The peak occurs in mid-May 2011 and we expect a downward trend until the beginning of 2012. At this point in the cycle analysis, we again move forward bar by bar and follow the carrier wave to detect shifts in the length or phase of the dominant cycle.

8.4 Following the vibration of the dominant cycle – September 2011

For the period from the peak in May until October 2011, we are able to follow the transformation of the active dominant cycle using the dynamic cycle explorer: As we progress bar by bar from October on, we see that the cycle contracts and that the phase slightly shifts, with the result that the projected ETA moves closer and closer to the current day.

Please watch a short video to review the non-interrupted dynamic behavior bar by bar at: http://www.whentotrade.com/dynamiccycles2/

The next chart presents the state of the cycle on 2 September 2011. We observe that the next ETA was updated based on the current state of the dominant cycle. The next ETA on the long-term chart is now expected to be 7 October 2011 instead of January 2012. Compare the last two cycle projections from May and September – you can see that it is still the same general dominant carrier wave: Three peaks and two valleys aligned to price behavior – and the next valley is expected to occur in October instead of January. This is the power of the dynamic approach – it analyzes the active dominant cycle with reference to current price behavior and vibration – it does not "curve-fit" the static cycle to the past! If we only considered our static projection from May, we would still be expecting a low in January 2012. As we are continuously monitoring the dominant cycle, we now know that this dominant cycle's dip is expected to arrive earlier.

8-3: Dynamic shift of the expected dip projection with updated ETA (2 September 2011)

If we look at the actual analysis of 2 September more closely we can see that we have already entered the cyclical trough period, which will last until mid-October. If you are familiar with cycle analysis, you know that an expected turning point will never occur precisely on the day/week of a sine wave peak or low. We should therefore be prepared for a possible upswing from this point on since we have moved into the bottom of the cycle. This juncture is interesting because the price already dropped 3 weeks ago. The main question at this point is: Has the cycle now perhaps reached the bottom?

8.5 Cycles within cycles – Sentiment in September 2011

To answer this question, we apply the cycles within cycles approach. To time the trade, we have to move to the next lower timeframe. To determine whether the bottom has already been reached, we have to analyze the dominant daily carrier wave. And to add an extra bonus to the cycles approach, I will use sentiment cycles on the daily timeframe instead of the daily S&P 500 to analyze our position in the market. Markets are driven by emotions. Therefore, if we are able to analyze the current sentiment cycle, we have the source and leading information for price behavior. The Volatility Index (VIX) is a useful measurement for the sentiment of the market.

Hence, to determine whether we are approaching or are already in a major low on 2 September 2011, we apply our cyclic work to the VIX on 2 September 2011.

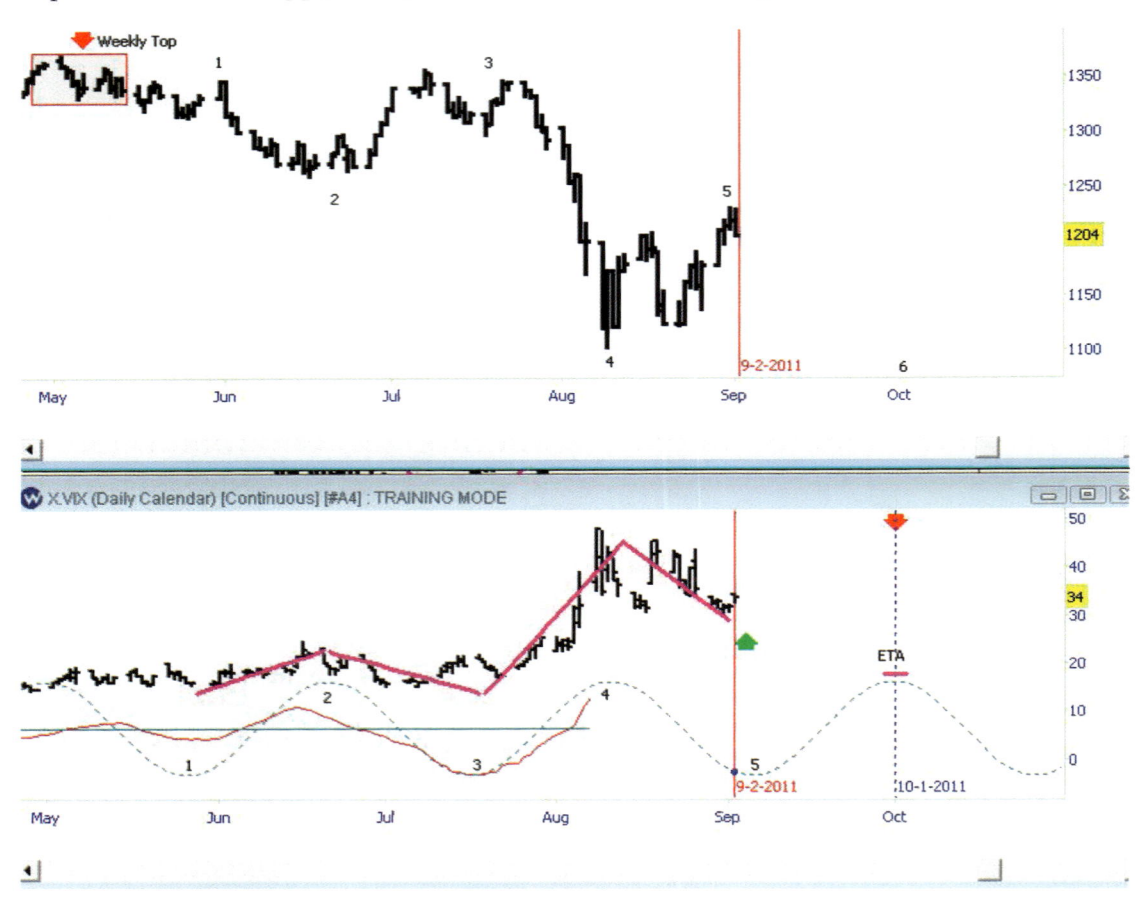

8-4: Daily S&P 500 with VIX and actual dominant sentiment cycle (2 September 2011)

The major market peak which we identified correctly using the weekly cycle analysis is represented by the small box on the upper S&P chart. We are short since May. We now attach the same indicator to the daily chart of the VIX (bottom chart). We apply the same standard settings, i.e., nothing special again. Simply drag the dynamic cycle explorer onto the chart. The algorithm detects and plots the current dominant carrier wave right onto the chart. The main swings of the detected cycle are marked with the numbers 1 to 5 on the

160

VIX and S&P chart. You can see that we have a vice-versa correlation of the sentiment cycle: A sentiment cycle's peak corresponds to a market low and vice-versa. This confirms that the automatically detected dominant cycle in the VIX is valid with regard to the market's major turning points. On 2 September 2011 – the date we shifted our attention away from the long-term cycle projection to determine whether the dip had already occurred – we clearly see that the actual turning point No. 5 occurs with an expected low in the sentiment index taking shape now (=market high). The next ETA projection is expected to occur during a period of high sentiment reading, topping on 1 October 2011 (Point 6). What does this mean with regard to our main question: Should we establish a long trade because the long-term cycle is forming a low right now? The answer is quite simple: The daily chart reveals that price has increased since the major low in August (Point 4). However, we know based on this current low sentiment cycle that the market has reached a daily peak at Point 5! Not a good time to place a long trade, because we expect the market to move down into the projected Point 6 as shown by the sentiment cycle ETA for 1 October 2011.

In addition, we can get a clear message now by combining long- and short-term dominant cycle analysis: If you only looked at the daily chart, you would go short now. However, based on your knowledge about the longer-term cycle, you know that we expect a major market low to take shape during this time – not the long-term situation we would necessarily like to place short trades in (only allowed in the aggressive mode)! So, the long-term analysis protects us from placing a short trade here. On the other hand, if you only used the long-term projection, you would probably want to go long now. In this case, the short-term analysis prevents us from going long now in the current situation of the market sentiment.

Support now comes from the cycles-within-cycles approach: We know from the long-term cycle that we can expect a low to take shape over the next few weeks into the beginning of October. The current short-term cycle projects the next market low to begin forming around 1 October. Here we have it: A fit of the long- and short-term projection, an expected major low around 1 October 2011. This is the timing on the daily timeframe now. Do not go long on 2 September 2011. Wait until the beginning of October before establishing the next major long position.

8.6 Current sentiment cycle fits into the long-term wave – October 2011

Again, let's move forward in time and track the dominant carrier sentiment wave day by day from 2 September onward. The next chart illustrates the situation on 4 October. The same dominant cycle is still active as the indicator demonstrates. Again only a slight shift took place, as indicated by Points 1-5 and the ETA mark with the blue line, which have not moved since our original analysis. The current cycle peak should have been reached as the analysis of 4 October shows.

8-5: Daily S&P 500 & VIX with updated cycle (4 October 2011)

We can observe that price dropped during the time sentiment on the VIX moved up into our ETA window. Just like it was projected by the identified dominant carrier wave. And now as we approach the projected ETA, our current cycle analysis confirms that we reached a high on the sentiment index on 4 October (=market low). Thus, based on the projection and the current state of the cycle, we have a picture-perfect and valid sentiment cycle whose peak is now projected for 4 October 2011. The market has dropped to a level that is even lower than the previous low back in August – hence, the sentiment projection of 2 September protected us from going long too early. A closely monitored, aggressive short trade would have given us additional profit during the sentiment ride.

Now we have our cycles within cycles alignment – it could not be more clear: The long-term weekly sentiment cycle projection ETA reveals a low on 7 October (see Chart 8-3). The short-term daily sentiment cycle projection ETA confirms this low on 4 October (Chart 8-4 & 8-5). We have a picture perfect cycle within cycles alignment. The only difference is that we would not have been able to detect this cycle alignment with traditional static cycle projection tools! We need the dynamic component which gives it that extra something. Furthermore, with the dynamic component we are now able to view the formation of the cycles in advance bar by bar and can prepare.

We have it in now: A major low on 4 October 2011 demonstrated by the cycles. Bear in mind: Not even price can give us this information for 4 October. No technical indicator, no trend line, no tool whatsoever would have indicated a major low based on price alone. The dynamic cycles on price and sentiment, however, have.

Let's move forward in time to see how this juncture plays out. The following chart shows the outcome on the right chart.

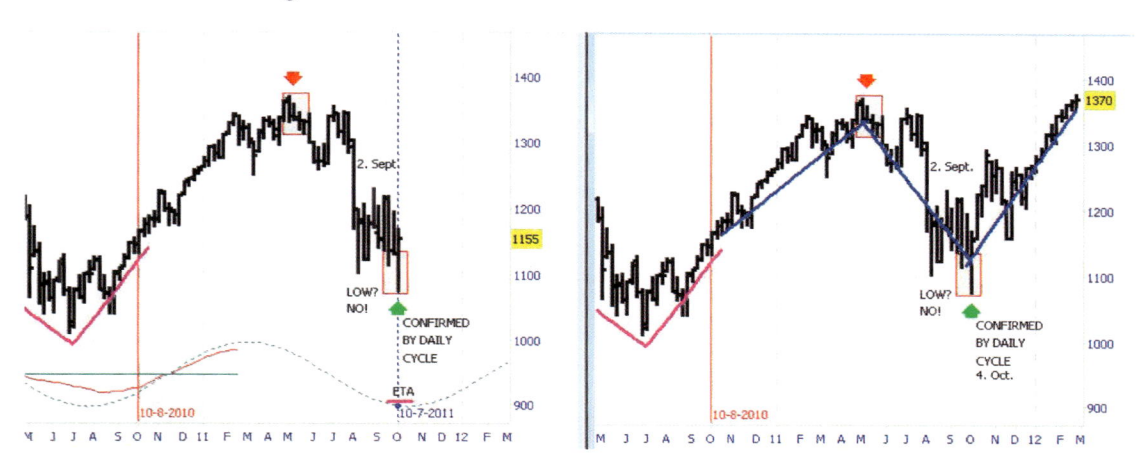

8-6: Daily S&P chart with identified market peak and market low updated to today

The projected low for 4-7 October 2011 occurred right on time. The market has moved up afterwards as projected by the long-term carrier wave.

The blue line on the right chart presents the trade summary of the example outlined here. We commenced with the running upswing in October, identified the major peak as projected in May and successfully fine-tuned the market low with the cycles within cycles approach in combination with the sentiment cycle in October. The complete example is based on the standard dynamic cycle explorer. No optimization or curve-fitting has been undertaken. And I am not cherry picking one specific situation here. A pure analysis of what the cycles within cycles approach showed us concerning the long-term perspective from October 2010 up to today.

This approach can be applied to any symbol on any timeframe. Even though this approach may look simple, discipline in dealing with moving projections and validating auto-detected cycles is required for it to be successful. With regard to intra-day trading, the dynamic cycles approach is more complicated than for daily charts. Why? Because there are a lot of interfering cycles active during the same time on intra-day timeframes like 5, 10 or 30 minutes, which makes it difficult to detect the single most active carrier wave. Dominant cycles jump over from one carrier wave to the next – they do not shift smoothly as they do on the daily charts. This is the area where additional research is necessary.

I hope that this chapter is an eye-opener to the fact that cycles breathe over time and don't stay fixed. If you accustom yourself with this fact and are able to develop or use tools that can convert this notion into tradable visual plots via optimized algorithms, cycle projections of this type will propel you onto the next level of trading and forecasting. In addition, try to detect and use dominant cycles on sentiment indicators like the VIX to identify major turning points in the market instead of solely focusing on the major index alone.

8.7 Video Lesson

Please review the outlined example in a non-interrupted bar-by-bar live video. Click video picture or link below:

Decoding The Hidden Market Rhythm – Part 1: Dynamic Cycles

Example Video Lesson
Weekly S&P 500 Index / Long Term Non-Interrupted Dominant Cycle

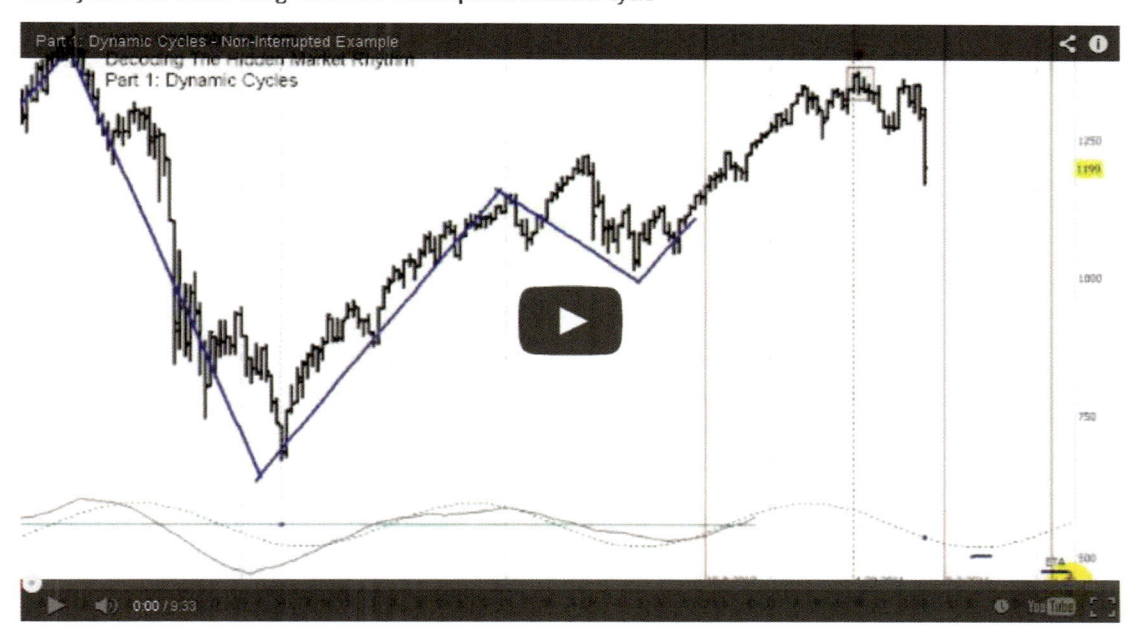

Review the bar-by-bar video:

http://www.whentotrade.com/dynamiccycles2/

---

9. Dynamic Cycles in Silver and Gold

On Monday April 15, 2013, the biggest one-day drop in the gold/silver markets prompted the following headline in the financial media.

Figure 1: Bloomberg Online News Headline, April 15, 2013 [2]

Gold and silver futures suffered their biggest one-day decline since the 1980s on April 15, 2013, with silver down 11% just for that day.

A brief review of the silver markets from a cycle analyst perspective shows that this event was expected and no surprise at all.

In 2011, silver futures experienced a parabolic up move. This scenario was monitored in public space and demonstrates the application of cycle tools to real time trading.

---

[2] Source: http://www.bloomberg.com/news/2013-04-15/gold-extends-bear-market-losses-as-investors-reduce-etp-holdings.html

9.1 Dynamic Cycles Projection: April/May 2011

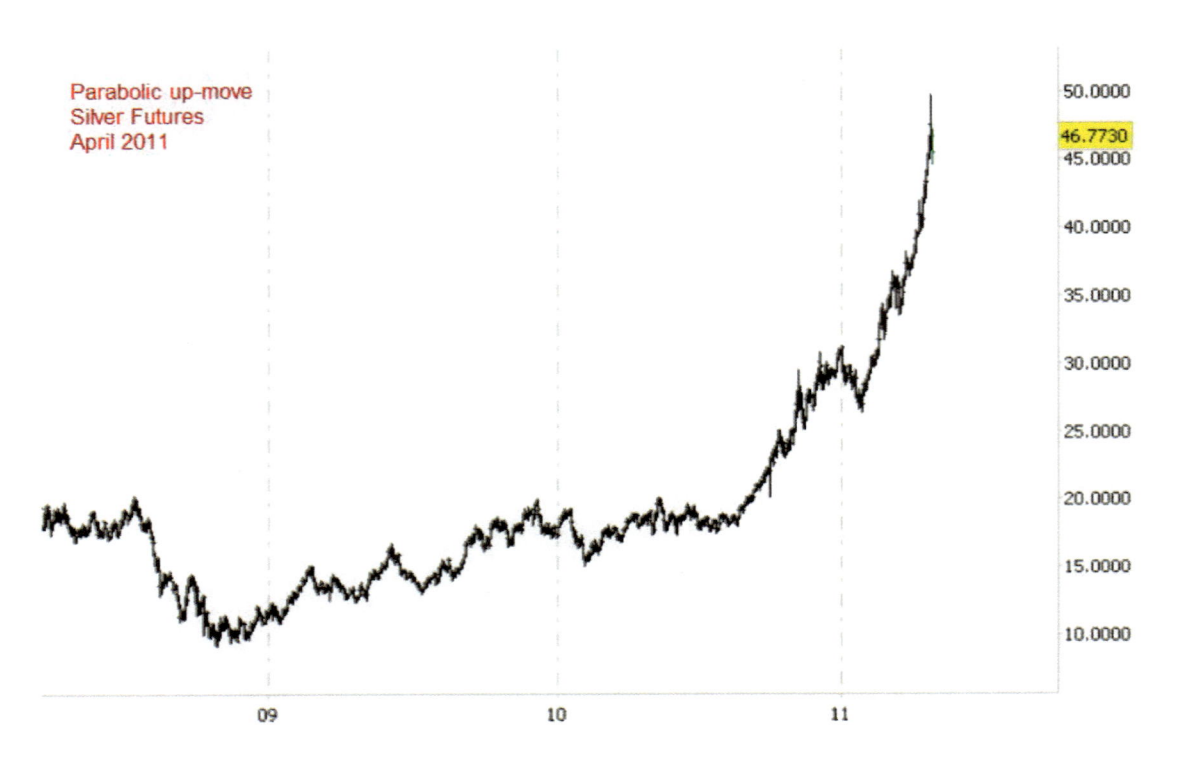

Figure 2: Parabolic Up Move of Silver Futures – April 27, 2011

The critical parabolic juncture in April 2011 was anticipated, and I issued a cycle analysis in advance to show this significant event.[3]

The analysis revealed a dominant cycle with a length of 117 trading days, which had been solid and stable since 2009! Therefore, there was a strong likelihood that this 117-day cycle could forecast the next significant turning points. The dominant cycle was already active and detected in 2009 (see Figure 3) – a bar-by-bar walkthrough from 2009 up to the day of the analysis (May 2011) revealed that this 117-day cycle projected all turning points from the year 2009 to 2011.

---

[3] Source: "Silver – parabolic move – what's next" / April 27 and May 3, 2011 postings.
  http://forum.wave59.com/idealbb/view.asp?topicID=5576

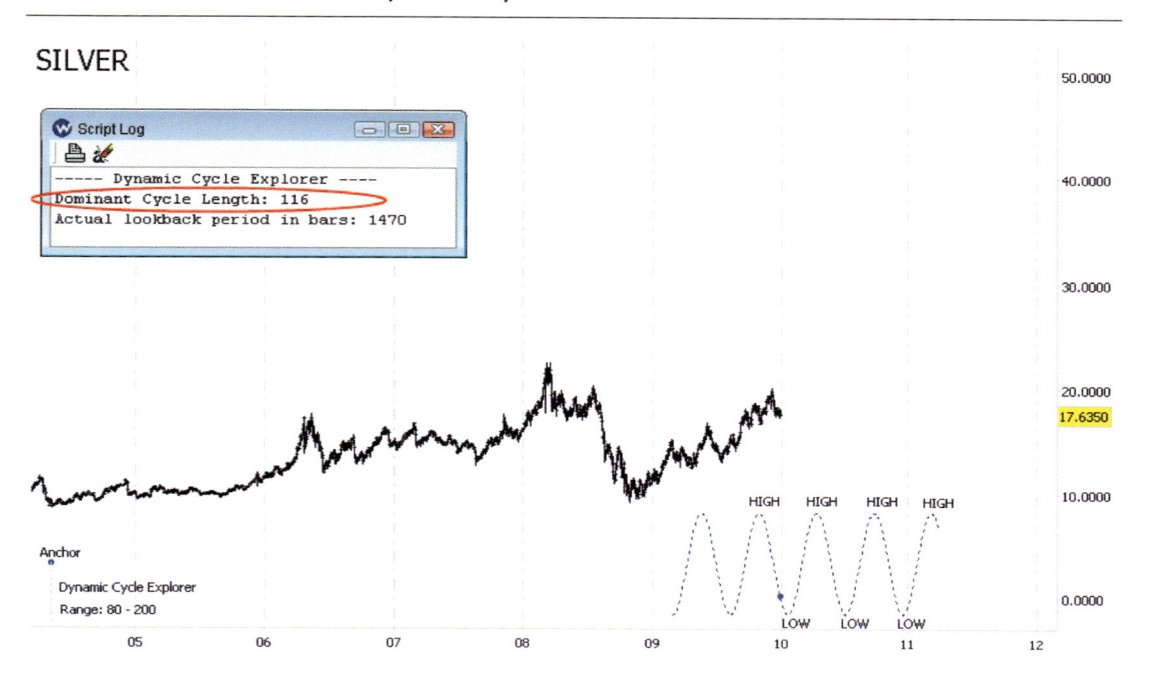

Figure 3: Detected 116-day Cycle at the End of 2009 (Posted on a Public Forum)[4]

The projected highs and lows are represented by the words HIGH/LOW on the cycle plotted into the year 2010/2011.

During the year 2010, the cycle remains active. The dynamic cycle explorer tracks the offset shifts (the cycle low causes a +/- movement in some bars) and the breathing of the cycle (lengths shift between 115 and 118 days).

Figure 4 shows the updated cycle progressed to May 2011. The anchor and dynamic cycle explorer indicator settings have not changed. The script log that detects the cycle length of 117 days shows that the cycle remains active. The dotted blue line is the current cycle projection based on the dynamic shifts for offset and breath.

The marked labels "HIGH" / "LOW" in Figure 4 have not been changed. These labels are placed based on the analysis and forward projection from the end of the year 2009 (see Figure 3). The dynamic shift is visible in this cycle because of a slight deviation between the dotted blue line indicated by the new projection and the old text markers (see Figure 4).

---

[4] Source: http://forum.wave59.com/idealbb/view.asp?topicID=5576

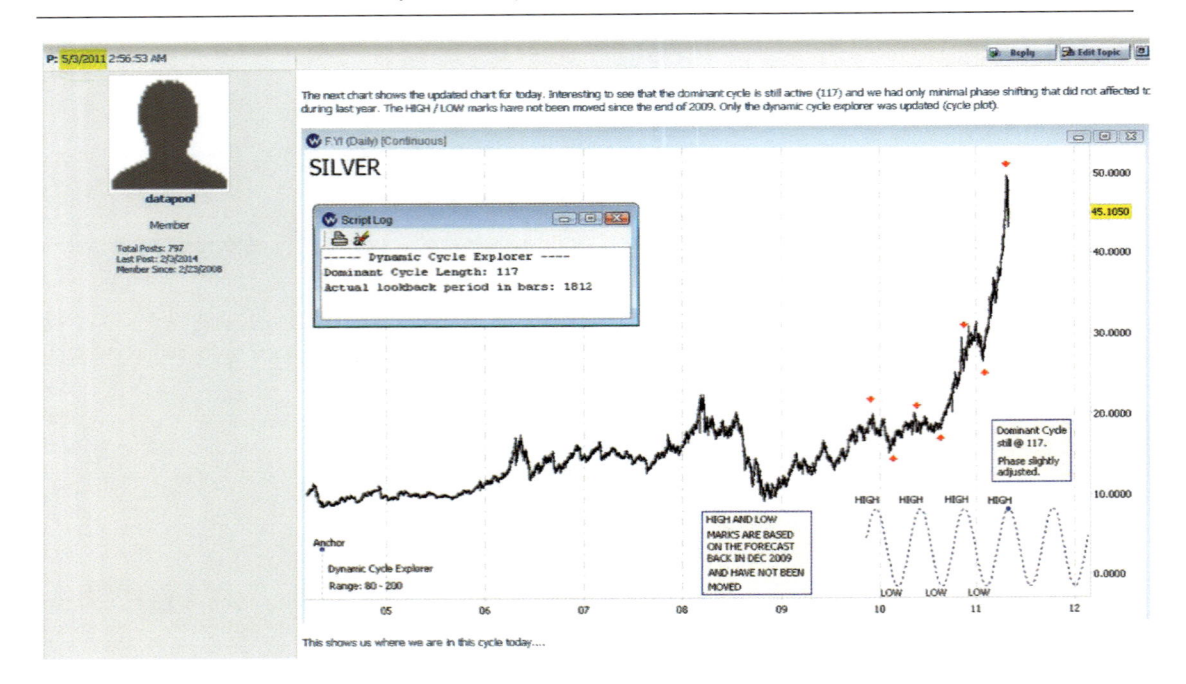

Figure 4: Real time Public Warning Concerning a Major Top Based on a 117-day Cycle (May 3, 2011); HIGH/LOW labels have been written to chart end 2009 [5]

Here the dynamic behavior is observed. Even with a consistent dominant cycle, a static projection must not be followed. The dynamic component must be updated following each new bar to align the "arrival" date of the next projected low or high based on the current shifts.

This same cycle, updated by the dynamic component, now projects an expected high in the silver futures on May 3, 2011. This analysis was done live and was posted to the Internet public forum. [6]

I was alarmed by the parabolic move of silver during the final weeks. Although, it is difficult to anticipate the end of a parabolic move. However, cycles can guide analysis by detecting and projecting the current dominant cycle. The dynamic cycle explorer is the appropriate tool.

---

[5] Source: http://forum.wave59.com/idealbb/view.asp?topicID=5576

[6] Source: http://forum.wave59.com/idealbb/view.asp?topicID=5576

The dynamic cycle explorer indicated the end of the parabolic move during the final days after the price started to drop. If a parabolic move ends and a dominant cycle projects a top, this is an interesting trade opportunity.

We were aware on 3rd May 2011 that this cycle projected all turning points in 2010. This prompted me to publicly share this analysis on May 3, 2011, after the silver price skyrocketed to over 45 US dollars and the dominant cycle projected a major top.

Over the next four days following the projection and the public cycle chart, silver futures fell 22% to 35 US dollars.

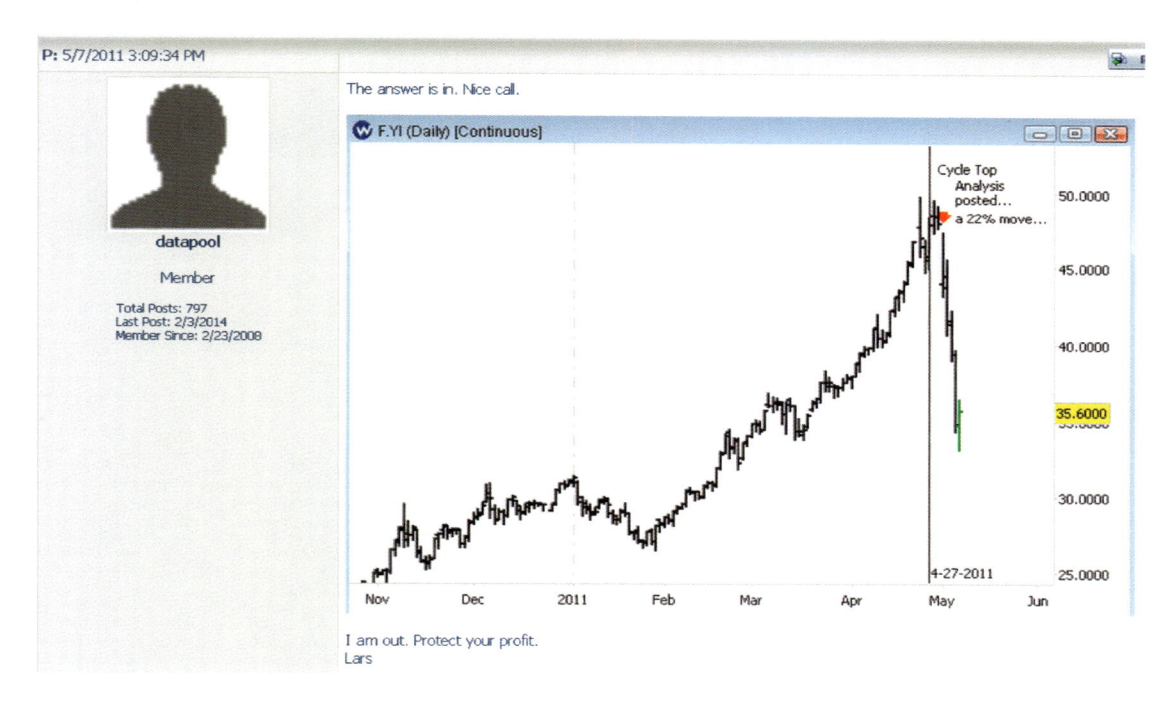

Figure 5: Price Update – Silver Futures Dropped 22% following the Call

This represents a perfect example of the detection and forecasting of cyclic market events. I recall this example because it was stable from 2009 and projected the major market top of 2011.

9.2 Dynamic Cycles Projection: August 2011

Three months later, on August 20, 2011, I posted a subsequent public cycle update with a warning concerning the next upcoming major high expected to occur during the next four weeks.

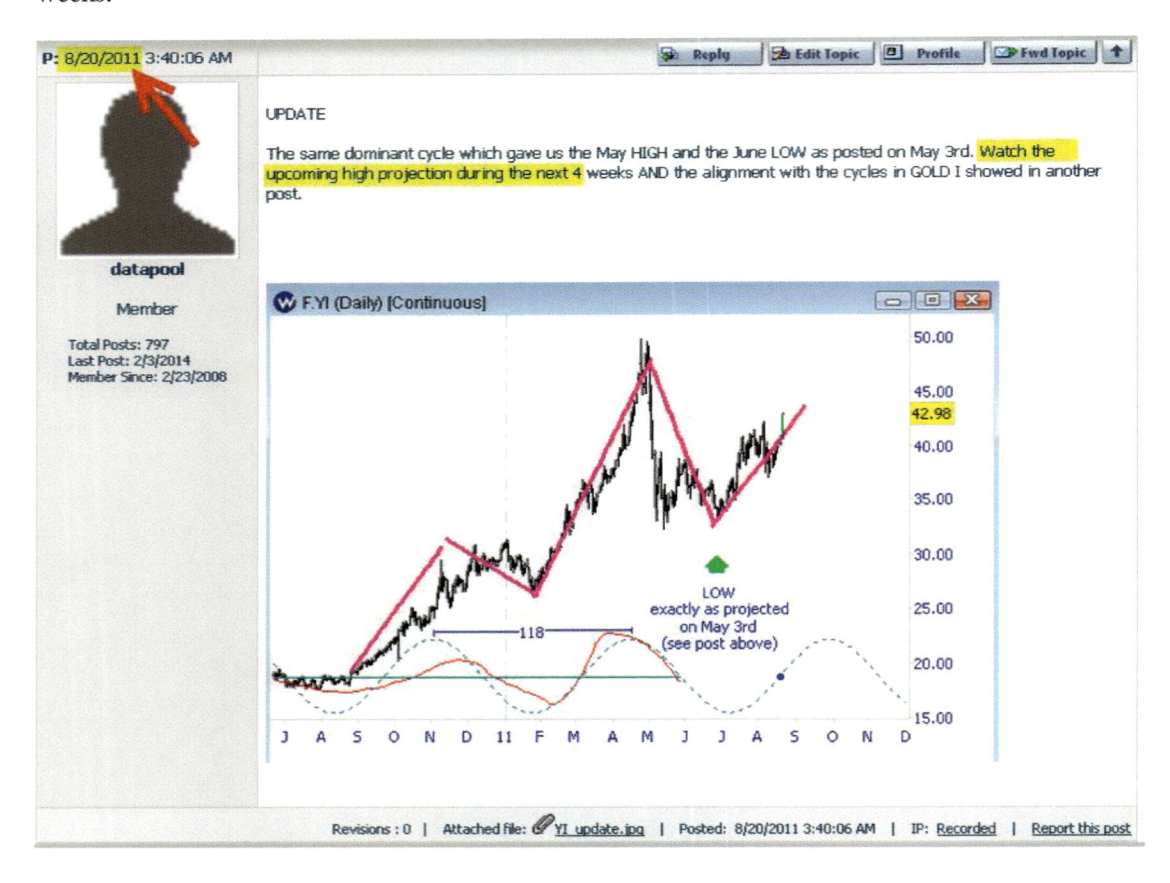

Figure 6: Forecasted Cycle Top Projection Within the Next Four Weeks (Posted August 20, 2011) [7]

To double check the validity of the silver cycle projection, a dominant-cycle cross-check with correlated markets is required. A similar cycle top should be projected for gold because there is a high correlation between gold and silver commodities. Therefore, I checked the

---

[7] Source:http://forum.wave59.com/idealbb/view.asp?mode=viewtopic&topicID=5576&num=20&pageNo=2

dynamic cycles for gold on August 20, 2011. The following post was published in the public internet forum:

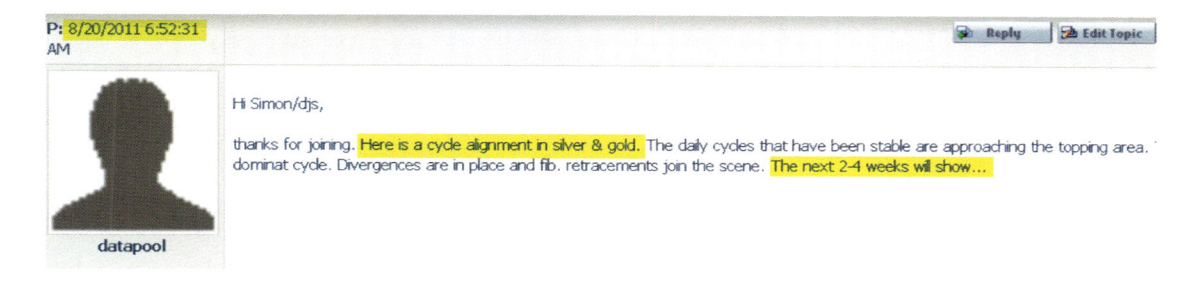

> **P: 8/20/2011 6:52:31 AM**
>
> Hi Simon/djs,
>
> thanks for joining. Here is a cycle alignment in silver & gold. The daily cycles that have been stable are approaching the topping area. dominat cycle. Divergences are in place and fib. retracements join the scene. The next 2-4 weeks will show...
>
> datapool

The following chart with the detected dominant cycle of the dynamic cycle explorer was attached to that public post.

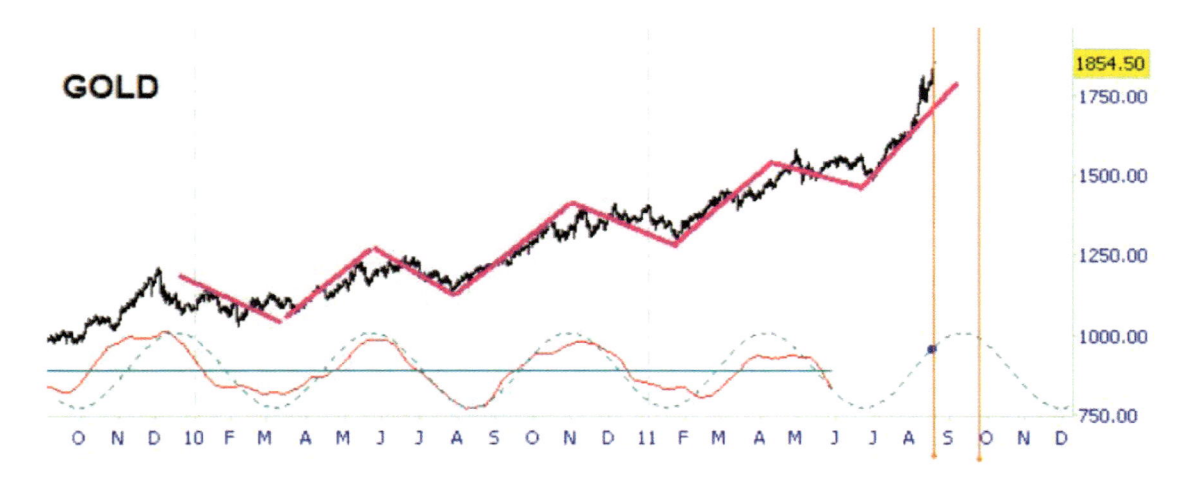

Figure 7: The Identified Dominant Cycle by the Dynamic Cycle Explorer on August 19, 2011 Projected a High for the First Half of September 2011 [8]

---

[8] Source: "The beat of gold," http://forum.wave59.com/idealbb/view.asp?topicID=5745

Exactly three weeks after the warning was posted, silver prices dropped by approximately 30% to 28 US dollars in September 2011.

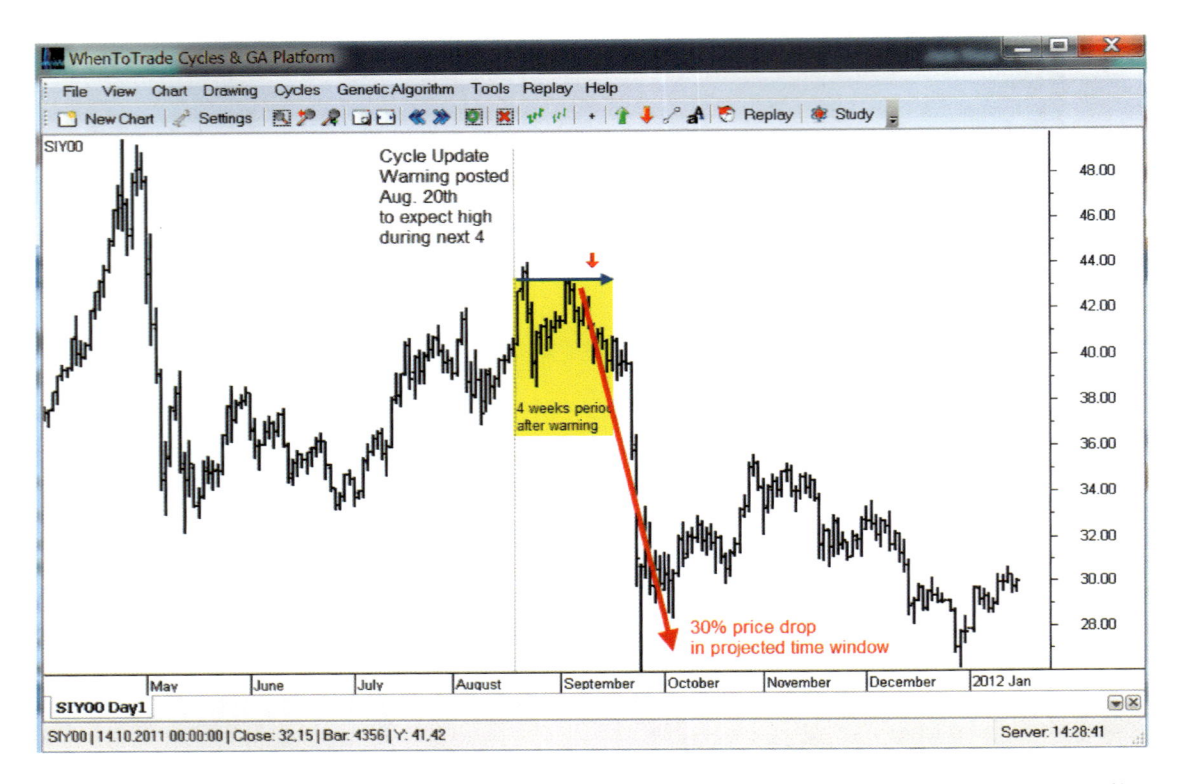

Figure 8: Silver Prices Dropped 30% in the Projected Time Window following the Public Call

Few cycle forecasters place their research in the public domain in advance because of the risk of failure. I use these same tools for my own trading and am confident in sharing examples in advance.

To conclude: The cycle was detected at the end of 2009. It was followed by the dynamic cycle explorer in 2010. Two accurate cycle projections were issued in advance in 2011 to the public community. Future prediction of the cycle should be straightforward.

9.3 Dynamic Cycles Projection: 2012 and March 2013

Now, coming back to the introduced Bloomberg news headline from the beginning of this chapter. Silver prices dropped over 10% in the course of one day in May 2013. The headlines shown at the beginning of the chapter reflected the surprise of the public and industry professionals. However, the reaction would have been quite different had the outlined dominant silver cycle received due recognition.

The identified and tracked cycle remained active in 2013. This implies that the dominant cycle with a length of 117 trading days forecasted all significant turning points between the years 2011 and 2013. The cycle revealed all tops and bottoms for another two years after the detection by the Dynamic Cycle Explorer and the public sharing in 2011.

Figure 9 illustrates a static cycle count to show that the distance of the tops and lows is approximately 117 bars. The cycle explorer guides you precisely through these points as shown by the examples.

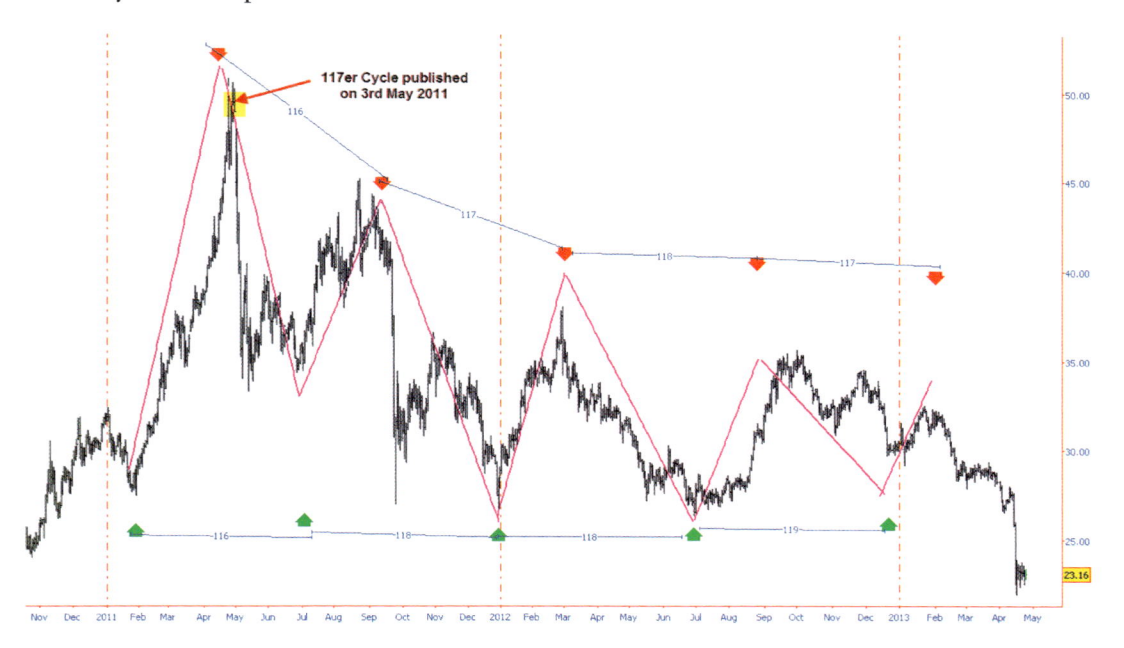

Figure 9: Static Cycles Review of the 117-day Dominant Cycle First Mentioned in May 2011

The drop in April 2013 was in the precise section of the expected cyclic downturn projected to begin in February 2013. The market complied. The market events with respect to silver have provided a classic textbook example of successful detection, projection, and trading for dominant cycles. This cycle was stable to the extent that even the static plot – as shown in Figure 9 – reflected an accurate cycle. If you followed this dominant cycle via the dynamic cycle explorer, the exact daily shifts of the top and bottom projections could be followed on time and updated bar by bar.

Let's start a detailed walkthrough beginning in February 2013. A dominant short-term cycle with a length of 40 days is active and shown for the gold market in Figure 10. This dynamic short-term cycle was monitored from December 2012 and was released publicly in the open forum on February 22, 2013 by a cycles toolkit client.[9] A preview of the expected low on February 22 and the expected high at the end of March was posted. The chart in Figure 10 was attached to the post and showed the detected cycle that projected a low on February 23 and expected the next high at the end of March.

Figure 10: Real-time Gold Cycle Analysis Projecting the Low in February / High in March[10]

---

[9] Source: http://forum.wave59.com/idealbb/view.asp?topicID=6193&num=20&pageNo=3

[10] Source: http://forum.wave59.com/idealbb/view.asp?topicID=6193&num=20&pageNo=3

So the public short-term gold cycle projection showed a situation to expect a market top in Gold at the end of March 2013.

Let us move back to our silver cycles. Figure 11 presents a detailed view of the dominant dynamic cycle at the end of March 2013. The Dynamic Cycle Explorer has again identified the dominant cycles automatically with standard settings. The 177er cycle showed up again in Silver.

Figure 11: Dynamic Cycle Explorer Analysis – March 2013

First, the 117er cycle originally mentioned in 2011 is still active. Second we observe a inter-market cycles-within-cycles' alignment between Silver and Gold for the short term cycle publicly shown in Feb. 2013. The 117-day cycle remains with respect to the silver futures. The long-term cycle was aligned at the low in the year 2004; the same indicator setting was used in May 2011 (see Figure 4) to project the 2011 major top with this long-term cycle.

Figure 11 shows a picture perfect cycles-within-cycles alignment. Both cycles project a major market top. Following this was the biggest drop in gold and silver seen during the past 33 years. [11]

Here is the chart updated after the drop in the gold and silver markets in April 2013.

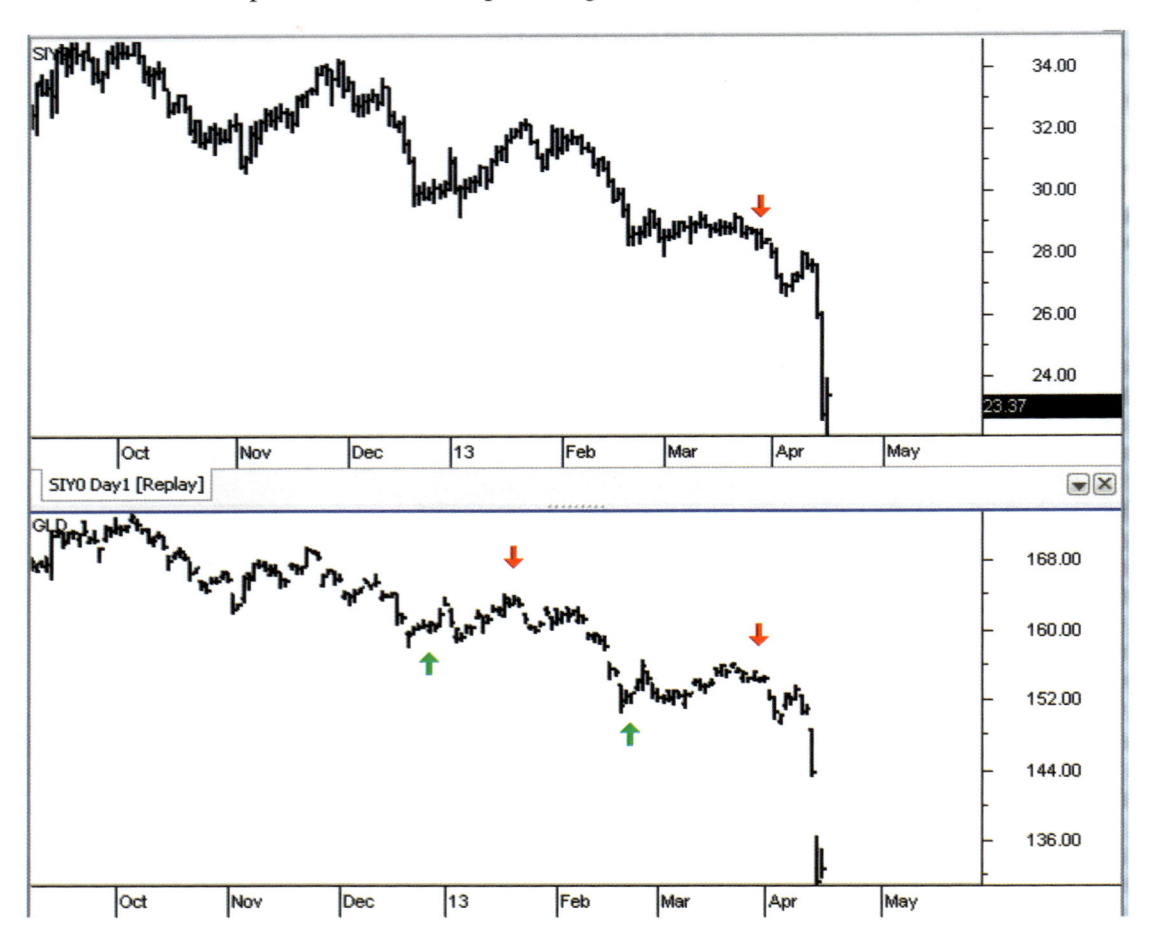

Figure 12: The Biggest Drop During the Last 33 years Following a Cycles-within-cycles Alignment

---

[11] Source: http://www.bloomberg.com/news/2013-04-15/gold-extends-bear-market-losses-as-investors-reduce-etp-holdings.html

This review should provide assurance that dominant cycles that are active for an extended period are significant. This full analysis was done in advance of the events during the past two years. Only real calls that were realized and publicly posted in advance are reviewed and I have not chosen biased examples.

The forum posts can be reviewed at the following sites.

"Silver - parabolic move - what's next?" *posted April 2011*
http://forum.wave59.com/idealbb/view.asp?topicID=5576

"Gold," – *"This cycle has caught the last two turns perfectly [...]", posted February 22, 2013*
http://forum.wave59.com/idealbb/view.asp?topicID=6193&num=20&pageNo=3

9.4 Video Lesson – Silver Cycles Live Calls

A step-by-step video of this analysis is available and includes all the details explained in this chapter:

Video Lesson:

Silver Cycles

http://www.whentotrade.com/silver-cycles/

10. Trading the swing of the dominant cycle – Next level momentum trading

So far, I have presented a technique that can be used to fine-tune standard indicators with the dominant cycle, a dynamic forecasting method based on different dominant cycles and how to build polarity forecasts for use as a market map.

Now, let's develop these ideas on cycles even further.

One of my personal goals was to build the "perfect" indicator. Just one indicator on my chart that is able to guide me through my trading. Just one indicator that points out high probability trades in real-time. Just one indicator that is visually easy to read. You know what I am taking about.

During my cycle research, I developed thousands of different indicators based on the fundamental cycle engine presented in the second chapter. Good ones, bad ones, and ones that were so-so.

And one day, when I least expected it, there it was! After developing and throwing out thousands of coded indicators, I came across this plot which was somehow extraordinary. It was obvious that this one was special. It took a lot of sleepless nights to carry out further evaluations. And it was worth all those sleepless nights. Today, I often trade using only this indicator.

I am not presenting thousands of indicator studies here. I could, however, fill hundreds of pages with ideas on indicator coding. But I only want to focus on and write about "things that work for trading".

Now is the right time to introduce my next idea, because it is a synthesis of the previous chapters. On the one hand, I will use the dominant cycle as the basic measurement vehicle, and, on the other, I want to build an oscillating indicator. So, instead of "fine-tuning" *old* indicators with the information about the actual dominant wavelength or building static cycle forecasts, I began to build a *new* indicator whose measurements are based on the identified ideal dominant cycle. It is not about forecasting the next important change in trend. I simply wanted to know in real-time what the actual state of the Dominant Market Vibration at this given bar is. It is not about projecting the ideal cycle in the future. It is about the actual state of the cycle on this respective bar.

I decided to focus on the measurement of where we are in the actual swing of the cycle. That is, instead of forecasting the ideal cycle in the future, I only wanted to know where we are in the swing of the dominant cycle. As I have already explained, my cycle engine is able to track the phase, amplitude, and wavelength shifts of the dominant cycle in accordance with the market vibration. Therefore, the actual swing's state can change from bar to bar. Hence, I did not expect a smooth sine-wave type ideal plot. But the plot should give me a visual idea of where we are in the actual swing.

10.1 Calculation of the cycle acceleration

The measurement of the cycle's state is achieved by measuring the momentum of the actual dominant cyclic component. To calculate the cyclic momentum, we need to forecast the cycle one bar ahead. Then we can build the momentum of the detrended cyclic component based on the following ideal formula: Cycle swing = acceleration of dominant cycle on the actual bar

The cycle swing information will be calculated on every bar. And because we are able to follow the shifting of the phase, amplitude, and wavelength on every bar, we have dynamic, updated information on the cycle's underlying forces – the cycle acceleration.

Keep in mind that this information is based on the detrended data. This indicator will show the cyclic force that swings around the actual trend.

The calculation is based on the acceleration of the actual dominant cycle, which is updated on each new bar. The output is plotted on the chart like any other indicator. The following picture summarizes the method:

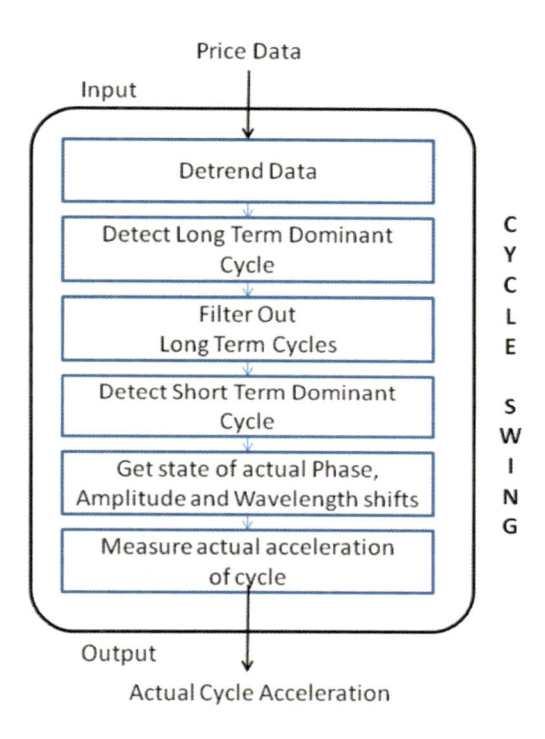

Figure 10-1: The Cycle Swing method

10.2 Evaluation criteria for the new Cycle Swing Indicator

To determine this indicator's effectiveness for use in the trading area, we need to establish our measurement criteria. Therefore, I will introduce five main parameters for reliable indicators and compare these to the best-in-class indicator available today. One of the best indicators out there is Wave59's Ultra Smooth Momentum curve. As the cycle swing concept is similar to the momentum of the price, I will use this indicator as a comparison guide.

The main criteria for technical indicators are:

- **Smoothness**

    There are two common ways to generate a smooth indicator curve:

    1) The length setting of the indicator calculation; 2) An additional smoothing algorithm: Simple moving average, exponential moving average or weighted moving average in addition to the indicator calculation. However, moving averages are based on past data, which means they will lag behind current data. For trading, we need timely signals and any lags will destroy profitable entry and exit points. Therefore, we have to keep an eye on the lag of the signal.

- **Zero lag**

    The conflicting goals pose major challenges:

    If you add standard smoothness to an indicator, you are also adding lag and will get late entries after most of the move has already occurred. On the other hand, if you want a lag-free indicator, you will lose the smoothness and produce a lot of whipsaw trades.

    Yet we need both: Smoothness to avoid whipsaw trades and lag-free signals for timely trades. To achieve both goals, we can use a few useful proprietary smoothing algorithms that are out there. The main drawback of these advanced algorithms is that even if you have a smooth and lag-free signal, you will still lose sharpness. Hence, we have the next criteria for indicator evaluation: Sharpness

- **Sharpness at turning points**

    When adding smoothness to an indicator, one frequent problem is that you lose sharpness in the visual plot. Even when you have zero lag, you often cannot see the turn/signal in accordance with the high smoothness of the curve. We therefore also need the third criteria: Smooth, lag-free, and sharp. This characteristic is often important – it is not only about smoothness. To trade in real-time you need a sharp peak on the smooth indicator to actually see the signal under real-time conditions. In real-time situations, you cannot see the "right" side of the indicator. A sharp turn of the indicator in real-time with no lag is a prerequisite for using it successfully in trading.

- **Robust and adaptive to market conditions**

    This criterion was already addressed in one of the first chapters on the fine-tuning of standard indicators. Most indicators need a length setting for the calculations. And the length setting is often very important for the indicator to be in sync with the vibration of the market. A false setting of the length parameter will considerably influence the signal quality. I have presented ways to use the cycle engine to select the correct settings before the trading day starts. But it would be even better if the indicator could automatically adapt to the actual market vibration. A robust indicator is not dependent on the length setting. But the best, of course, would be an adaptive indicator that sets the right length in accordance with the dominant market vibration on its own.

- **Accurate divergence detection**

    A lot of indicators' high probability signals are discernible by the divergences between the oscillator and the price curve (momentum, RSI). Therefore, if an indicator is able to detect market extremes with good divergence plots on the indicator, the better qualified it is for trading usage.

There are several advanced indicators out there with optimized algorithms to add smoothness without lag. These indicators can be found in Wave59: Adaptive Moving Average (AMA) and Ultra Smooth Momentum (USM). There is also the well-known indicator kit developed by Jurikes research. These indicators like the VEL and JMA are very similar.

Here is an overview of these advanced indicators in consideration of the introduced criteria.

Simple Indicator	Advanced Indicator (AMA, USM, Vel, JMA)	Leading Indicator „Cycle Swing"
Noise: too much false signals	Proprietary Calculation Wave59: USM / AMA Jurik: Vel / JMA	Proprietary Calculation plus using leading momentum based on dominant cycles
Smoothness: adding lag reduced sharpness	Result: Smooth without adding lag but losing sharpness at turning points	Result: same smoothness BUT + more sharpeness + leading / ahead of USM + more divergences
Fixed length: no one knows the length in advance	Fixed length: no one knows the length in advance	adaptive length: auto-dynamic adjustment

Figure 10-2: Criteria comparison for technical indicator evaluation

When you think you have found a better indicator, you have to compare it with the best-in-class indicators out there. I do not choose the USM here to prove it's a "bad" indicator. Don't get me wrong. In fact, the USM is one of the best indicators out there. I am only using this comparison to check whether the new indicator really has additional value.

Now let's evaluate the new Cycle Swing Indicator step-by-step against the introduced criteria. I will choose different types of financial instruments and time frames to show that this concept works on any market and for any time frame.

10.3 Super smooth with no lag – The cycle's acceleration is the leading price momentum

Let's move on to the chart and review the characteristics of the Cycle Swing Indicator. A chart can say more than a thousand words. I will use the current month of trading, i.e., while writing this. I do not have to cherry pick a date from the past on which this has worked. In fact, it works every time. Over and over again. That's the reason I can use the current price data – no cherry picking here!

I will also use an uncut amount of time and not only focus on a few days. I will use the uncut history of last month's trading behavior of the E-mini S&P 500 futures contract. We can now determine and study the signals from swing to swing.

First cycle swing characteristic

> **Super smooth**
>
> **The Cycle Swing Indicator has the same smoothness as – for comparison purposes - the Ultra Smooth Momentum curve. The smooth curve is paired with a leading zero lag movement. This will result in a reduced amount of whipsaw trades.**

The following chart presents the Ultra Smooth Momentum curve and the Cycle Swing Indicator on a 30-minute intraday chart of the S&P 500 E-mini futures contract. The red and green arrows with the price indication represent trade signals generated by the Cycle Swing Indicator in real-time. These occurrences are marked on the chart for easy reading. You can clearly see how well the indicator is able to spot all major swings in the market. We will go over these signals when I explain the chart. Let's turn to the first important criterion of the indicators – smoothness.

This chart visually demonstrates that the Swing Indicator looks very similar to the Ultra Smooth Momentum.

This chart is only used here to demonstrate that the cycle swing is a very smooth indicator. A smooth indicator is crucial for real-time trading.

Figure 10-3: Cycle swing – Super smooth

Instead of measuring price momentum, the cycle swing measures the strength of the dominant cyclic phase. It therefore looks similar, but has some "built-in" advantages based on the distinct calculation approach used here.

Second cycle swing characteristic

> ### Leading, zero lag & on time
>
> **The cycle swing is precisely on time with reference to the turning points on the indicator and the market. Compared to the "best-in-class" USM, the cycle swing leads by an average of 2-3 bars.**

We will use the same chart as above to review this criterion. But now the turning points of the Cycle Swing and USM Indicator are linked with the bar counter tool on the chart. The corresponding turns of the cycle swing and the USM are interconnected with the blue lines. The number indicates the number of bars that lie between the connected turns.

All important turns are indicated. We can now see that the turns on the cycle swing are visible 2-3 bars earlier than on the USM curve. This is particularly significant because the USM curve is already a "zero lag" indicator – despite being super smooth. For those who are familiar with the tools based on Jurikes research, it's the same as comparing the turns with the RSX or VEL indicator.

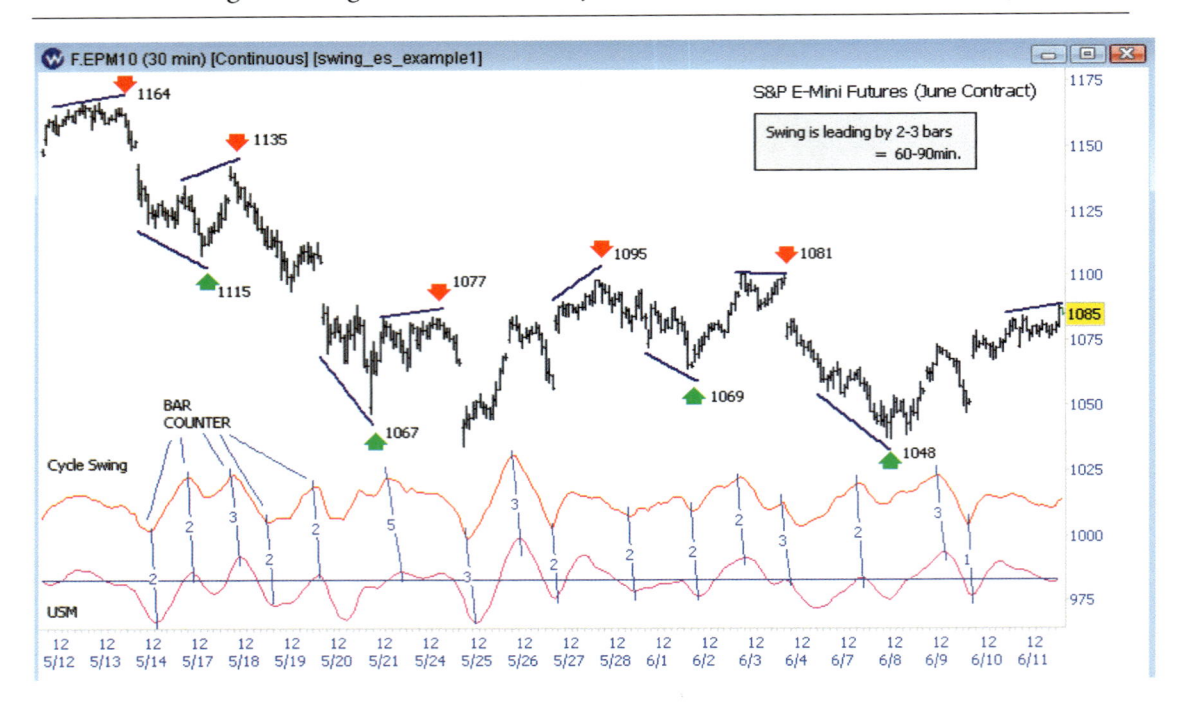

Figure 10-4: Chart 2 - Cycle swing leads by 2-3 bars

This really fast performance of the Cycle Swing Indicator combined with the ultra smoothness will give you a new competitive advantage in trading. On the 30-minute chart it means that you will be able to enter your trades 60-90 minutes earlier than the trader who uses the best-in-class indicators like the USM. This can significantly improve your trading profit.

To better understand the value of this performance, we will now examine the first three trades from May 12 – 18, 2010 in detail.

I. Zoom-in on first signal on May 13:

This is a close-up of the first trade signal from the Cycle Swing Indicator. The chart that illustrates the signal which appears on the Cycle Swing Indicator in real-time is seen on the left side. The chart on the right side displays the point at which the trade signal would have been visible on the USM indicator.

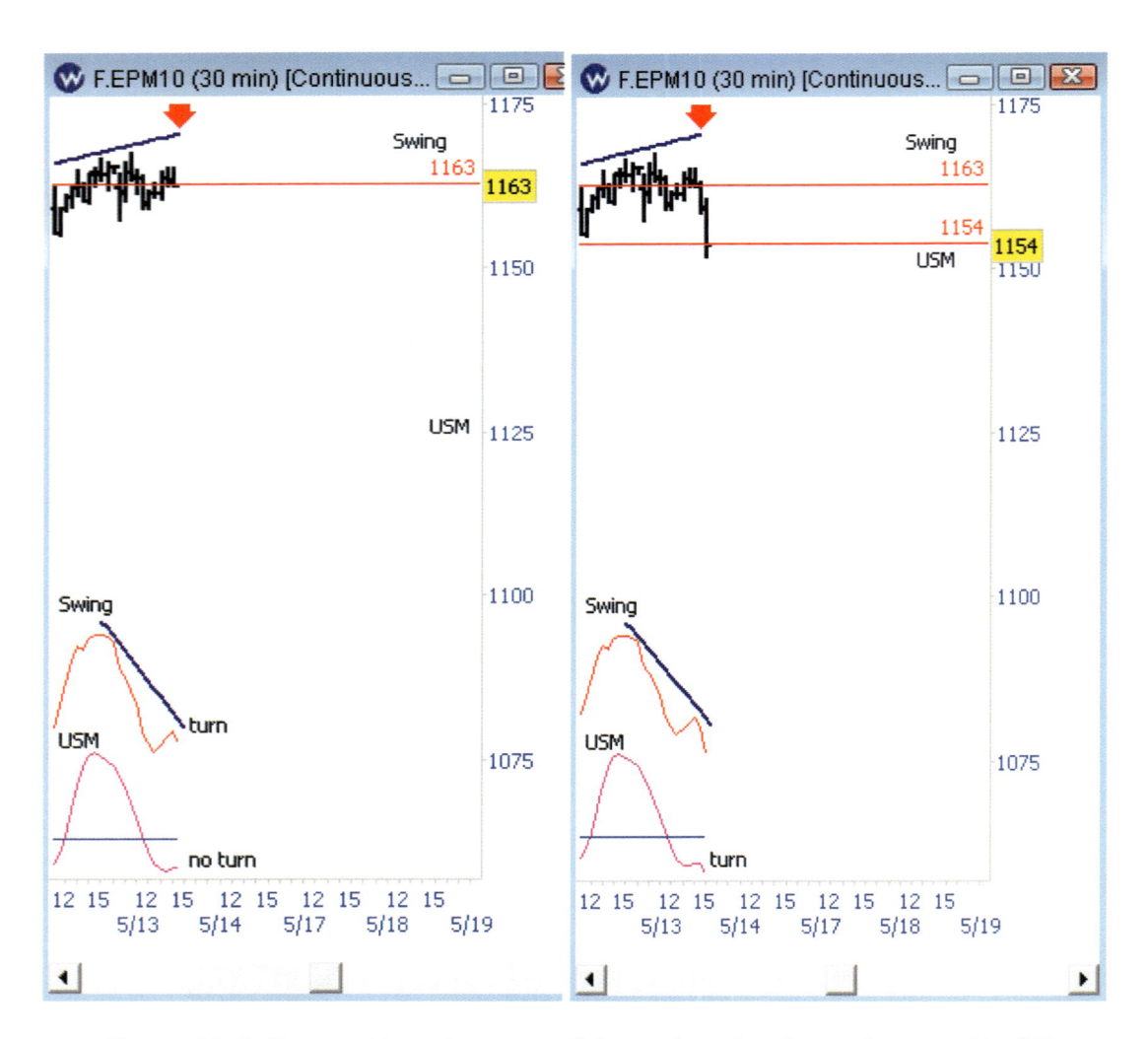

Figure 10-5: Competitive advantage of the cycle swing for trade entry (1 of 3)

We will analyze the difference between the two signals next.

1. Signal on the cycle swing (left chart)

    The trade signal was visible on the cycle swing in accordance with the clear divergence that formed between the price and indicator. The futures have moved to a higher high while the cycle swing recorded a lower high with the close of the actual bar.

    Had we only used the USM indicator, we would have gotten no clear divergence signal. The USM did not show us a turn now. Hence, the entry on the cycle swing signal would have been at 1163 points, whereas there was no signal on the USM.

2. Signal on the USM (right chart)

    The right chart displays an incidence involving 2 bars (= 60 minutes) later. Only now do we see the divergence on the USM curve. The USM only recorded a lower high on this bar and would now have indicated this divergence signal on the USM curve.

    The cycle swing is now lower, but recorded the turn 2 bars earlier. That is, the futures contract is now trading at 1154, 9 points below the cycle swing's entry signal.

    This is the point in time when all other traders are able to spot this trade signal with the actual "best-in-class" ultra smooth momentum oscillators.

You can now clearly see the significance of being 2-3 bars ahead. By the time other traders would have begun entering for the expected downturn based on the divergence signal, we would have already booked a respectable profit of 9 points 60 minutes earlier.

The full swing of this signal encompassed 1164 to 1115 points – a considerable 50 point jump. Using the cycle swing to time this trade would have given you an advantage of 9 points. This equals 18% of the full swing! The cycle swing would have increased your profit on this trade alone by 18% compared with the current best-in-class indicators like the USM, VEL or RSX.

Please note: To precisely trade the full swing is, of course, hypothetical. But this is used to measure the advantage of the cycle swing in real trading with reference to price movement, not just in terms of measurement of bars.

II. Zoom-in on second signal on May 17:

We will move on to the next divergence signal recorded by the cycle swing. The left chart shows the situation two trading days later when a bullish divergence signal was recorded on the Cycle Swing Indicator.

Figure 10-6: Competitive advantage of cycle swing for trade entry (2 of 3)

1. <u>Signal on the cycle swing (left chart)</u>

   The futures have recorded a lower low while the cycle swing recorded a higher low with the close of the actual bar. The cycle swing turned up and the divergence signal was set on the Cycle Swing Indicator. And again –no divergence signal is visible on the Ultra Smooth Momentum curve at that point in time. The USM is still turning downward and has not recorded a high low here.

   The entry for this buy signal on the cycle swing is at 1119 points.

2. <u>Signal on the USM (right chart)</u>

   The right chart presents the situation at 1 bar (= 30 minutes) later. Now the divergence is also recorded on the USM curve with the upturn and the high low forming on the USM.

   At this point in time, the futures contract is already 6 points up and trading is at 1125 points.

This trade again demonstrates the advantage of the cycle swing - the cycle swing would have triggered the trade 6 points earlier. In other words, we would have a 6 point profit "booked" once others begin to even notice this signal.

This second upswing jumped from 1115 to 1135 points – a 20 point move. The advantage of capturing 6 points more of this 20 point upswing using the cycle swing is equal to a 30% advantage compared to when using the other indicators. Even if it is only one bar in this second trade – compared to the complete swing, this results in a profit increase of 30%.

III. Zoom-in on third signal on May 18:

This is the next, uncut third trading signal recorded by the cycle swing. The chart illustrates the next situation in which a clear bearish divergence appeared on the Cycle Swing Indicator.

Figure 10-7: Competitive advantage of cycle swing for trade entry (3 of 3)

1. <u>Signal on the cycle swing (left chart)</u>

   The futures have moved to a higher high as of the actual closing bar. The Cycle Swing Indicator is also turning down – ultra smooth but on-time with the market. But the cycle swing did not move to a higher high on this turn. Therefore, a bearish set-up is now evidently visible at the close of this bar. The futures contract is trading at 1137 points.

   This time, there is no turn on the Ultra Smooth Momentum curve. And– what also differs from the first two swings – the momentum curve is already higher than the last high. So there is no turn or divergence on the USM.

2. <u>Turn on the USM (right chart)</u>

   The right chart illustrates the situation at 3 bars (= 90 minutes) later. Now the turn is also registered on the USM curve with the downturn of the indicator plot. But the USM curve has also moved to a higher high like the price. Therefore, NO divergence signal appears on the Ultra Smooth Momentum curve.

Please review this third situation illustrated in the first chart (see Figure 10-3 on page 188). This was one of the largest swings for the entire previous month. The swing began at 1135 points and moved down to 1067 points only two days later: A substantial 68 point move in total. This move and corresponding entry was NOT recorded by the Ultra Smooth Momentum curve. Instead, using the cycle swing, our real-time entry would have been 1137 points, as shown above.

When we compared the first two swings, the cycle swing gave us a profit increase of +18% and +30%. With regard to the third turn, it was only visible with the cycle swing. That is, the trader using only the advanced indicator would have perhaps completely missed this great trade entry.

This brings us to the third very important characteristic of the Cycle Swing Indicator.

Third cycle swing characteristic:

> ### Adaptive Divergence Detection
>
> **The cycle swing self-adapts to the Dominant Market Vibration. Therefore, it has no "length" setting. The benefit is that it is able to spot each divergence signal between price and indicator with uncanny precision. We are thus able to identify more high probability trade set-ups.**

These divergence signals are usually in alignment which each major turn of the given instrument you are measuring with the Cycle Swing Indicator. Due to the nature of the algorithm - "measuring the momentum of the dominant cycle, not the price" – you will never miss an important turn in the market.

My research shows that each important turning point in the market is accompanied by a divergence signal on the cycle swing. There is thus a high probability that a significant turn will follow when you "see" a divergence on the cycle swing.

These three characteristics make the Cycle Swing Indicator especially unique. There is no indicator out there that is able to combine all these characteristics into just one indicator. That is the reason why I frequently only trade using this single indicator. A clean chart and just one indicator on it. Wait until the divergence comes – and simply push the button.

These characteristics will show up on any financial instrument. We will now examine this behavior and this type of trading signal on the S&P 500, gold, and forex market.

10.4 Adaptive divergence detection on any market: Repeating patterns at cycle tops and bottoms

The main purpose of the Cycle Swing Indicator is to spot the high probability trade set-ups that occur at cycle tops and bottoms. These cycle tops have a common pattern:

When a cycle tops out, the price lags, because the emotions that drive the price at extreme turning points restrain the energy of the pure cycle. Consequently, you will see the price forming a higher high (or lower low) in accordance with the "overshooting emotions" of market participants. Despite the fact that the energy which drives these emotions is already decreasing and forming a lower high (or higher low). This is very common behavior at cycle extremes.

Using the Cycle Swing Indicator, we are now able to precisely measure these situations. This is the pattern that will show up at every important turning point: A divergence between the price and the cycle swing.

The explanation for this is straightforward and clear:

When the incoming cycle energy slows down (measured by the cycle swing) while the emotions of market participants are at extremes (price movement), there is an imbalance between cyclic forces and price movements that will be resolved very quickly. These are the high probability trade set-ups we are all looking for.

I have chosen three different financial instruments to demonstrate the precision of this pattern at cycle extremes.

- Example 1: S&P E-mini Futures / 30 min.
- Example 2: Gold Futures / 30 min.
- Example 3: GBP/USD Forex / 5min.

Please study the following three charts thoroughly to familiarize yourself with this trading pattern and the advantages of the Cycle Swing Indicator.

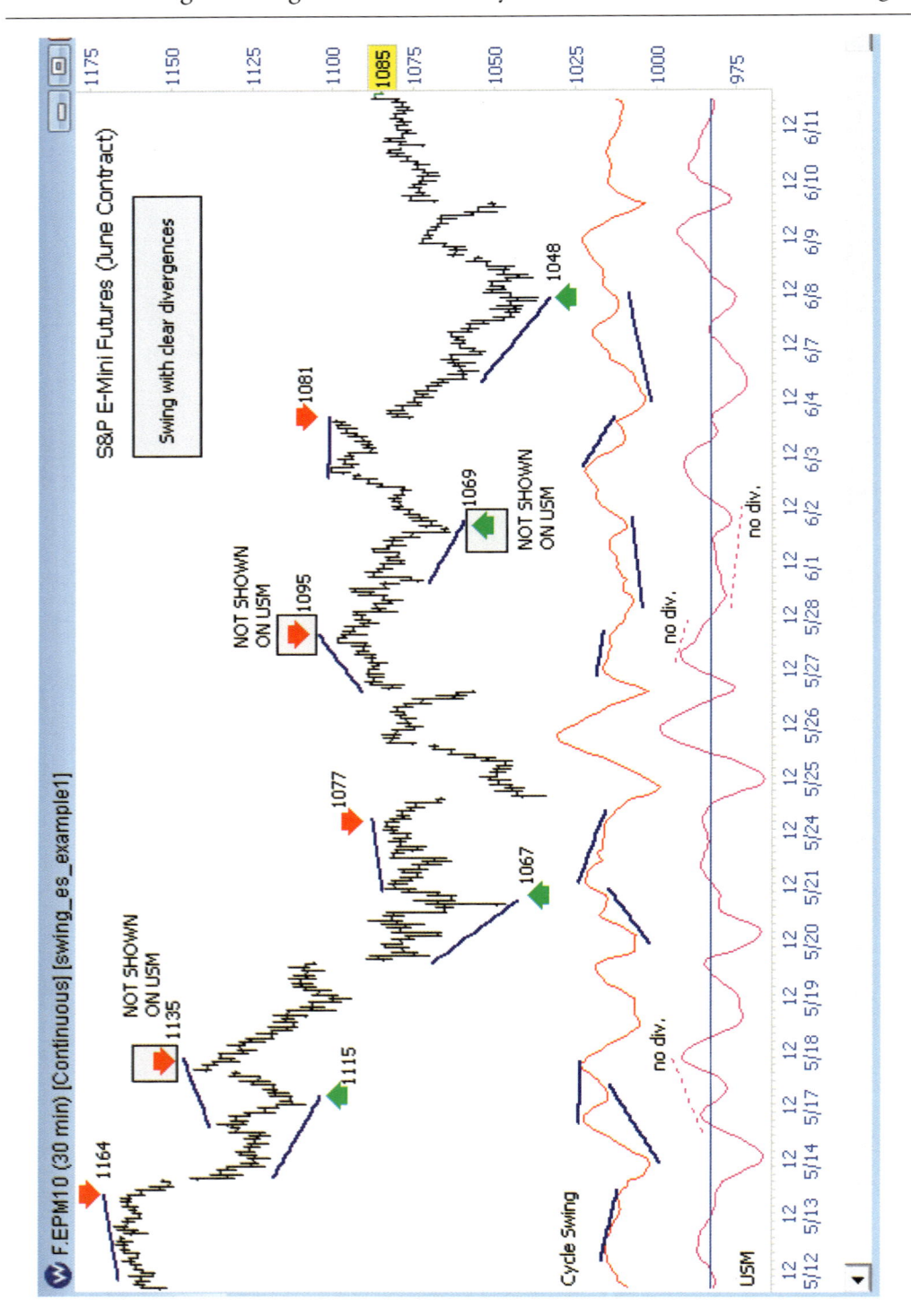

Figure 10-8: Example 1 / Cycle Swing Divergence Signals - S&P E-mini Futures / 30min

1. Review of the Cycle Swing Indicator on a 30-minute S&P 500 E-mini futures contract

The 30-minute chart on the E-mini futures contract was used in the examples above (Figure 10-8). Each major turning point was captured by a divergence pattern using the Cycle Swing Indicator.

There were three situations when the trade set-ups only appeared on the cycle swing:

a) <u>The bearish set-up at 1135 points on May 18</u>

This signal indicated the beginning of the biggest swing during the select period. The Ultra Smooth Momentum recorded a higher high, not a lower high.

b) <u>The bearish set-up at 1095 points on May 27</u>

This signal was the result of the "sharp" characteristics of the cycle swing. Often, when an indicator is too smooth, you will lose the ability to see turns. This is one example. The cycle swing, however, remains sharp – even when the indicator is smooth. However, the signal on smoothness was not visible on the Ultra Smooth Momentum.

c) <u>The bullish set-up at 1069 points on June 2</u>

This signal was followed by a straight 12 point upturn. Another good trade possibility that was again only visible on the Cycle Swing Indicator. This is attributable to the adaptive nature of the algorithm. The cycle swing is always in vibration with the market.

These three signals indicated the beginning of three swings over the last month:

- First swing: 68 point move (straight down move for three days)
- Second swing: 26 point move (straight down move for two days)
- Third swing: 12 point move (straight up move for one day).

Three high probability set-ups with a total of around 110 points that were only visible on the cycle swing.

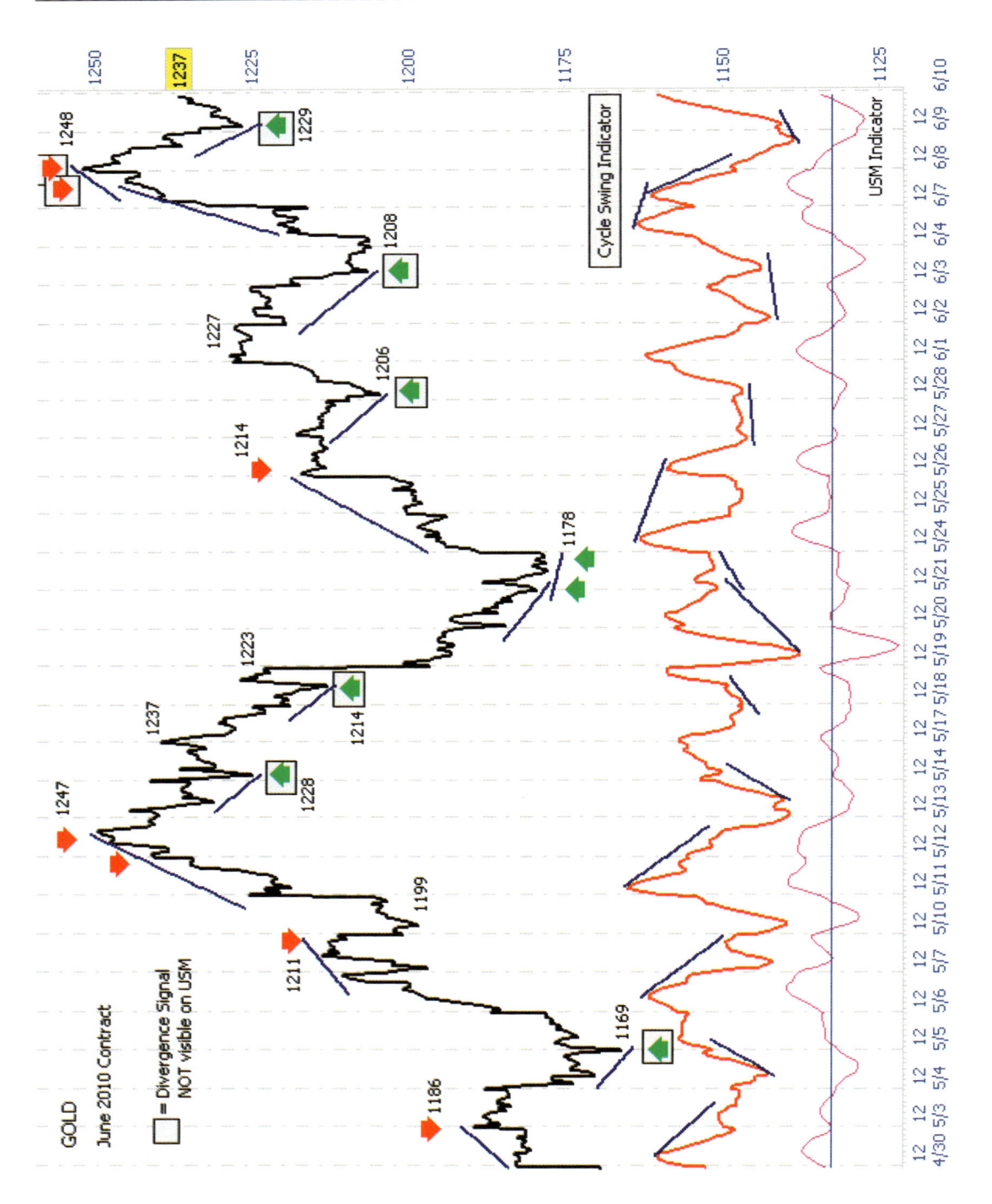

Figure 10-9: Example 2 / Cycle Swing Divergence Signals - Gold Futures / 30 min

2. Review of the Cycle Swing Indicator on a 30-minute gold futures contract

The next chart shows the YG / gold futures contract on a 30 minute time frame (Figure 10-9). The divergence signals are highlighted on the chart. The trading signals are again marked with green and red arrows. The signals that would have only been visible on the cycle swing are highlighted with a small box around the arrows.

In this chart, the cycle swing was able to capture 15 trade set-ups with the divergence pattern. All trade set-ups have been followed by a price reversal of higher magnitude (= tradable set-ups).

However, 8 of the 15 trade signals have only been identified by the cycle swing. Or, in other words: The current state-of-the-art indicators would have missed 50% of the entry signals. That is, you get a lot higher probability set-ups with this new Cycle Swing Indicator.

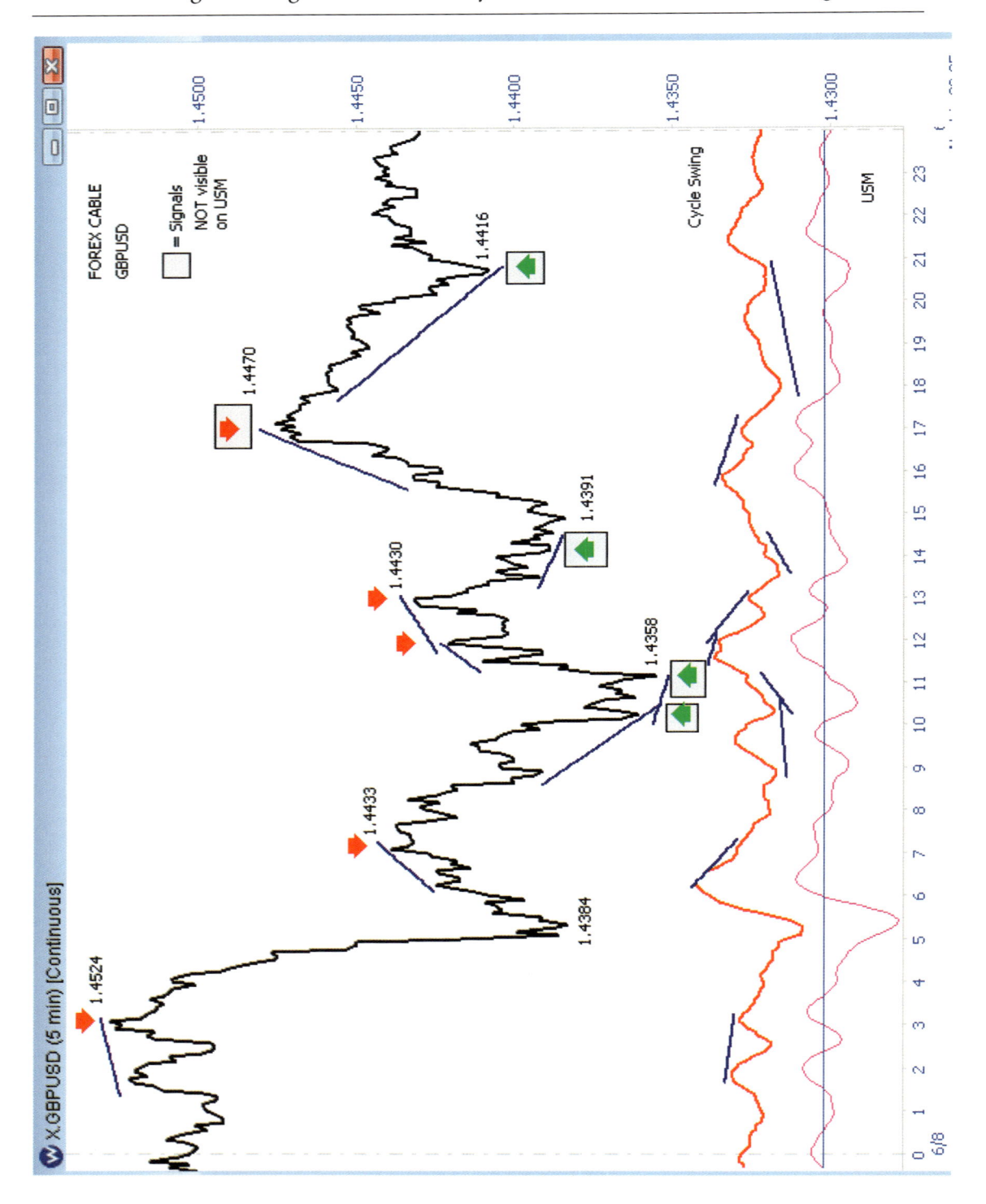

Trading the swing of the dominant cycle – Next level momentum trading

Figure 10-10: Example 3 / Cycle Swing Divergence Signals - GBP/USD Forex

3. Review of the Cycle Swing Indicator on a 5-minute GBP/USD currency pair

The third chart (Figure 10-10) shows the Cycle Swing Indicator on the forex market. The "cable" pair – GBP against the USD – is used here. I am using a 5-minute intraday example to exemplify a different time frame. Also, forex traders often only trade small time frames.

All divergences are highlighted on the Cycle Swing Indicator with blue lines and corresponding red and green arrows on the price chart. Again, a box is placed around the arrows when the signal was only visible on the cycle swing.

We can conclude that the swings at the end of the day appeared only on the Cycle Swing Indicator. These three swings around 14:00, 17:00, and 20:30 were major turns with high probability trade set-ups. However, these swings would have only been tradable with the cycle swings.

These three financial instrument types were used here to demonstrate that this technique works on any instrument and any time frame.

10.5 Trading the turns of the cycle swing – Staying in vibration with the market

There are, of course, additional and different ways of using the Cycle Swing Indicator for trading. You can use any technique that is used with oscillator signals. I will introduce another very important method now. One major advantage of the cycle swing is that it is fast, sharp, and smooth. Therefore, it sounds interesting to use only the turns of the Cycle Swing Indicator for trading. Hence, we try to trade every cyclic high and low of the indicator.

This idea is very similar to the idea of trading overbought / oversold situations from classical oscillating indicators like the RSI or Stochastic. Bands are used on normal indicators to indicate an overbought or oversold market situation. When the indicators break above or below these bands, it is used as a "trading signal".

Let's combine these two ideas:

- Trade the cycle extremes (compared to overbought / oversold situations)

- Use bands to indicate when the price changes from the cycle high to the next cycle low and vice versa.

The Cycle Swing Indicator has no static scale from 1 to 100. The parameter scale can change according to the amplitude and strength of the cycles. We therefore need "adaptive bands" that are able to adjust to this situation. We have to re-calculate the oscillator zone which is dynamically set based on the recent behavior of the underlying Cycle Swing Indicator. In the WhenToTrade Platform, we do not need to code this separately, we can use the built-in function to realize this idea.

Ok, now that we are ready, we can turn to the signals:

- **SELL**

    When the Cycle Swing Indicator breaks down below the upper adaptive band. We can refer to this as a sell because there is a high probability that the cycle has reached and just passed its crest. According to the nature of cycles, the subsequent cyclic move has to be down.

- **BUY**

    When the Cycle Swing Indicator breaks up above the lower adaptive band.

    We can refer to this as a buy because there is a high probability that the cycle has reached and passed its trough. Therefore, the next cyclic phase with an expected move upward has to follow.

The next chart shows an intraday example of this idea for the E-mini futures contract. The Cycle Swing Indicator is plotted with the adaptive bands. The signals are highlighted in the chart according to the rules.

I would, of course, not recommend using it as a stand-alone swing trading system. But you can recognize that the cycle swing extremes have a high correlation to changes in price trend. Hence, these signals indicate high probability trade set-ups.

You can even increase the accuracy of these signals when you watch for cycle extremes (turn above/below the bands) followed by a divergence signal. These are very powerful set-ups.

This is another example to demonstrate how you can use the Cycle Swing Indicator for trading. To give you some ideas which you can expand on your own, I would like to introduce a simple automated trading system as a starting point in the next chapter.

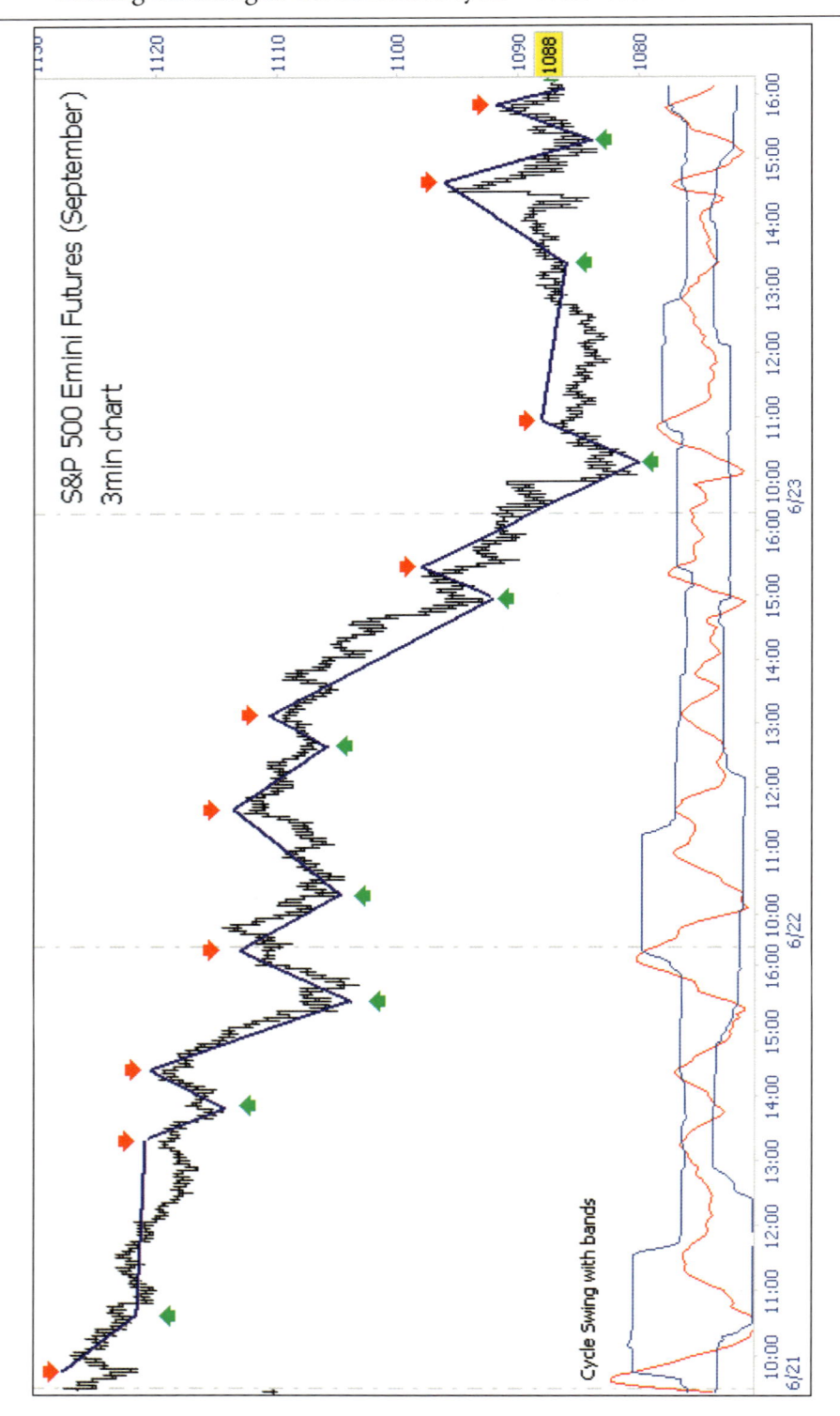

Trading the swing of the dominant cycle – Next level momentum trading

Figure 10-11: Cycle swing with bands & signals

10.6 Developing automated trading systems based on the Cycle Swing Indicator

The idea is to use the introduced cycle's extreme method and build a swing trading system around this single indicator. The system will trade each buy/sell signal. I have added a "take profit" rule to protect the profit. It is a simple rule that will close the trade if the profit reaches the average true range.

This is quite straightforward and presented here for demonstration purposes only. It will exemplify how to start building automated trading strategies around this single indicator. For the system evaluation, I will use the last three months of a 3-minute intraday history for the ES (E-mini futures contract).

Here are the facts for this study:

System evaluation period:	last 3 months (April – June 2010) / 3-minute chart
Bars for analysis:	7820 bars
Instrument:	S&P 500 E-mini futures contract (ES)
Trading:	One contract
Entry rule:	Buy / Sell signals from cycle swing bands break
Take profit rule:	Close trade if profit = ATR
Exit/Stop loss rule:	none

And here are the system statistics:

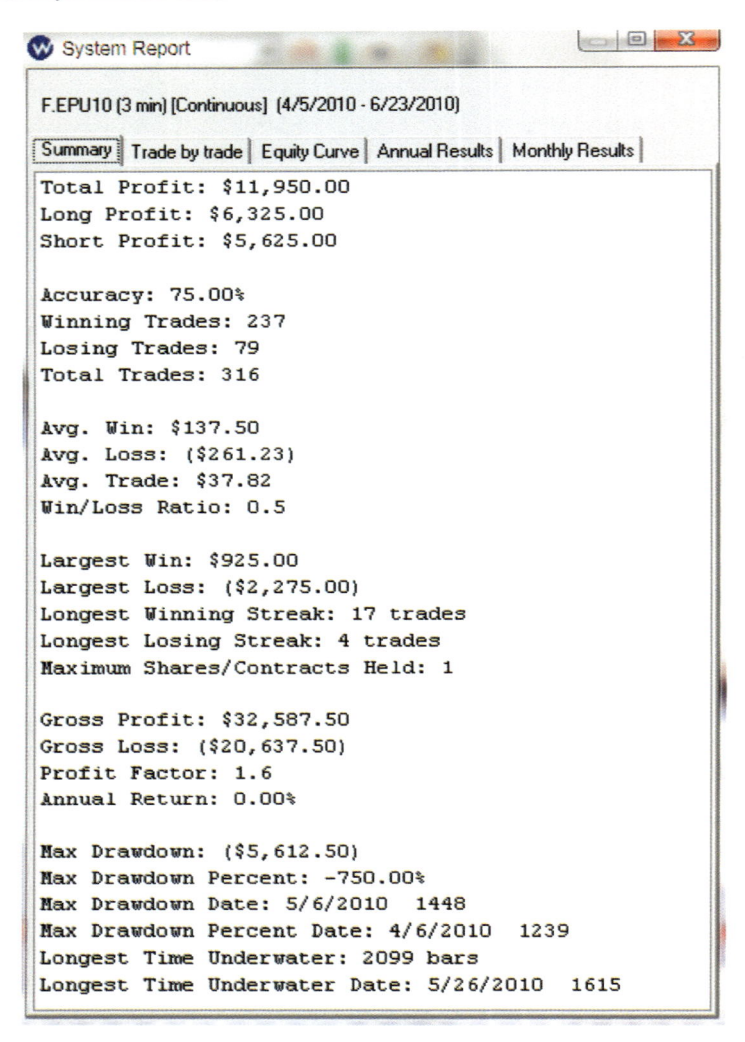

```
System Report
F.EPU10 (3 min) [Continuous]  (4/5/2010 - 6/23/2010)
Summary | Trade by trade | Equity Curve | Annual Results | Monthly Results

Total Profit: $11,950.00
Long Profit: $6,325.00
Short Profit: $5,625.00

Accuracy: 75.00%
Winning Trades: 237
Losing Trades: 79
Total Trades: 316

Avg. Win: $137.50
Avg. Loss: ($261.23)
Avg. Trade: $37.82
Win/Loss Ratio: 0.5

Largest Win: $925.00
Largest Loss: ($2,275.00)
Longest Winning Streak: 17 trades
Longest Losing Streak: 4 trades
Maximum Shares/Contracts Held: 1

Gross Profit: $32,587.50
Gross Loss: ($20,637.50)
Profit Factor: 1.6
Annual Return: 0.00%

Max Drawdown: ($5,612.50)
Max Drawdown Percent: -750.00%
Max Drawdown Date: 5/6/2010    1448
Max Drawdown Percent Date: 4/6/2010    1239
Longest Time Underwater: 2099 bars
Longest Time Underwater Date: 5/26/2010    1615
```

Figure 10-12: System report (cycle swing test)

First, what's impressive is the accuracy rate of 75%. It is very rare to achieve such a high accuracy score with only one single indicator and a simple set of rules.

Second, the distribution of the short and long profit is equally well-distributed. Half of the profit came from short and the other half from long trades. That's very balanced.

On the other hand, the win/loss ratio of 0.5 is not acceptable. It is attributable to the fact that we have not used an exit/stop loss rule here. This would be the next step to optimize our results.

The profit factor of 1.6 is quite reasonable.

The overall profit for trading one contract is, of course, acceptable. With 316 trades distributed over 57 trading days, we have an average of approximately five trades per day. That's satisfactory for a 3-minute time frame, but already at a maximum that would be acceptable. Perhaps we should add a filter rule to avoid some trades.

The absolute drawdown seems a little too high. The reason for this is that we have not applied a stop loss rule to the system. As already mentioned, a stop loss rule has to be applied to enhance the win/loss ratio and keep the drawdown lower.

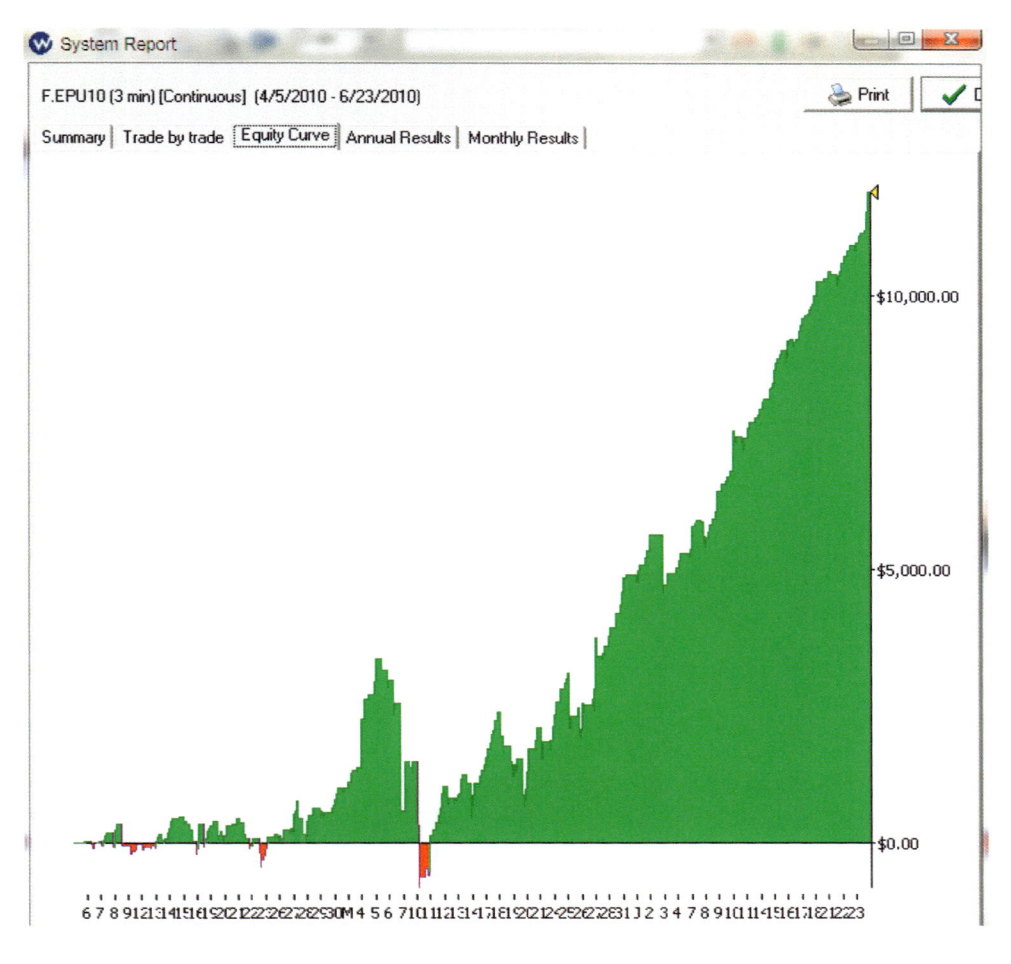

Figure 10-13: Equity curve

The equity curve looks good. An analysis of the "flat" range in April is in alignment with the market, i.e., the market was also flat during this period. Market volatility increased throughout May and June. We can see that the system performs very well in volatile markets in which the cycle swings can be identified and traded agreeably. But it is also interesting that during flat periods the system profit does not decrease. This would normally be observed with standard indicators where we would have a lot of whipsaw trades. This is not the case with the cycle swing. The system remained flat during this period and did not enter negative territory. And that's just fine!

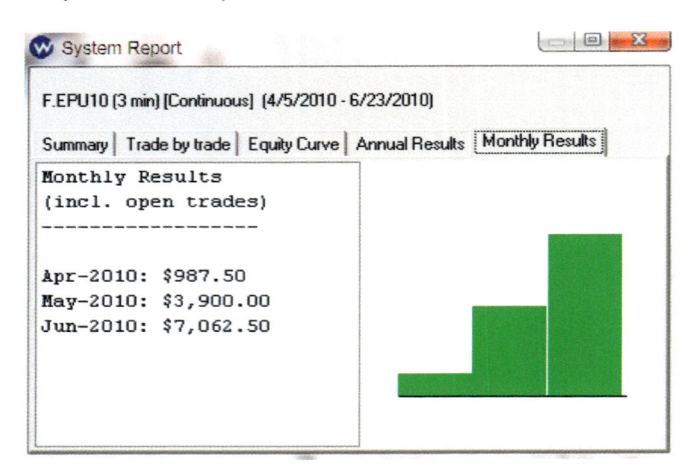

Figure 10-14: Monthly profit of system study

There is no month that ended with a loss. All three months would have been profitable.

This is only a demonstration on how to start building a trading system around this indicator. It would be a good starting point to expand on this idea. The QScript is included in the toolbox and can be used for further research and trade system development.

10.7 Cycle Swing Indicator parameter and usage

Using the cycle swing is really simple. You only need to turn on the Cycle Swing Indicator in the "Cycles" menu.

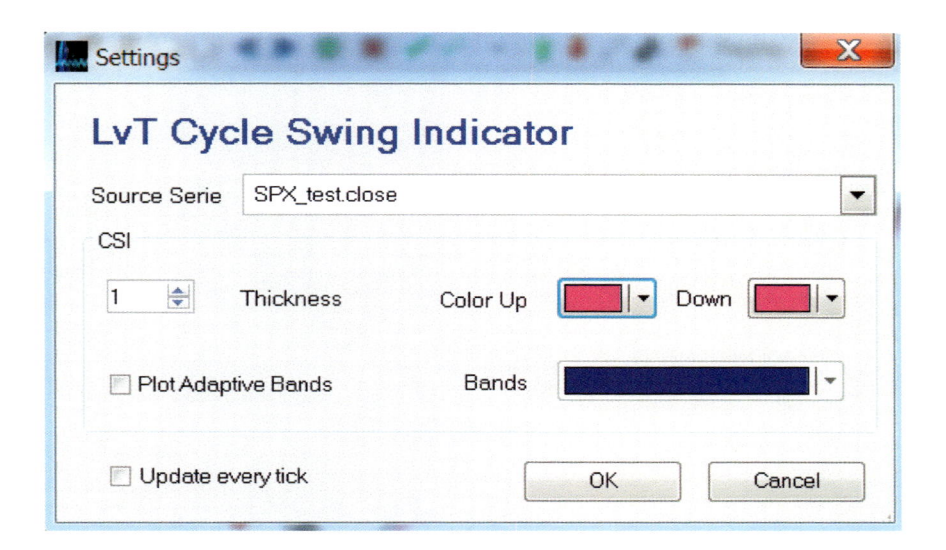

11. Multiple Cycle-Frame Trading

The advantages of applying multiple timeframe analysis when using technical indicators are well documented. When signals from a higher and lower timeframe concur, the effectiveness and probability of technical signals increases considerably. When we add cycle-based analysis to our trading arsenal, we can add another multiple chart frame technique which is very similar to the multiple timeframes approach.

Cycles are not only manifested in the form of time. A number of cycles are important during trading. Our time-based charts only provide the time-based view on cycles. By applying cycle analysis tools to the price chart, we try to detect dominant time based-cycles and aim to identify the expected change in trend based on time.

The change in trends (CITs) that are evident on the price chart during an intraday session are not attributable to time-based cycles only. That is an important as well as compelling factor why you will not be able to spot most CITs by using cycle tools on a time-based chart.

A new trading technique emerges if we combine time-based cycle analysis with other important market cycles.

11.1 Volume Cycles

One of the most important forms of cyclic behavior, especially on intraday future charts, is volume. If you look at one single day, there is a fixed amount of money or "traders" that try to move in and out of the market. For example, if all market participants are fully invested on the long side based on the available volume, the market will decline, regardless of signals or not from the time-based technical analysis. There is no volume left to push the current condition any higher. Volume tells us that we will see a drop before the market can start growing again. Such of signals are only perceptible when you can find, detect and project the dominant cycle in terms of volume currently available for trading.

First, to apply this form of volume cycle analysis, we need a volume-based chart rather than time-based charts. A charting tool which allows plotting the chart as a volume-based chart is needed. This implies that each bar contains a fixed amount of volume. A new bar will be plotted if the traded volume moves beyond the volume cut-off level allowed for each bar.

Second, a charting tool is necessary which allows the detection, monitoring and forecasting of the dominant cycles which represent the underlying force of the plotted price movements. A dominant cycle forecast on a volume chart gives you some idea about future turning points with reference to the next bars. But these future bars do not refer to time in the future – these projections refer to an amount of volume traded at a point at which the next turning point might be expected. Even if the charts of time- and volume-based bars look similar in terms of their visual form – they measure and plot two entirely independent factors: time and volume. Volume charts are an ideal form of applying cycle tools because volume cycles play an important role, especially on intraday charts.

Let's look at an example of how to combine cycle signals on time- and volume-based charts. First, we will only use one cycle tool: the Cycle Swing Indicator (CSI). This indicator measures momentum based on the current active dominant cycle instead of using the raw price data. It detects the active cycles and uses the acceleration of the underlying dominant cycle to indicate momentum. This results in an ultra-sharp, non-lagging and smooth momentum indicator based on cycle analysis.

The next chart illustrates this cycle analysis technique on a volume chart of the eMini futures during one full week from February 11 to 15. Each bar holds a volume of 15k. The derived trading signals are marked on the chart based on divergence and extreme turns of the cycle swing indicator. This indicator can, in particular, be used for divergences because it is a leading indicator which is sharp at the turns and smooth during noisy periods. This characteristic is not available among standard indicators which usually make trading of divergences impossible when using normal indicators. By applying the CSI, the divergence is typically seen 1-2 bars before the turn unfolds its force.

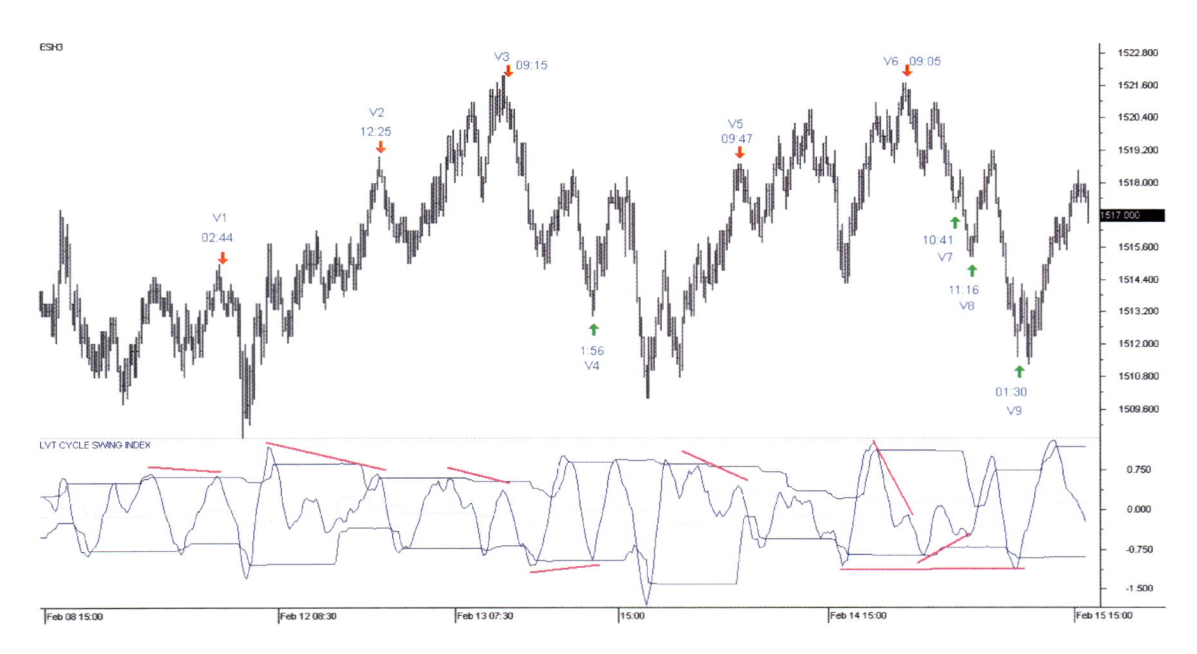

Chart 1: One week volume bar chart on the eMini futures (ESH3, 15k/bar, 11-15 Feb.)

The trading signals are marked on the chart with arrows and the time they became visible.

As shown on the chart, an important move followed in the proposed direction after every signal. This already is evidence of the potential of cyclic analysis based on pure volume charts. We can now see the turns expected on the dominant volume cycles. The divergence indicates at which point the volume flow must move in the other direction to resolve the current volume extremes – in such situations, price will simply follow the volume. Traders must therefore switch from long to short positions to free enough volume to let a new up-move unfold. Without the possible volume for a new long position, price must decline first – and vice versa. This is a very important cycle which should be followed on volume-based charts.

11.2 Price Range Cycles

Another important cycle that can be measured is based on price alone. Besides volume- and time-based cycles, each instrument follows its intrinsic price pattern. A contract switches from one price range to another in the form of cycles. These are cycles on the "vertical" where price is plotted, not on the "horizontal" where volume or time is recorded. To detect these cycles, we need to switch to price range charts. This is a chart which plots a new bar after a specific price range in trading has been exceeded. This implies that a contract will move in constant price steps – up and down. Now, the cycle toolset is introduced, which allows us to detect the underlying dominant price range of our trading vehicle. By applying cycle tools, we can now measure another complete independent cycle: price range cycles which are not connected to either volume or time. This is what makes cycle analysis so unique!

The following chart presents the eMini futures for the same period, just plotted in range bars. Each bar holds a range of 1.5 points.

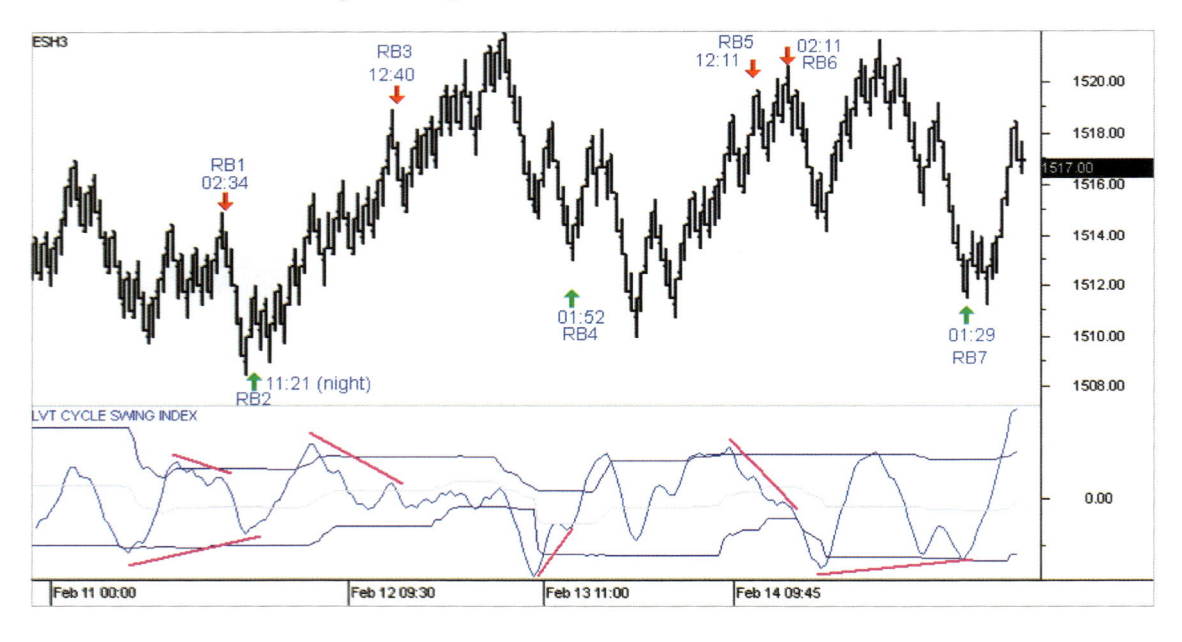

Chart 2: One week price range bar chart on the eMini futures (1.5 points/bar, 11-15 Feb.)

Again, the trading signals have been marked on the chart with arrows and the time they became visible. And again, after every signal, an important move followed in the proposed direction – in this case, however, based purely on price range cycles.

11.3 Time Cycles & Cycle Cluster

The next chart shows the same period for the eMini futures contract on a time-based chart with 10 minutes for each bar during trading hours. We will use the same Cycle Swing Indicator to spot important turns based on the dominant time-based cycles. Now, all three signal types are combined into this time-based chart. The signals from the volume chart are marked with V, the price range chart with RB and the time-based signals with T.

Chart 3: One week time-based chart on the eMini futures with all signals (10min, 11-15 Feb.)

Now, the full potential of trading multiple cycle frames unfolds: we see that nearly all important changes in trends have been detected by our cycle indicator. It is important to map the signals in the time-based chart because we live and trade in the time-based domain. Hence, these three chart types (volume, price range, time) should be monitored in the real trading environment in parallel with the cycle's indicators. The signals are then mapped onto the time-based chart which is the primary trade execution chart.

This approach shows that all turns are mainly based on cyclic behavior, i.e., on pure natural law which is now observable on the price chart. However, time-based cycles are not the only factor that influence market behavior. And this is the reason why a lot of important turning points are hidden on the time-based charts. This explains the triple divergences on time-based charts: these are attributable to the fact that the volume and/or price cycles are not yet where the time cycles are – they still need to keep moving. However, when volume and price cycles are in sync with time, it's time for your move. In other words, do not concentrate on time-based cycles only. If you add volume and price range cycles to time-based cycles, you can decipher nearly all market moves on intraday charts. You will be able to see and decode such important trading signals if you apply the potential of cycles to volume and range charts. It is important to analyze cycles on these three chart types, and not just the purely technical indicators. Cycles are the driving force, and not price plotted.

To summarize: the highest potential unfolds when time, volume and price range cycles are in sync and form a cycle cluster. These occurrences are marked in yellow on the time-based chart numbered from 1 to 4. After each alignment, the most significant moves of the full week start to unfold. This is what you want to look for in the real-time trading environment. The chart shows one week of non-interrupted intraday trading action and reveals four clusters. You will be rewarded if you pay close attention to all three cycle frames and wait until they are aligned when cycles come into play. This is the time you want to place your intraday trades.

12. The CSI and cRSI Combo Trading Technique (Intraday)

The following trading strategy demonstrates the cycle swing indicator (CSI) in combination with the cyclic-smoothed RSI indicator (cRSI) on a 2-minute chart. I will introduce a simple standard rule-set for the detection of the right and wrong entry points.

I will use the Nasdaq 100 E-Mini Futures contract (ENQ) on a two-minute chart to demonstrate this technique. We will use three uninterrupted days on a 2-minute chart to illustrate the result (March 21 to 23, 2012).

The basic technique is the following:

1. Look for divergences on the CSI and/or the cRSI.

2. The other indicator must confirm the divergence.

3. Watch closely the relationship between the Cycle Swing dynamic bands and the current value to differentiate correct from misleading signals.

The Cycle Swing is one of the most powerful "momentum-like" indicators because it relies on cycle acceleration instead of price behavior. Consequently, the CSI is fast, sharp, and without lag.

The cRSI and the distance of the current CSI value to the dynamic bands provide additional trade advice. This technique identifies high probability trade entry signals. Paired with trade and risk management rule-sets, this is a powerful algorithm. It is easy to apply and does not contain a myriad of rules or expectations. A straightforward approach is necessary for a fast moving 2-minute real time chart.

Figure 12.1 presents a two-minute ENQ chart for March 21, 2012. The CSI appears on the base of the chart and the cRSI on the top of the chart. Both indicators use the standard, out-of-the-box settings. The points of interest are marked with numbers. A step-by-step review of the events explains this technique.

12.1 Day 1: March 21, 2012

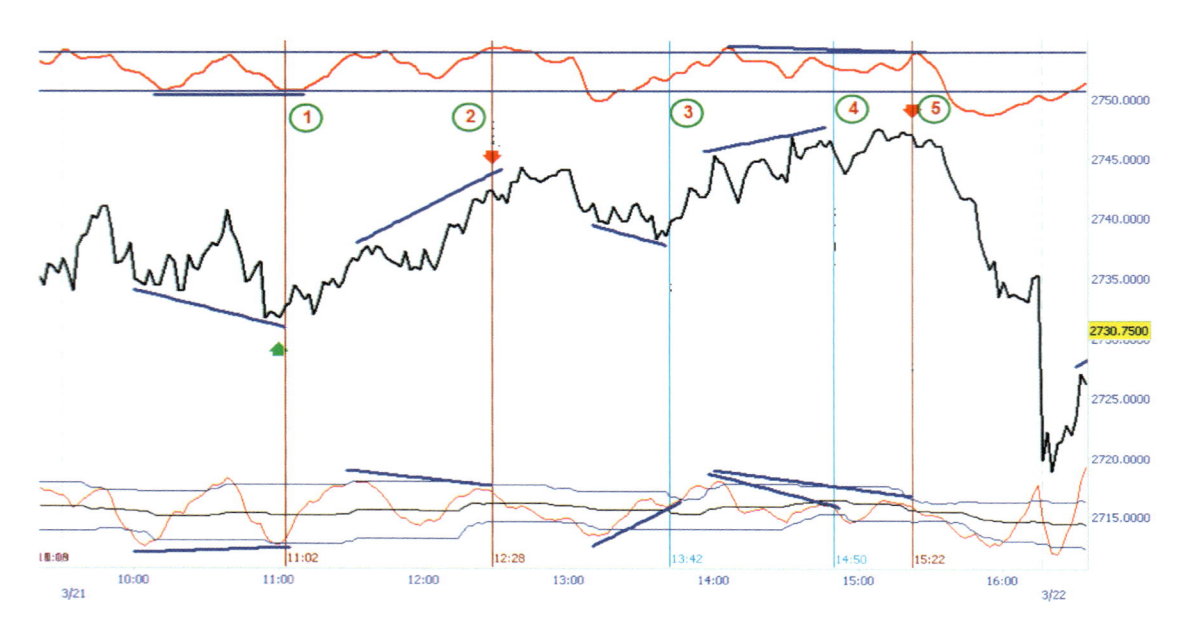

Figure 12-1: Two-minute NASDAQ eMini Futures / March 21, 2012

Situation 1: Classic Buy Signal (11:02)

CSI: The Cycle Swing shows a bullish divergence with values below the lower band.

cRSI: The cRSI confirms the bullish situation with a simultaneous bullish divergence.

Both indicators show a bullish entry signal with the CSI absolute position at a value where there is room for the upside. We go long with respect to the market.

Situation 2: Classic Sell Signal (12:28)

CSI: The Cycle Swing shows a bearish divergence with the values touching the upper band.

cRSI: The cRSI shows no divergence. However, the cRSI shows an extreme condition that confirms the bearish divergence of the CSI.

The bearish divergence is confirmed by the extreme cRSI overbought situation. We close the long position and go short with respect to the market.

Situation 3: False Buy Signal – Close Short Only (13:42)

CSI: The Cycle Swing again shows a bullish divergence. However, the absolute position of the CSI is already at its upper dynamic band. This invalidates the bullish signal because there is insufficient room for the upside based on the cycle's momentum. Instead, cycle acceleration is in a position where we expect downward pressure in the near future. This is not a situation to go long.

cRSI: Although a divergence on the cRSI is in place. The absence of room for the CSI already invalidates a bullish divergence.

The conclusion is simple. Ignore the bullish divergence; do not go long. Close the established short position now and wait for the next sure situation.

Situation 4: False Sell Signal (14:50)

CSI: This is the opposite of the observations from Situation 3. The Cycle Swing now shows a bearish divergence. However, the absolute position of the CSI is close to its lower dynamic bands. This invalidates the bearish signal because there is insufficient room for the downside based on the cycle momentum. Instead, cycle acceleration is in a position where we expect upward pressure. This is not a situation to go short.

cRSI: Although a divergence on the cRSI is in place. The absence of room for the downside on the CSI already invalidates a bearish signal. Therefore, we ignore the cRSI.

Again, we use the same rule-set. Ignore the bearish divergence; do not go short. (If you are long in the market, close your long position now.)

Situation 5: Sell Signal (15:22)

CSI: Situation 5 is similar to that of Situation 4. The bearish divergence is in place and is actively signaled by the indicator plot. However, contrastingly, the absolute value of the CSI is not at the lower band. The CSI is positioned above the midline. This is significant because the bearish divergence is no longer disabled by the position. Instead, room on the CSI on the downside allows a short trade. We must verify that the cRSI can confirm the bearish signal.

cRSI: The cRSI shows a bearish divergence and it is positioned in an overbought situation.

The sell signal from the CSI is confirmed by the cRSI, which shows a valid sell signal.

A Summary of the Trades for March 21, 2012

We observed three confirmed trade signals, all of which have been profitable and tradable. The signals caught the main turning points—the low and high of the day. The CSI can pinpoint the significant daily events with simple, additional rules to validate or invalidate the market situation.

12.2 Day 2: March 22, 2012

The next day shows the trading technique with an uninterrupted two-day example. Figure 12.2 demonstrates the technique's ability to catch the main swings of the majority of trading days.

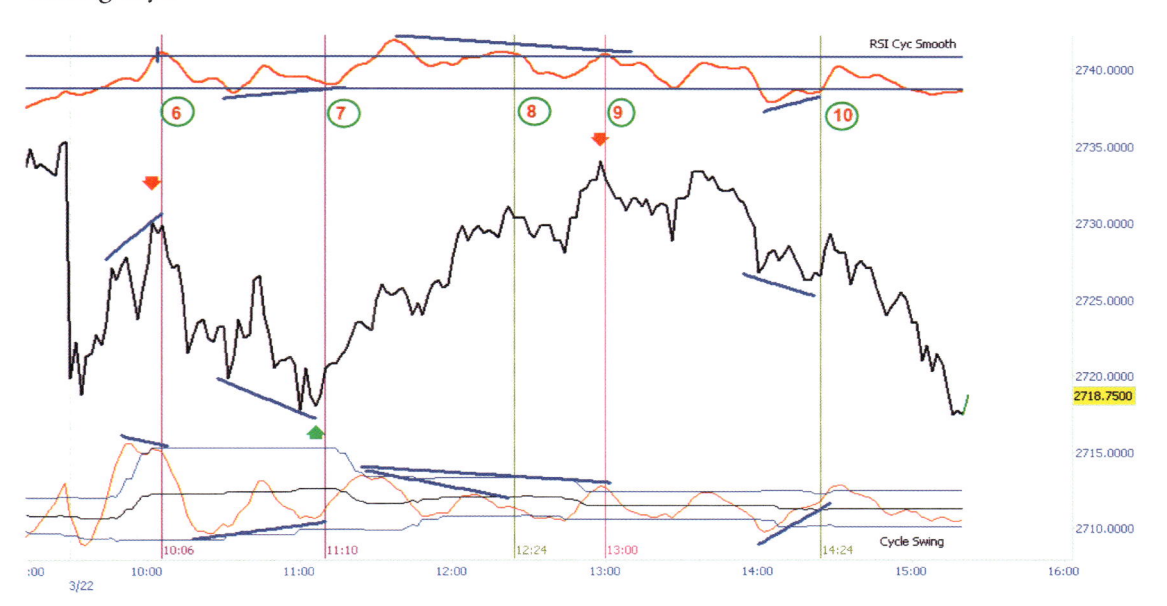

12-2: Two-minute NASDAQ eMini Futures / March 22, 2012

Situation 6: Classic Sell Signal (10:06)

CSI: The Cycle Swing shows a definite bearish divergence with the values at the upper band.

cRSI: The cRSI does not show a divergence. However, the cRSI shows an extreme overbought condition that confirms the bearish divergence of the CSI.

The bearish divergence of the CSI is confirmed by the cRSI overbought situation. This represents a classic sell signal to establish the next short trade.

Situation 7: Classic Buy Signal (11:10)

CSI: The Cycle Swing shows a definite bullish divergence with the absolute value placed at the lower band.

cRSI: The cRSI confirms the CSI buy signal by showing a similar bullish divergence simultaneously with an additional absolute oversold condition.

Both indicators show a bullish entry signal. We close the previous short position and establish a new long position at the same time.

Situation 8: Invalid Sell Signal (12:24)

CSI: The Cycle Swing now signals a bearish divergence. However, the absolute position of the CSI is neither above the midbands nor close to the upper band. This is required to confirm the bearish divergence. Therefore, the absolute position at/below the midband invalidates the sell signal from the bearish divergence. The position of the CSI does not allow the establishment of a short trade.

cRSI: Although a bearish divergence on the cRSI is in place, the absence of room for the downside on the CSI invalidates a bearish signal. Therefore, we ignore the cRSI as a confirming indicator.

We ignore the bearish divergence and do not go short. However, we close any long trade.

Situation 9: Valid Sell Signal (13:00)

CSI: Situation 9 is similar. A new bearish divergence is in place and is visible at the top of the current CSI plot. Contrastingly, however, the absolute value of the CSI is above the midband and the CSI is positioned above the upper dynamic band. This is the ideal situation – a divergence with the absolute position above the upper dynamic band. We must ensure that the cRSI confirms the bearish signal.

cRSI: The cRSI is positioned in an extreme overbought situation.

The sell signal from the CSI is confirmed by the cRSI, which gives us a valid sell signal.

Situation 10: Invalid Buy Signal (14:24)

CSI: The Cycle Swing signals a bullish divergence. However, the absolute position of the CSI is close to the upper dynamic band above the midline. This implies that the cyclic momentum will imminently roll over to the downside, which is not a situation to go long. Therefore, the absolute position of the CSI invalidates the bullish divergence.

cRSI: Although a bullish divergence on the cRSI is in place, the absence of room on the upside on the CSI invalidates a buy signal. We ignore the cRSI as a confirming indicator.

We ignore the bullish divergence and do not go long. However, we close any short trade.

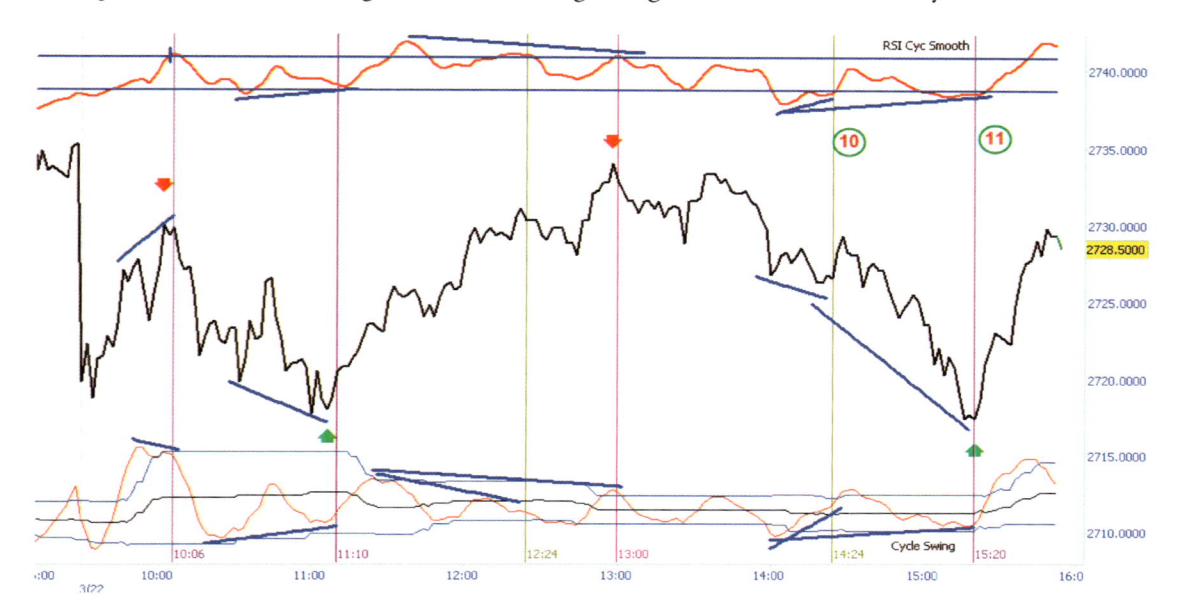

12-3: Two Similar Situations: Invalid Buy at 14:24 and a Valid Buy at 15:20

Situation 11: Valid Buy Signal (15:20)

CSI: Now, the cycle swing shows another bullish divergence and the absolute position of the CSI is at the lower dynamic bands. This is not the same situation observed before, and we now have a valid buy signal. We must obtain confirmation from the cRSI.

cRSI: The cyclic smoothed RSI confirms the CSI buy signal with a bullish divergence observed simultaneously with an absolute oversold situation.

Both indicators show a bullish entry signal, and we establish the next long position.

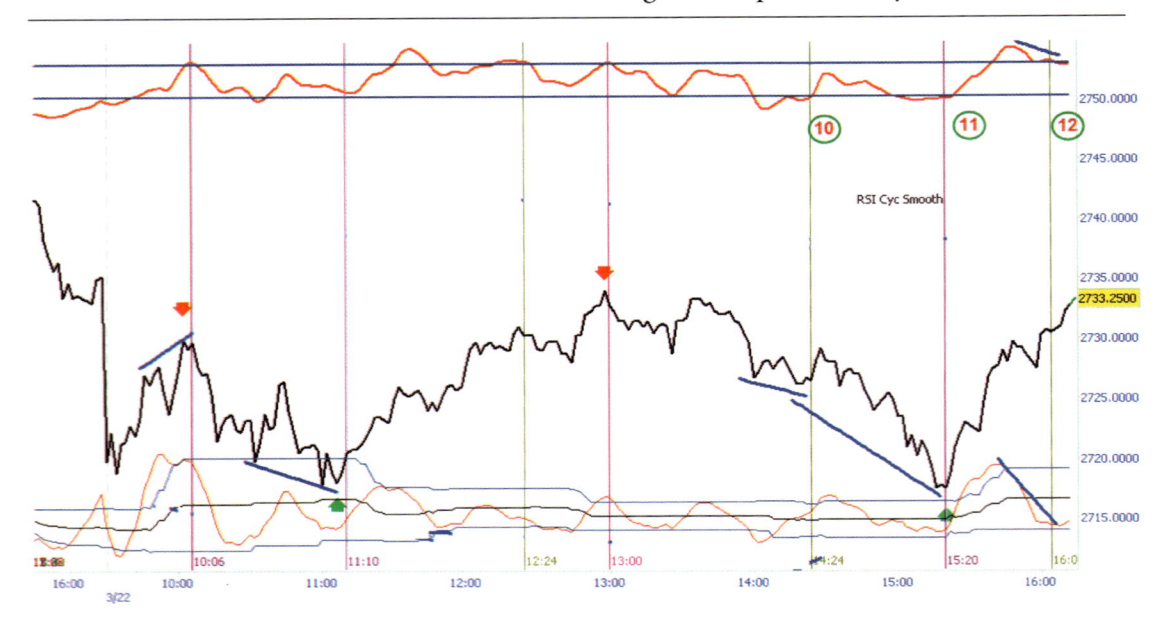

12-4: Follow Up: No Valid Sell Signal at 16:00 / Close Long Only

Situation 12: no sell signal (16:04)

CSI: The CSI shows a divergence; however, the absolute position is too close to the lower band to allow a bearish signal. We expect the cycle momentum to turn upward, which does not allow a short trade.

cRSI: The cRSI shows a bearish divergence. However, this is not count based on the already invalidated sell signal from the CSI position.

The result suggests simply closing the long trade and not going short.

A Summary of the Trades for March 22, 2012

We observed four confirmed trade signals—two long signals at 11:10 and 15:20 and two short signals at 10:06 and 13:00. The signals reflected the major lows and highs of the day. Moreover, all signals have been profitable and tradable.

12.3 Day 3: March 23, 2012

We examine the third uninterrupted day in the sequence applying the trading technique.

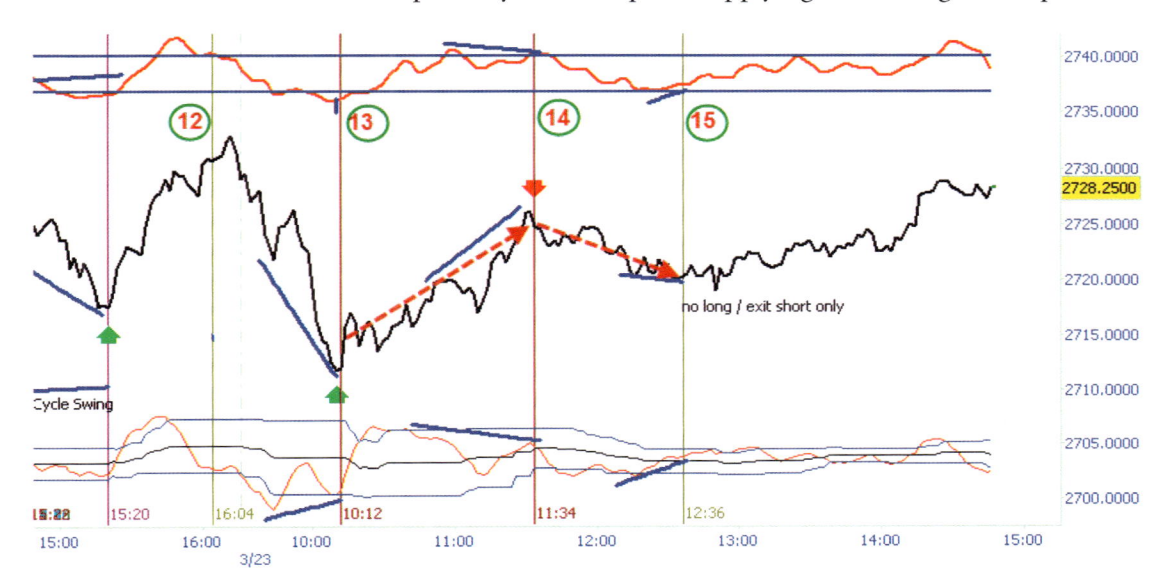

12-5: Two-minute NASDAQ eMini Futures / March 23, 2012

The events for March 23, 2012 are summarized now that the indicator readings have been explained.

A buy signal is observed at 10:12 with a CSI divergence confirmed by the absolute position and the cRSI (Situation 13). Approximately one hour later, at 11:34, we observe a sell signal that reverses the current long position into a short position (Situation 14). One hour later again, at 12:36, the cRSI signals a bullish divergence. However, the absolute position of the CSI close to the upper band permits a long position. Therefore, we close the running short trade and take the profit. We do not go long.

Finally, on the third day of trading using this technique, we have one long and one short trade, both of which have been profitable. The three days of 2-minute eMini futures on the Nasdaq 100 signaled nine trades, all of which have been profitable in an uninterrupted sequence.

This example was extracted from a live training session conducted during the three days of the cycle trading method.

13. Cycles Toolbox and Charting Platform

This book uses the scripts and codes available in the WhenToTrade Standalone Charting Platform. The Cycles Module is also available for existing Wave59 customers. However, the WTT module has additional research and analysis functionalities such as a Genetic Engineering Module. The module interacts with the cycles tools and offers new areas of cycle research in addition to that described in this book. The main cycle engine is built into high-speed code based on C++. The core algorithms use heavy mathematics and signal processing algorithms. These calculations cannot be done in a script language because of coding limitations and executing speed.

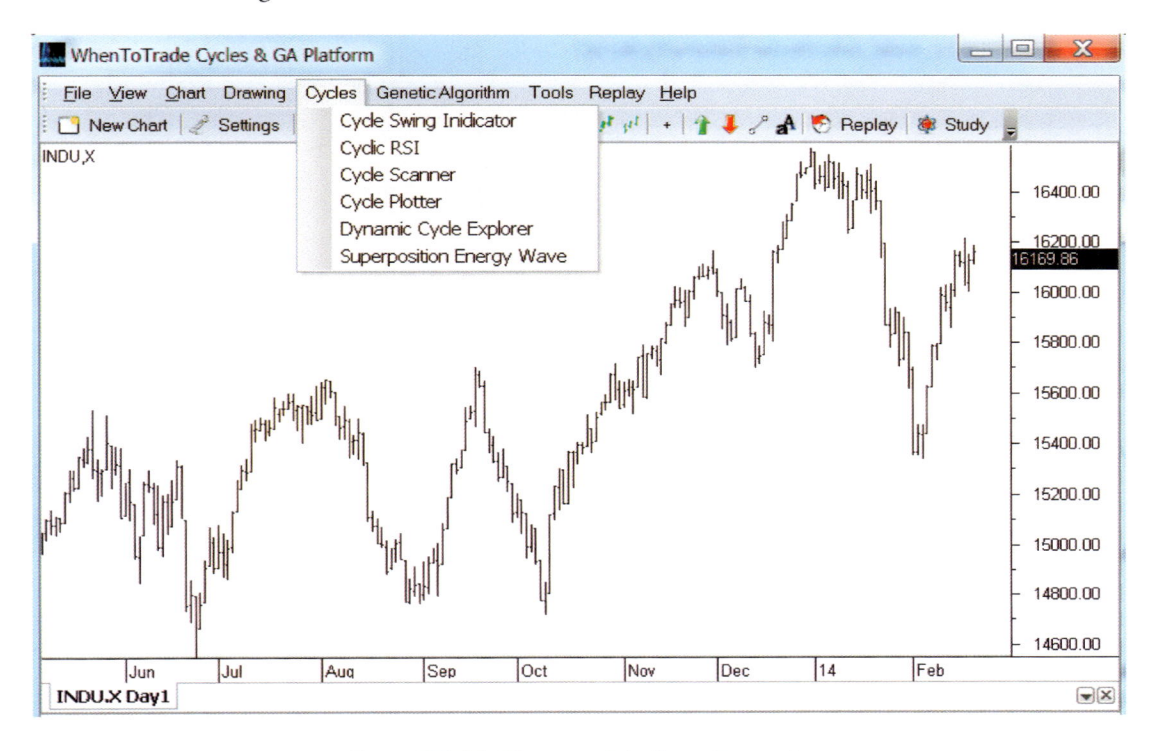

The WTT Charting Platform Module is available from the WhenToTrade.com website.

Chart: WTT Charting Platform Screenshot

231

The cycle functions can also be accessed from the Wave59 menu if you are an existing Wave59 customer. The cycle plug-in must be purchased and activated. The W59 Cycles menu is only visible after you have registered for the additional WTT cycle plug-in.

Chart: Wave59 Cycle Menu Screenshot

My aim is to provide you with professional cycles tools that can be used for your own trading and research purposes. Therefore, the cycles toolbox is not limited to the information presented here. You can use these cyclic tools to expand and research your own ideas.

14. Bibliography

Ackert L., Church B., Deaves R. (2003): "Emotion and Financial Markets", Federal Reserve Bank of Atlanta, Economic Review, Second Quarter 2003, Page 33-41.

Bartels, R. (1982): "The Rank Version of von Neumann's Ratio Test for Randomness", Journal of the American Statistical Association, Vol. 77, No. 377, (Mar., 1982), pp. 40-46.

Bressert, Walter (1991): "The Power of Oscillator/Cycle Combinations", Published by Bressert Marketing Group, Chicago.

Carolan, C. (1993): "The Spiral Calendar and Its Effect on Financial Markets and Human Events", New Classics Library.

Freeth, Tony (2009): "Decoding an Ancient Computer: New explorations have revealed how the antikythera mechanism modeled lunar motion and predicted eclipses, among other sophisticated tricks", SCIENTIFIC AMERICAN, December 2009, Page 76-83.

Hurst, J.M. (1970): "The Profit MAGIC of Stock Transaction Timing", Traders Press, Reprinted February 2000.

Jackson, M. (2003): "Out, Dammed Spot!", The IRM Quarterly, Volume 13 Number 1.

Krivelyova, A., Robotti, C. (2003): "Playing the Field: Geomagnetic Storms and the Stock Market", Working Paper, October 2003, Federal Reserve Bank of Atlanta. http://www.frbatlanta.org/filelegacydocs/wp0305b.pdf

Kolesnik, A.; Borodin, A.; Pobachenko, S.; Kolesnik, S. (2005): "An electromagnetic mechanism of solar-terrestrial relations", Discussion paper, INTERNATIONAL JOURNAL OF GEOMAGNETISM AND AERONOMY, VOL. 6, 18 October 2005.

Lo, A.; Mamaysky, H.; Wang, J. (2000): "Foundations of Technical Analysis: Computational Algorithms, Statistical Inference and Empirical Implementation", Working

Paper 7613, National Bureau of Economic Research, MIT laboratory for Financial Engineering.

Merriman, R. (1997): "The Ultimate Book on Stock Market Timing, Vol. IV: Solar-Lunar Correlations to Short-Term Trading Cycles", Seek It Publications.

Meyer, D. (2003): "MESA vs Goertzel-DFT", Working Paper, http://www.meyersanalytics.com/publications/MesaVsGDFT.pdf

Millard, B. (1999): "Channels & Cycles: A Tribute to J.M. Hurst", Traders Press.

Muller, R., Rohde R. (2005): "Biodiversity Comes and Goes", University of California at Berkeley, http://www.lbl.gov/Science-Articles/Archive/Phys-fossil-biodiversity.html

NOAA Space Weather Prediction Center (2010): "A Profile of Space Weather", http://www.swpc.noaa.gov/primer/primer_2010.pdf

Palmer, S.; Rycroft, M.; Cermack, M. (2006): "Solar and geomagnetic activity, extremely low frequency magnetic and electric fields and human health at the Earth's surface", Surveys in Geophysics, Volume 27, Number 5, page 557-595.

Puetz, Stephen J. (2009): "The Unified Cycle Theory: How Cycles Dominate the Structure of the Universe and Influence Life on Earth", Outskirts Press.

Phillips, T. (2008): "The Moon and the Magnetotail." NASA Goddard Space Flight Center, www.nasa.gov/topics/moonmars/features/magnetotail_080416.html

Schwarzschild, B. (2007): "Varying cosmic-ray flux may explain cycles of biodiversity", Physics Today, American Institute of Physics, October 2007, Page 18-20. http://www.physics.ku.edu/top/PTO000018.pdf

Taylor, R. (2006): "Paradigm", Savas Beatie.

Tomes, R. (1989): "Towards a Unified Theory of Cycles", Foundation for the Study of Cycles, Conference Proceedings February 1990, Cycles Research Institute.